Political Economy and American Capitalism

Political Economy and American Capitalism

Rodney D. Peterson
Professor of Economics

Colorado State University
Fort Collins, Colorado

Kluwer Academic Publishers
Boston / Dordrecht / London

Distributors for North America:
Kluwer Academic Publishers
101 Philip Drive
Assinippi Park
Norwell, Massachusetts 02061 USA

Distributors for all other countries:
Kluwer Academic Publishers Group
Distribution Centre
Post Office Box 322
3300 AH Dordrecht, THE NETHERLANDS

Library of Congress Cataloging-in-Publication Data

Peterson, Rodney D.
    Political economy and American capitalism / Rodney D. Peterson.
      p.   cm.
    Includes bibliographical references and index.
    ISBN 0-7923-9142-X (alk. paper)
      1. Capitalism—United States.   2. Macroeconomics.   3. Comparative
    economics.   I. Title.
    HB501.P4157   1991
    330.12'2'0973—dc20   90-26711
                                                              CIP

Printed on acid-free paper.

Printed in the United States of America

Contents

List of Tables

PREFACE

We are now witness to the waning years of the 1900s. Soon, we shall embark upon a bold journey into the uncharted territory of the twenty-first century. Futurists of various persuasions have speculated as to what the oncoming decades might bestow upon us. Not surprising, most predictions are closely tied to advances in technology, especially in astrophysics, biochemistry, electronics, and genetics. But what about the economic system? Whatever happens, forces have undoubtedly already been set in motion which will mold (or remold) the structure and character of American capitalism.

American capitalism has been, is, and will undoubtedly continue to be a system in transition. Technology perennially changes, albeit at a faster or slower pace sometimes than others, and society's institutions continually adjust to these technological changes. Such adjustments alter the character of our politico-economic system when statutes are enacted, court decisions rendered, administrative agency rules promulgated, and cultural mores realigned to supplant old ones. Other adaptations are brought about when small-group collective action is successful in causing a special status of privilege to be conferred on some members of society, but restrictions to be levied on others.

What kinds of institutional adjustments to advancing technology will develop to assign property rights, allocate resources, and distribute income? How tight will linkages between market and State be forged? How far to the right (or to the left) will American capitalism move? Can the industrial sector of the U. S. economy be expected to become more concentrated than it currently is, or less so? And what of the growing inequality in the distribution of income, wealth, and social power? By which mechanisms will all members of our democratic society be allowed an effective voice into setting the national agenda, if at all? Will government, law-enforcement, and social programs become kinder and gentler, or harsher and more restrictive? The list of questions concerning what the future American economy might be is virtually endless. Obviously, only a few can be treated here.

As the title indicates, this book is about political economy and its relation to American capitalism. The central hypothesis guiding its preparation is that our economic system, being based on the market, benefits (or perhaps, suffers) from substantial nourishment (or perhaps, interferences) by the State. In short, American capitalism is a political economy. But what does that mean? Political economy can ordinarily be understood by examining the existence of power and status which inevitably leads to privilege and disparities. A number of paths can be followed to gain insight into how political economy is practiced in American capitalism.

One revealing focus for observation, investigation, and description is that of economic systems. Indeed, the essence of American capitalism can be contemplated by observing it unfold in the course of its historical development, and by noting its kinship to arrangements found in feudalism, mercantilism, fascism, and socialism. Another view involves taking a sector-by-sector look at how different parts of the economy function because of connections between State and market. This effort helps to note actual mechanisms by which power developed and gained its foothold, and how the State has been involved in forging and perpetuating such power positions. Both approaches are used below as complementary ways to begin to understand the nature of our economy. Only a cursory glimpse at politico-economic systems is provided, and only a few sectors are examined. Nevertheless, on this basis, a general picture emerges as to what constitutes capitalism.

My concern over the nature of our economic system began more than 30 years ago as graduate studies began in economics at South Dakota State University. A course titled "American Capitalism" focused on J. K. Galbraith's "countervailing power" and his "affluent society" as well as on *Monopoly in America* by W. Adams and H. Gray. These tracts, coupled later on with materials on *The American Economy* and *Economic Issues of the 1960s* by A. H. Hansen, lighted the way for exploring various corners of the American business scene. Other scholarly works have also contributed to this intellectual development: Schumpeter's *Capitalism, Socialism and Democracy*; Chamberlin's *The Theory of Monopolistic Competition*; and R. McCloskey's *American Conservatism in the Age of Enterprise, 1865-1910*. Often, as a young professor, I made course assignments in books by R. Heilbroner (*The Making of Economic Society* and *The Limits of American Capitalism*) and J. K. Galbraith (*The New Industrial State* and *Economics and The Public Purpose*). A number of other excellent studies on the nature of American capitalism also captured my imagination. Among them are M. Reagan's *The Managed Economy*, R. Averrit's *The Dual Economy*, J.

Weinstein's *The Corporate Ideal in the Liberal State 1900-1918*; T. Lowi's *The End of Liberalism*, R. Solo's *The Political Authority of the Market System*; and *The Irony of Democracy* by T. Dye and H. Zeigler. We all learn from one another through observing, reading, and listening. The influence and impact of these and other related works will undoubtedly be noted in the pages which follow.

During the quest to become trained broadly in both business and economics, a vexing question continually arose: "What is the American economic system like, where has it been, and where might it be heading?" Knowledge and insight from the fields of industrial organization and macroeconomics helped provide some answers. Industrial organization analysis deals with identifying the structure, conduct, and performance of firms in industries, many of which are concentrated to various degrees of intensity. Indeed, the field of industry economics is largely about power, and so is political economy. Therein can be found a vital connection between political economy and American capitalism.

The field of business cycles, as it relates the development of Keynesian macroeconomics, also provides some answers. During the Great Depression and the New Deal there was no small amount of concern about economic systems. Was capitalism failing? Is socialism the answer? Does the American economy require a policy of mercantilist protection and controls? Are New Deal business and social agencies an early stage of fascism?

As noted, a number of excellent treatises contain thoughtful insight into the nature of our economic system. The present book provides yet another view on how modern American capitalism operates. The message is simple, but hopefully not simplistic: American capitalism appears to be a mixture of economic systems, and some of the mixing can be noted clearly in selected sectors of the economy.

In grade school and to some extent, high school, it is not uncommon to inculcate the young and impressionable about the nature of American capitalism by organizing a cookie sale, selling greeting cards, or setting up a lemonade stand. But it is both foolish and misleading to pretend that the American economic system is based on business endeavors of that type, and that productive capacity in the United States is typified by such small, simplified units. Rarely, if ever, are these methods of teaching about capitalism related to the corporate form of business, working with governmental agencies, or lobbying to gain favorable status, receive subsidies, and obtain protection from foreign competition. But these matters are in the realm of political economy, a topic which is discussed below. And the question of what capitalism "really" is and whether it is tinged with socialism, fascism, mercantilism, or feudalism are also matters of political economy which need to be explored. Hopefully, professors of economics, business, and various social science subjects will find the contents of this book useful to themselves and to both graduate and undergraduate students for discerning some aspects of political economy in American capitalism.

ACKNOWLEDGEMENTS

This book culminates an academic career of reading, teaching, writing, and reflecting. We all learn from one another and whatever I've assimilated in a lifetime of scholarship as a university professor I owe to teachers, students, writers, colleagues, family, and people from various walks of life. A number of special persons have provided encouragement, stimulated my thinking, listened patiently to ideas (some bad and some hopefully good), tried to straighten me out when I went down the wrong path, and been "there" when I've needed them. I cannot possibly name all who have helped, but there are several who stand out.

To begin with, my mother instilled in me a zeal for education. From that, I could not have chosen a more exciting and rewarding profession than that of an educator. Many of the good ideas I have explored were obtained from my devoted wife and companion, Evelyn. She has always been helpful and critical with her questions and comments, and moreover, usually correct. Each of our three sons--Douglas, Russell, and Stuart--has tolerated my ramblings, read various manuscripts and articles, and communicated his reactions to numerous drafts of my written materials. A teacher and friend, Wallace C. Peterson, has always been a helpful sounding board for ideas and proposals. Several colleagues have read many of my manuscripts at different stages of development and offered excellent suggestions: Craig R. MacPhee, John R. McKean, and Robert R. Keller. While at the University of Idaho in the mid-1960s, Max E. Fletcher contributed much to my intellectual development. Since 1968, when I joined the faculty at Colorado State, Robert L. Darcy continually provided counsel on institutional economics and has remained a faithful friend. On various occasions, I selfishly picked the brain of an unselfish historian, George Dennison, and a helpful political scientist, Wayne Peak. Harry Rosenberg, David Allen, John Richard Felton, Fred Enssle, and Ann Mari May also read parts of this manuscript and made valuable suggestions. Despite all this assistance, I must assume responsibility for any error or misstatement. While at Colorado State

University, several outstanding members of the secretarial staff in the Department of Economics have tolerated my occasional impatience while patiently provided typing support. Each one deserves my sincere thanks for accurately reading my illegible handwriting and giving rapid turnaround of neatly prepared manuscript: Phyllis Johnson, Mary Huwa, Nancy J. Harris, Waneta Boyce, and Mary Olivas.

The preparation of this book essentially began more than fifteen years ago while I was on sabbatical leave at Simon Fraser University in British Columbia, Canada. It was there that I did background reading for the chapters on fascism, mercantilism, and capitalism which were first published as journal articles. While in law school at the University of Denver during the early 1980s, I prepared papers on rail and air transport for Professor Paul Stephen Dempsey, an outstanding teacher and scholar. All these, coupled with some papers presented at professional meetings, provided a framework and impetus for additional work. On balance, approximately half of the chapters in this book appeared previously in one form or another as academic, refereed articles. These contributions must be recognized. Accordingly, I gratefully acknowledge permission from the following organizations to present various portions of materials previously contained in their publications:

University of Akron:
R. D. Peterson, "Pluralist Democracy, Political Economy, and Modern American Capitalism," *Akron Business and Economic Review*, Vol. 9, No. 2, Summer 1978, pp. 14-19.

Western Illinois University:
R. D. Peterson, "Views of Fascism and Modern American Capitalism," *The Journal of Behavioral Economics*, Vol. VII, No. 1, Summer 1978, pp. 155-189.
R. D. Peterson, "Political Economy: Janus or Hydra?" *Western Illinois University Journal of Business*, Fall 1989, pp. 1-17.

University of Washington:
R. D. Peterson, "Is There Neomercantilism in America?" *Journal of Contemporary Business*, Vol. 10, No. 2, August 1981, pp. 97-112.

University of Denver:
R. D. Peterson, "An Economic Analysis of Statutory Changes in Rail Carrier Entry and Exit," *Transportation Law Journal*, Vol. 13, 1984, pp. 189-226.

Francis Neilson Fund and Robert Schalkenbach Foundation:
R. D. Peterson, "The CAB's Struggle to Establish Price and Route Rivalry in World Air Transport," *The American Journal of Economics and Sociology*, Vol. 49, No. 1, January 1990, pp. 65-80.

Kluwer Academic Publishers:
R. D. Peterson, "Industrial Power: Meaning and Measurement," (Chapter 1) in Wallace C. Peterson, editor, *Market Power and the Economy*, Boston: Kluwer, 1988, pp. 1-26.

Finally, I must recognize the research facilities at several universities where I was a student, or a Visiting Scholar, or a faculty member: The University of Nebraska at Lincoln; Simon Fraser University, Burnaby, British Columbia; and Colorado State University. I am deeply indebted to the taxpayers who have thoughtfully supported these academic institutions.

R. D. Peterson
Fort Collins, Colorado

1   OVERVIEW

INTRODUCTION

> The private market works within patterns of unequal distribution of economic, social, and political power. [J. W. Hurst, *Law and Markets in United States History*, Madison: University of Wisconsin Press, 1982, p. 138.]

Modern American capitalism is often represented by academic and popular writers as something quite different from the way the system actually works in the United States. Characteristics of capitalism are usually described by citing several basic features, but by neglecting interaction among key institutional arrangements. An example of this kind of incomplete description is to propose capitalism as the epitome of a market economy in which the typical firm is a one-owner, one-product, one-plant enterprise. Except for brief analyses of oligopoly, rarely is the economics of corporate organization handled meaningfully in basic business and economics texts. Unfortunately, these publications are ordinarily the primary sources which leave a lasting impression on many of the nation's citizens. Some authors mention lobbying by trade associations, pressuring of legislators to seek import quotas, tariffs, or other special privileges, or working with governmental agencies to secure control over entry into certain markets. However, there are few treatments of the historical development of specific grants of privilege, or the internal dynamics and external symbiosis in large industrial corporations.

It is recognized that American capitalism is difficult to define, describe, and explain. Rather than speak of "modern American capitalism" perhaps a neutral term, such as "the American economic system," ought to be used to minimize any definitional concerns? Yet, there are far too many references to the operations of "American capitalism" in library holdings than to seek an Orwellian "right-think" rephrasing or adopt the

1

book-burning tactics of *Fahrenheit 451*. Indeed, sufficient materials are housed in existing archives to expose countless intricacies within America's contemporary economic system. Some of these sources are cited below in a brief review of literature.

Diverse Perceptions

Numerous attempts have been made in recent years to give modern American capitalism greater form and substance, to identify relevant functions, operations, and results, as it were. Some accounts are incomplete whereas others are rather accurate and comprehensive. On the positive side, five distinguished scholars of the American economy have captured the essence, albeit in different ways, of the pith and ken of American capitalism. Their insights describe the private sector of our economic system as a complex of organizations in which, alternatively, the following institutions and motivations are predominant: the competitive market; a well organized, protective industrial system; an urgency for amassing and controlling wealth; economic coordination by the managerial corporation; and a post-industrial society with the corporation as a social institution. These works serve as connecting links for contrasting views, each of which identifies key institutions of modern American capitalism, especially the market, the corporation, and the State.

More than a generation ago, Milton Friedman, dean of 19th century classical liberalism in economics, sketched how market forces of supply and demand, competition, and political and economic freedoms cause the American economy to function most effectively. These conditions were established in his venerable tract, *Capitalism & Freedom*,[1] in addition to magazine columns,[2] speeches, and an educational series for television. Friedman consistently argues that governmental intrusions into the market ultimately work against private well-being. By pursuing one's own self-interest within a policy of laissez faire, he contends that efficiency and justice will necessarily result. Although the existence of a government-flavored political economy is recognized, he expects it to be minimized.

The presence of a political economy is not only recognized but accepted in the Galbraithian trilogy,[3] a bold expose of an intractable nexus between State and market. John Kenneth Galbraith identifies goals, activities, and effects of the practice of capitalism in America, especially of fundamental dichotomies among oligopolistic blocs, the public and private sectors, and large and small business organizations. These contradictions in American capitalism have created checks and balances which allow a system of large enterprises and public agencies to operate effectively. At the same time, prime market forces tend to be obviated, despite the development of disparities between basic sectors of the economy and among members of the citizenry.

Written from a philosophical standpoint, Robert L. Heilbroner's *The Nature and Logic of Capitalism*[4] is an abstract inquiry into how and why the American economy functions as it does. Whereas Galbraith focuses on broad operational tactics and strategies of large-size business firms, Heilbroner intellectualizes the institutional arrangements operating behind the scenes. These interconnections irreversibly shape the position of the State, the role of the citizen, and the way that business absorbs society. Capitalism in the United States is a product of a unique American culture which has created a system of class domination. Those subscribing to capitalist values have become obsessed with using power to acquire and accumulate wealth. This quest has become a relentless, self-reinforcing mechanism.

Since the 1940s, Peter Drucker has written about management theory, the corporation, and the role of government in fostering free enterprise.[5] For Drucker, the American economy is an integrated system of power centers. The large industrial corporation is the dominant social institution engaged in a process of "governing" which affects all members of society. Yet, big business need not be feared if its power to govern is legitimized through shared responsibilities between labor and management. Indeed, the union has a vital role in the "political duality" of industrial enterprise. To achieve all these goals, government must allow corporations the flexibility to pursue their managerial decision making.

As a social theorist, Daniel Bell believes that trends within industrial capitalism portend vast changes in American social institutions. In *The Coming of Post-Industrial Society*[6] and *The Cultural Contradictions of Capitalism*[7] he suggests that technology and modernization are polarizing American attitudes and beliefs: rationality and efficiency versus feeling for self-fulfillment; rural versus urban values; bourgeois versus adversary cultures. Tensions exist between a cult of efficiency (wrought by large corporations) and social needs (wrought by the impersonality and bureaucracy). A basic contradiction is that American capitalism spawned a work ethic which created economic security for some but only rising expectations for others. A decline in a willingness to work hard and make demands on oneself suggests that those expectations will not be realized. However, Bell suggests that the corporation is in the process of being subordinated to social responsibilities, and could become a primary mechanism for achieving social justice.

Objectives of Political Economy and American Capitalism

Capitalism can be discussed meaningfully in terms of its historical experience.[8] The pages which follow are guided by a working hypothesis that one enlightening way to understand the essence of modern American capitalism lies in the field of comparative economic systems. The genesis of this approach is not new, but has been suggested in different ways by several authors. In *The Making of Economic Society*[9], Heilbroner describes economic systems historically in terms of three fundamental but broad organizational patterns which have been followed over the centuries: Tradition, Command, and Market. In his *Behind the Veil of Economics,*[10] Heilbroner warns that these categories do not contain separate or discrete epochs because one logically but slowly merges with another. They are not mutually exclusive because each exists historically on a continuum. In *The New Industrial State,*[11] Galbraith infers that American capitalism contains neo-mercantilist and neo-fascist tendencies. Other writers have made similar points about those models, as well as about socialist and feudalist features within the social fabric of the United States.[12]

Several objectives are pursued in this book. First, being an inquiry into the nature and meaning of political economy, an important goal is to examine modern American capitalism as a "mixed economy," as a blending of a market economy with a political economy. Next, American capitalism is contrasted with several popularly contemplated economic systems to note how the former might compare to each of the latter. A final goal is to observe the specific mixture of the market with political economy in several important sectors of modern American capitalism.

A BACKWARD GLANCE

The chief business of the American people is business.   [C. Coolidge, Speech to the American Society of Newspaper Editors, January 17, 1925.]

Business and capitalism are not synonymous; the former existed long before the latter began to play a role on the economic stage. Nevertheless, business and capitalism have much in common. The background of the contemporary economic system in the United States can be related to three streams of experience: the history of business enterprise, the rise of industrial capitalism, and the basic characteristics of traditional capitalism. These parts form a backdrop against which to widen the meaning of modern American capitalism.

Business History, Briefly

It is no joke that the word business refers essentially to a state of "busy-ness."[13] The crucial question is, however, "busy doing what?" A simple answer is that it relates to being busy engaging in economic activity. Yet, there are numerous ways by which economic activity might be organized, such as by military dictatorship, direction by religious authority, or planning by governmental officials. In everyday parlance, business refers to commercial, industrial, and professional dealings in which producing, buying, and selling are conducted for private monetary gain (usually called "profit"). Reflection on this point suggests that two needs logically follow from the quest for private gain: a standard for basing profit calculations and a way to measure any gain. Indeed, record-keeping and a monetary unit are naturally related to any system of "business."

In ancient times, most of the population was economically self-sufficient with only a few persons engaged in commerce. Then, economic activity for private gain "was confined largely to what would now be classified as finance and commerce as opposed to industry."[14] Some bazaars and small-size individual proprietors existed, and most trade and exchange was transacted through barter. Money came to be used by the Chinese; the Romans developed some banking; and the Babylonians had a basic system of bookkeeping. Nevertheless, money, credit, and transportation were in a primitive state then because technology was simple. Political instability also existed, especially after the fall of the Roman Empire. Life and property were often not safe, so trade was unable to thrive and survive.[15]

Trade was revived in the Middle Ages. Towns and manors settled within city walls. Hand fabrication in cottage industries was common, and this form of production evolved into specialization based on division of labor. The factory method and territorial expansion ultimately took place. Townspeople started producing and exchanging among themselves. Soon, commercial trade routes were established and caravans carried goods between towns. Markets were set up at which both locally made and imported goods were exchanged, not only by barter but with money. Eventually, production and trade by craftsmen, artisans, and family enterprises were transformed into extended processes in which workers were hired. From that evolved the merchant and craft guilds, the forerunners of factories and labor unions. Moreover, unique forms of individual cooperation gave rise to various types of "business" ownership. Finally, increasing specialization and advances in technology set the stage for the next act in the history of private interests carrying on economic activity for profit.[16]

Rise of Industrial Capitalism

Several key attributes of capitalism were present in ancient Egypt, Babylonia, Carthage, Greece, and Rome: private property, individual enterprise, money lending, and trade. However, the exercise of governmental powers under the Roman Empire in medieval Europe forestalled complete development of a business class.[17] When feudalism declined toward the end of the Middle Ages, a merchant class arose when towns grew, commerce expanded, and the use of money became widespread.

With the advent of the industrial revolution in mid-18th century England, business activity was extended to mechanized plants--the factory method--especially for making textiles. Large amounts of money were needed to acquire equipment. In addition, transportation facilities--from vessels and vehicles to sea lanes and roads--had to be developed, requiring further infusions of capital. Indeed, the former basic indicator of "business"--the use of private property for production and sale for profit--had been augmented by the use of machines and hired workers. Industrial capitalism had arrived!

Capitalism has passed through several stages in the history of its development.[18] First, there were the craftsmen, artisans, and small storekeepers who had some rudimentary equipment, but were largely family enterprises with little or no hired labor. After that came the merchant capitalists: importers, exporters, wholesalers, retailers, and ship owners. About this time, insurance, banking, and money lending became important, and businessmen began to pool their wealth to form joint stock companies (a forerunner of the corporation).

Next, the early industrial capitalist entered, using machine techniques and producing for inventory rather than to fill special orders. Specialization and division of labor continued to increase. This development allowed larger-scale production and distribution than before, with additional emphasis on controlling costs, setting prices, training workers, expanding markets, and securing profits. Indeed, what later became the primary functional areas of modern business were born during that era.

Traditional Beliefs About Capitalism

Alternative views and definitions of capitalism are not scarce. Most introductory economics and business textbooks contain a few paragraphs which list features, requirements, characteristics, elements, or objectives.[19] Written accounts generally stress a limited number of traits of capitalism including an explanation of the role of each: private property, personal incentives, freedom of choice, a profit motive, competitive markets, and to some extent, laissez faire. A bit of caution must be exercised, however, whenever enumerating the basic attributes of capitalism. Some requirements are minimum, whereas others are merely corollaries of essential characteristics.

Obvious duplication occurs when items which naturally flow from minimum and inescapable features are added, such as the market, a price system, individualism, consumer sovereignty, free enterprise, private enterprise, and a right to make personal decisions. This tendency is also compounded by expanding freedom of choice to encompass freedom to use property, to produce, purchase, and consume goods, to pursue an occupation, to work at any job offered, and to retain whatever is earned. Other co-incidental features may be added, such as ability to make binding contracts, the use of capital equipment, and inheritance (especially of real property). Finally, technology and democracy have also been cited as elements of capitalism. However, the institutions of privately owned property and multi-faceted individual economic choice in free markets are probably the most fundamental qualities.

Despite a tendency to increase the number of features describing capitalism, one item frequently listed but not expanded or extended is the role of government. The concept of a "mixed" economy is usually shortchanged, although a few authors may acknowledge that: "all organizations, public and private, are directly or indirectly affected by statutory law, government policies, public opinion, organized labor and a host of other forces."[20] While discussing laissez faire some explanations imply that government should have no role (or at most, a minimum role) in business affairs, that the State ought not interfere with private decision making under capitalism, and that, above all, the State must not "confiscate" what private business produces.

Several crucial questions must be asked at this point. What are the sources and mechanisms for establishing market-exchange rules, enforcing contracts, protecting property, insuring freedom of choice, building fairness into the market-and-price system, assuring the right to compete, and hearing and redressing violations on these matters? Some governmental entity, hopefully democratically elected and administered, would presumably be an appropriate body for achieving the aforementioned goals. Furthermore, how are these tasks to be supported if not by taxation coordinated by some level of government? Obviously, there is more to capitalism than the minimal State implied by laissez faire when the relation between business and government is contemplated. As will be noted, the role of the State in fostering, subsidizing, and protecting business, often at its own request, somehow obviates the naive convention that government has a minor role in capitalism!

THE VIEW AHEAD

[T]he more complicated industrial production became, the more
numerous were the elements of industry the supply of which had to
be safeguarded. [K. Polanyi, *The Great Transformation*, Boston:
Beacon, 1962, p.75.]

The presentation of materials falls logically into three parts. Part One
covers some preliminary considerations supporting the main analysis. Part
Two focuses on historical economic systems which might be compared or
contrasted with American capitalism. Part Three features applications of
political economy to four specific sectors of the American economy. A final
chapter summarizes and concludes the discussion of political economy and
modern American capitalism.

Part One

Whereas the present chapter introduces the subject matter of this book
by overview, the three chapters of Part One develop several definitions and
descriptions which lay a foundation for political economy and modern
American capitalism.

Any form of economic organization, such as mercantilism or fascism or
capitalism, is ostensibly a system of *political economy*, a term enjoying much
popularity in recent years among social scientists. Chapter 2 reviews various
usages of this concept by economists of various methodological persuasions.

An important ingredient of political economy is *power*. This topic has
of late been the subject of numerous articles and books by economists.
Chapter 3 suggests that power is more pervasive and insidious than sheer
force or violence, and has become an integral part of business and economic
life in the American economic system.

A primary repository of power in systems of political economy, especially
capitalism, is the corporate form of organization. The *legitimacy* of this type
of business ownership has been challenged and questioned on moral
grounds. Toward this end, Chapter 4 provides a philosophical inquiry into
the role of the corporation in modern American capitalism.

Part Two

Chapter 5 initiates an examination of several so-called economic
systems--perhaps systems of political economy--which existed during the last
thousand years in parts of Europe, Asia, and Africa, and in America. The
first, a discussion of *feudalism*, provides a point of departure for
understanding the evolution of American capitalism.

Continuing an investigation into systems, Chapter 6 treats *mercantilism*, the mechanism for political economy which developed from feudalism. At this point certain comparisons begin to appear for appraising the historical backdrop of American capitalism.

The analysis heats up in Chapter 7, on *fascism*, where parallels become even more bold than in the previous chapter. Seeds of suspicion planted here may lead readers to draw some vexing conclusions about modern American capitalism!

Another system of political economy, *socialism*, is discussed in Chapter 8. Despite fears and warnings about increasing expenditures on various governmental programs in the United States, it is concluded that American capitalism is surely not becoming socialistic.

Chapter 9 presents an analysis of how political economy operates in *modern American capitalism*. The discussion focuses on the activities of voluntary associations and their efforts to influence legislation and governmental agencies to grant special privileges which design authority and assign power.

Part Three

The final part of the book concentrates on four specific sectors of American capitalism in which political economy is highly prominent. Chapter 10 describes the *military-industrial complex*, a coalition within the American economy comprised of a broad spectrum of diverse market participants. Members seek public support and then interact with branches of government to improve their economic position with taxpayer funding.

Chapter 11 appraises the political economy of two components of the *transportation* sector: for rails, protective entry and exit legislation for more than a century has not improved the status of this industry; and for international air carriage, a half-century policy of entry control and sanctioning price fixing ended in deregulation in an industry which has remained oligopolistic.

Technological advances in modern American capitalism have led firms in the industrial sector to need well-trained technicians, scientists, and managers. Chapter 12 discusses *higher education* in terms of how colleges and universities respond to the political economy.

Chapter 13, on *medical care*, discusses how physicians' groups sought authority from the State and obtained passage of power-generating legislation to control the production and distribution of medical care. The success of these political efforts is not unrelated to America's second-rate overall health status.

Finally, Chapter 14 presents a brief summary and conclusion of *impressions* gotten from previous chapters as well as some implications for the future of modern American capitalism.

CONCLUDING REMARKS

[I]t is one thing to reach the logical conclusion that institutional atavisms are the seat of all our trouble and quite another to determine methodologically what to do about it. [C. E. Ayres, *The Theory of Economic Progress*, New York: Schocken, 1962, p. 251.]

This overview of *Political Economy and American Capitalism* suggests that insight might be gained into the economic culture of the United States by noting similarities to institutional arrangements from the past, and by observing specific instances of how political economy is practiced in certain industries and markets.

The pages which follow constitute a heroic attempt to add to the already existing, often excellent literature on the subject of American capitalism. The chapters paint a limited but hopefully accurate picture of the American economic landscape which has not always been viewed in the perspective and colors applied here. Most of the presentation is analytically descriptive, without conventional analysis of statistical models, empirical tests of hypotheses, or tabulations of data from questionnaires or other primary sources. Instead, the narrative is both a collage and a montage: it synthesizes existing views, along with some subjective interpretations, while at the same time guiding the reader toward certain warranted conclusions.

Whereas the following analysis is both positive and normative, it does not reach policy conclusions, i.e., what to do about whatever might be wrong with modern American capitalism. It is predominantly positive, in the sense of describing some of the attributes of political economy in the American business system. Yet, a normative flavor emerges, as for example, when one considers the selection of phenomena which are reported in various chapters. There are obviously other ideas of what capitalism is supposedly about. Some of them have already been noted in the brief review of literature above, and numerous other views can be found in books, journal articles, pamphlets, and speeches available in libraries across the nation.

It will soon be apparent that several topics are neglected which might have been included: the growth of conglomerate and multinational corporations; direct foreign investment abroad and the American policy of subtle imperialism; protected-class discrimination, poverty, and problems of income distribution; the environment, pollution, conservation, and resource depletion; the sizes of the public debt and of the deficit in the international balance of trade; inner-city blight and the need for continued urban renewal; low productivity, worker participation in management decisions, and the decline of organized labor; the savings and loan crisis and the unpaid debt (and even interest on that debt) of developing nations south of our borders. These important topics, and others, must be left for later analysis.

Hopefully, the narrative which follows will be successful in registering the intended messages. The American system of concentrated industrial capitalism, which evolved out of feudalism and mercantilism and still contains some remnants of both, may be currently evolving into a unique form of state capitalism, sometimes described by the term "fascism." However, the economy is probably not moving toward socialism, at least not in the immediate future. Moreover, modern American capitalism is not merely a market economy but is a complicated mixture of the market with the political economy, not by an authoritarian government acting on its own but one which responds to large-scale, well organized groups by supporting their self-interested requests with state-agency action. As will be noted, these interrelations can be observed in many industries and markets in modern American capitalism.

NOTES

1.   M. Friedman, *Capitalism and Freedom*, Chicago: Phoenix, 1962.

2.   Many of his *Newsweek* magazine columns are reprinted in M. Friedman, *An Economist's Protest*, Glenridge: Horton, 1972.

3.   Whereas the composition of the list may be disputed, the "Galbraithian Trilogy" as discussed here consists of: (1) J. K. Galbraith, *American Capitalism*, Boston: Houghton Mifflin, 1952; (2) J. K. Galbraith, *The Affluent Society*, Boston: Houghton Mifflin, 1958; and (3) J. K. Galbraith, *The New Industrial State*, Boston: Houghton Mifflin, 1967. A fourth book, J. K. Galbraith, *Economics and the Public Purpose*, Boston: Houghton Mifflin, 1973, constitutes an elaboration and extension of ideas presented in the three earlier books.

4.   R. L. Heilbroner, *The Nature and Logic of Capitalism*, New York: Norton, 1985.

5.   P. F. Drucker has written many books and articles about managerial capitalism. Three important ones are: (1) P. F. Drucker, *Concept of the Corporation*, New York: John Day, 1946; (2) P. F. Drucker, *The New Society*, New York: Harper & Row, 1949; and (3) P. F. Drucker, *Technology, Management and Society*, New York: Harper & Row, 1958.

6.   D. Bell, *The Coming of Post-Industrial Society*, New York: Basic, 1973.

7.   D. Bell, *The Cultural Contradictions of Capitalism*, New York: Basic, 1976.

8.   J. A. Schumpeter, *History of Economic Analysis*, New York: Oxford, 1954, pp. 12-23 and 33-40.

9.   R. L. Heilbroner, *The Making of Economic Society*, Englewood Cliffs: Prentice-Hall, 1962.

10.   R. L. Heilbroner, *Behind the Veil of Economics*, New York: Norton, 1988.

11.   Galbraith, *The New Industrial State, op.cit.*

12.   As examples, see: (1) J. Burnham, *The Managerial Revolution*, New York: John Day, 1941; and (2) M. D. Reagan, *The Managed Economy*, New York: Oxford, 1963.

13. D. M. Keezer, "Business," in E. Seligman and A. Johnson, *Encyclopedia of the Social Sciences*, Vol. 3, New York: Macmillan, 1968, p. 81.

14. *Ibid.*, p. 82.

15. These events, and others, are reported in R. Cameron, *A Concise Economic History of the World*, New York: Oxford, 1989.

16. C. M. Hicks, *Introduction to Business*, New York: Johnsen, 1961, pp. 15-18.

17. H. Plotkin, "Capitalism," *Academic Americana Encyclopedia*, Vol. 2, Danbury: Grolier, 1989, p. 124.

18. N. S. B. Gras, *Business and Capitalism*, New York: Kelley, 1971, pp. 175-90.

19. As examples, see: (1) K. Davis, *The Challenge of Business*, New York: McGraw-Hill, 1975, pp. 25-36; (2) J. B. Poe, *An Introduction to the American Business Enterprise*, Homewood: Irwin, 1972, pp. 9-16; and (3) T. J. Sielaff and J. W. Aberle, *Introduction to Business*, Belmont: Wadsworth, 1969, pp. 9-14.

20. W. Rudelius, W. B. Erickson, and W. J. Bakula, Jr., *An Introduction to Contemporary Business*, New York: Harcourt Brace Jovanovich, 1973, p. 29.

2   POLITICAL ECONOMY

INTRODUCTION

The very term 'political economy' is fraught with ambiguity."[R. Gilpin, *The Political Economy of International Relations*, Princeton: Princeton University Press, 1987, p. 8.]

Political economy has been known for more than 50 years as the nineteenth century term for what was called "economics" during most of the twentieth century. Lately, the term political economy has portrayed situations with implications which are not altogether consistent with one another. A title search of articles and texts published over the past several years yields hundreds proclaiming "the political economy of" diverse subjects. Scholars have traced the origin of the term and changes in its meaning and orientation. Given the recent attention paid to political economy, one wonders whether anything new can be added to the subject. Yet, political economy is not even listed separately by the American Economic Association, and the *International Encyclopedia of Social Science* does not contain an entry for the term. Except for brief descriptions found in business and economics dictionaries, few comprehensive definitions of political economy exist. Two interrelated issues continue to haunt economics: Given the widespread use of the term, does political economy stand on equal footing with other schools of economic thought as a distinguishable area of inquiry?

What is the meaning of political economy? Which topics are included? Does it embody a separate theoretical structure with a distinct methodology? Does it have a paradigm? Is it normative or positive? Reductionist or holist? Compatible with orthodox economics? Where does it stand, ideologically, left or right? How does it relate to various economic systems? This chapter considers such questions by examining different uses of that venerable term, political economy.

ECONOMICS AND POLITICAL ECONOMY

Political Economy [is] the interrelationship between the practical
aspects of political action and the pure theory of economics."[D.
Pearce, *The Dictionary of Modern Economics*, Cambridge: MIT Press,
1981, p. 336.]

Until recently, economists lived in a two-part world. Political economy
was referred to as the old name for what was being called "economics" and
meant scientific economic--logical positivist, Neoclassical analysis. Political
economy often implied something less rigorous with little or no empirical
testing of hypotheses using quantitative data. Such inquiries were regarded
as descriptive presentations of historical background on the development of
institutional arrangements, of how government interfaces with the market
system, or of what the writer thought about economic problems and the
ideas of other economists toward those problems. It has been claimed that
economics possesses a positive features but *political economy* exhibits
normative tendencies.

As a discipline, the profession has vacillated between using the terms
economics and political economy for some time. Political economy "is
derived from the Greek *polis*, meaning a city as a political unit, and
oikonomia, denoting the management of a household."[1] It can also mean
estate management and public administration, "a usage that maintained some
continuity for more than two thousand years before the discipline became
known as political economy."[2] For the latter concept, "Andreades traced
[it]. . .to . . . Montchretien's Traite de l'oeconomie politique published in
1615."[3] Groenewegen, however, reports "prior use in Mayerne-Turquet" in
1611 and later use by Petty in England in 1691.[4] However, "Sir James
Steuart [was] first . . . to put 'political economy' into the title of a book" in
1767.[5] These uses predated Adam Smith, the recognized father of political
economy, even though he did not use those words in the title of his
celebrated book. Alfred Marshall adopted the term "economics" rather than
political economy, considering the former term to be somewhat broader than
the latter. Some economists now contend that political economy is the more
inclusive term.

For J. Schumpeter, political economy is "the analysis of the behavior of
individual firms . . . [vis-a-vis] . . . the behavior of governments."[6] Likewise,
R. Gilpin states that "without both state and market there could be no
political economy."[7] He uses "the term ". . . to indicate a set of questions
to be examined by means of an eclectic mixture of analytic methods and
theoretical perspectives."[8] D. Fusfeld contends that "political economy [is]
the analysis of economic power, its sources, limits, and uses."[9] E. Phelps
defines political economy as "the study of the effects of various mechanisms,
and systems of mechanisms, used . . . by societies to operate their social
economy."[10] Business and economic dictionaries also emphasize the

connections among government, business, and the economy to define political economy.[11]

In general, political economy examines the interface of State and market. It investigates the possession of power by large organizations such as corporations, the military, trade associations, and labor unions in terms of who was responsible for consolidating that power, and when, how, and why it was created and transmitted. Political economy traces the historical development of institutional arrangements which assign property rights, allocate resources, and distribute income, then perpetuate contradictions and class conflicts. Specific variations of political economy, however, may emphasize various aspects in different ways.

The State is necessarily involved in any type of market economy. Because a market is based on private property and voluntary exchange for private gain, at a minimum the State must protect these arrangements if the market is to continue to function. In the extreme, the State may foster, promote, control, and even perform economic activity. Political economy therefore describes the degree of connection between State and market. The question is whether the relation is direct or indirect, and active or passive. Debates about political economy involve the extent of State influences on markets. These debates have ideological overtones because matters of control and freedom--intervention versus laissez faire--inevitably arise. Indeed, feudalism, mercantilism, fascism, capitalism, socialism, and communism can each be described as a system of political economy.

Political economy is not incompatible with orthodox economics but complements rather than substitutes for it. To illustrate, whereas Neoclassical economics might estimate investor preference functions for corporate securities, political economy would trace the evolution of the legal duty which leads corporate officers to maximize net stockholder wealth. Obviously, both tasks are necessary in order to understand fully the market for stocks and bonds.

TYPES OF POLITICAL ECONOMY

For some writers, 'political economy' seems to be a formal label applicable to any and all studies dealing with aspects of public policy. [M. Staniland, *What Is Political Economy?*, New Haven: Yale University Press, 1985, p. 2.]

Political economy has been used recently by a growing number of economists to label their analyses, but not everyone uses it the same way. R. D. G. Black reports at least seven variations.[12] B. Frey presents four[13] and D. Greenwald lists five.[14] L. Wade[15] and R. Gilpin[16] both describe three "paradigms" and "ideologies," respectively. In this chapter, seven concepts of political economy are discussed. Economists who are Classical, Marxian, Neoclassical, Institutional, Post-Keynesian, Public Choice, and Radical each profess their scholarship to constitute political economy.

A common set of criteria characterizes many professing political economy: A concern for the social, political, and economic connections between State and market, especially the historical development of organized power mechanisms and institutional arrangements that create and perpetuate class differences in income distribution and other relations needing policy intervention in order to restructure economic affairs.

Classical Political Economy

"classical political economy . . .stressed individualism, free trade, self-interest, and the security of property." [P. Newman, *The Development of Economic Thought*, Englewood Cliffs: Prentice-Hall, 1952, p. 101.]

That political economy is the old name for economics usually means Classical Economics. Political economy of the eighteenth and nineteenth centuries was based on natural law philosophy and Newtonian mechanics. Economic affairs were said to be governed by immutable laws of nature, and the task of economists was to determine how these laws affected economic activity and influenced economic policy. Classical political economists established several economic laws to explain that natural-law forces inevitably resulted in equilibria which should not be altered by human intervention. Only a policy of individual liberty and free competition, interacting with private property and self-interest, led to a rational social order.[17] Classical Political Economy was prominent during the mercantilist era. "Political" as an adjective referred to the active role that government played in private economic affairs. Adam Smith called it an interference, but its role was also civil. One student of the era points out that "classical economists attacked the dominant social classes of the time" and "opposed the contemporary wars in which their countries were engaged."[18] Moreover, most Classical economists "favored some legislation aimed at the abuses of industrialism and urbanism."[19]

Marxian Political Economy

"Any bibliography of political economy reveals . . . at least half . . . using the term as synonymous with Marxism." [M. Staniland, *What Is Political Economy?* New Haven: Yale University Press, 1985, p. 2.]

Marx reportedly ". . . always used the term political economy . . . and his followers have never departed from that usage."[20] For O. Lange, "political economy or social economy [is] the study of the social laws governing the production and distribution of the material means of satisfying human needs."[21] In Lenin's view, it deals "with the social relations between people in production."[22] Analyses based on Marxian Political Economy start broadly (with population), focus on its components (such as social classes), examine the social relations among them (such as exchange value), and ultimately move to higher levels of abstraction (such as the state and its interrelations with the world economy).[23] Indeed, "Marxists have always claimed that comprehensiveness--the connection of all kinds of . . . distinct social institutions--is a special merit of their approach."[24]

There are two strands of Marxian political economy: evolutionary and revolutionary; L. Wade believes that there are several.[25] R. Heilbroner identifies "four essential elements in the overall corpus of Marxist writings": (1) a dialectical approach to conflict and class struggles having no harmony and no equilibrium; (2) a materialist approach to the history of the class struggle over the economic surplus; (3) a general view of capitalist development; and (4) a normative commitment to socialism.[26]

Neoclassical Political Economy

"a number of scholars . . . have defined political economy as the application of the methodology of . . . the so-called rational actor model, to all types of human behavior." [R. Gilpin, *The Political Economy of International Relations*, Princeton: Princeton University Press, 1987, p. 8.]

Although two branches have emerged--orthodox economics (meaning Neoclassical analysis) and political economy (meaning historical and descriptive presentations)--there is a lingering tendency for some Neoclassical economists to regard their work as political economy. In the late 1950s the Public Choice view emerged, but prior to that Neoclassical Political Economy existed primarily within the Chicago School. This view persists. To one of its students the Chicago School (F. Knight, H. Simons, *et al.*) is Neoclassical[27] and a leading member ostensibly admits it.[28] Neoclassical Political Economy via the Chicago School (G. Stigler, M. Friedman, *et al.*) focuses on the minimum relation between state and market--namely, that government ought to insure safety, freedom, defense, and property, but reduce the concentration of power. The older Chicago School was quite policy oriented in its desire to forge and recast competitive institutions. The newer Chicago School not only focuses on public policy, but is also quite empirically based (reflecting a philosophical posture tied to logical positivism). A recent view is that "a broader research . . . called neoclassical political economy . . . involves the analysis of individuals' attempts to escape the invisible hand of the market and to redirect policy proposals for their own advantage."[29]

Institutional Political Economy

"institutional economists generally are . . . political economists." [T. Hutchison, *A Review of Economic Doctrines*, Oxford: Clarendon, 1953, p. 3.]

Institutional economics involves "areas in which political and sociological elements are intimately intertwined with strictly economic ones" such as organized groups and "the economic behavior of the state."[30]   John R. Commons recognizes that "political economy is not merely a matter of governance; it is . . .. a question of power, of dominance and subservience in the determination and legitimization of goals, rules, and policies."[31] Adolphe Lowe believes that institutional economics cum political economy must be policy oriented to "discover what 'premises', . . . behavioral forces, . . . technological constraints, [and] . . . institutions--would be necessary to attain targets or goals."[32]

Institutionalists contend that large enterprises dominate economic activity[33] and see important social problems which must be solved by political means. They have reacted against the Classical-Neoclassical axis for nearly a century for using Newtonian static equilibrium as a standard for analysis.   Being concerned with how institutions adjust to changes in technology, Institutional economists question how and why technology moved in certain directions, under whose control, and for the benefit of whom. Examining how institutional adjustment occurs involves determining if the presence of power hampers the process. To accelerate institutional adjustment to enhance social welfare, institutionalists have been pragmatic in proposing imaginative public policy measures to reallocate resources and redistribute income.

Post-Keynesian Political Economy

"Post-Keynesian economics [is] political economy according to the Cambridge-in-the East." [E. Malizia, *Review of Radical Political Economy*, Winter, 1975, p. 91.]

Post-Keynesian economics began shortly after Keynes published the *General Theory*, and contains "the work of a heterogeneous group of economists . . ."[34] Three "strands" of Post-Keynesian thought have been identified: from followers of Marx, Marshall, and Keynes.[35] These roots have given rise to diverse terms such as "Post-Keynesian Institutionalism,"[36] "The Kaleckian/Post-Keynesian Model,"[37] and "The Post-Keynesian/Marxian Approach."[38] Most economists calling themselves Post-Keynesians share a common "dislike for mainstream neoclassical theory" and seek to develop "coherent alternative approaches to economic analysis."[39] Post-Keynesians strive to introduce time into economic analysis and to link Keynes's short-run analysis "to long-period theory of Classical economics."[40] Post-Keynesians want to reconstruct economic analysis by combining Classical economics with a "theory of effective demand in a monetary economy."[41] Their public policy focuses on means to monitor inflation, redistribute income, and stabilize production costs by establishing wage and price controls."[42]

Public Choice as Political Economy

"Public choice . . . sometimes . . . is just called 'political economy' in the United States." [B. Frey, *Modern Political Economy*, New York: Wiley, 1978, p. 66.]

Public (or Collective, or Social) Choice emerged as an area of economics in the late 1950s, and studies governmental decisions for raising and spending public funds. Public Choice economists study non-market decisions by applying microeconomics to the political process, and draw heavily from public finance, welfare economics, game theory, and econometrics.[43] Neoclassical optimization is central to Public Choice Political Economy. Human beings are assumed to be "rational utility maximizers in all their behavioral capacities."[44] The "voter is thought of as a customer and the politician as a businessman-entrepreneur. Voters use political institutions to shop . . . for publicly supplied services [and] politicians seek to maximize their own utilities."[45] Yet, "political institutions are highly imperfect reflectors of preferences, . . . [government] is a monopolistic supplier, [and its] agencies do not have incentives to minimize costs."[46] Public Choice scholars believe that social welfare would be improved if many governmental activities were contracted to private companies.

Radical Political Economy

"The New Left, or . . . 'Radical Economics', is the modern variant of Marxist political economy . . ." [B. Frey, *Modern Political Economy*, New York: Wiley, 1978, p. 41.]

Radical Political Economy is a product of "the student uprising of the late 1960s."[47] Views of radical political economy are found in the editorial policy of *The Review of Radical Political Economics* (RRPE) and writings of the Union for Radical Political Economy (URPE). Although URPE members exhibit "a full range of positions"[48]--some are Marxist and some are Libertarian--their "basic common concerns . . . are inequality and imperialism."[49] They share in common a distrust of orthodox economics, and many want to restructure American capitalism through a transition to market socialism.[50] Exhibiting a historical "pro working class perspective," they are concerned about the struggle of employees against their employers.[51] Radical political economists would use the State to eliminate such unacceptable capitalist practices as monopoly power, discrimination, and environmental ruin by freeing the State from its capture by the ruling class.[52]

SCIENTIFIC DIMENSIONS OF POLITICAL ECONOMY

I know not when we shall have a perfect system of statistics, . . . it is the only . . . obstacle in the way of making Political Economy an exact science. [W. Jevons, *The Theory of Political Economy*, London: Macmillan, 1871, p. 14.]

Questions arise as to the scientific character of political economy, of whether it presents a cohesive theoretical structure with a distinct methodology, and whether it constitutes a Kuhnian paradigm. Determining if political economy is normative or positive, analytical or descriptive, reductionist or holist, and left or right are also important topics for scientific inquiry. These questions relate to political economy broadly rather than to examining any of its specific variations.

Preliminary Considerations

. . . political economy [is an] . . . exposition of a comprehensive set of economic policies that its author advocates on the strength of certain unifying (normative) principles. [J. Schumpeter, *History of Economic Analysis*, New York: Oxford University Press, 1954, p. 38.]

If positive means establishing what is and normative what ought to be, political economy is both positive and normative. Most scholars of political economy, regardless of allegiance, are concerned with the historical background of how certain economic relations arose and with their present impact. Followers of political economy often call for specific courses of action to alter the impact of certain social problems. Political economy has tended to be normative, especially when revelations of the way power positions were created, continue to function, and burden certain members of society shock one's conscience into demanding corrective action.

Most scholars subscribing to political economy affirm democratic principles; some, however, are politically conservative whereas others are liberal. Indeed, political economy is the property of neither the left nor the right, and policies across the ideological spectrum have been identified by those who profess political economy.

Being analytical means to break down into constituent parts to discover their interaction. Being descriptive means to define, portray, and explain the existence and structure of occurrences. On these grounds, political economy is both descriptive and analytical. In their zeal to focus on the historical background of problems, scholars of political economy strive to describe the evolution and status of events. Yet, by tracing cause-and-effect relations and their impact on human conditions, specific factors are isolated and ultimately related to the broad environment from which they arose.

The analytical-descriptive dichotomy parallels the concern over reductionism and holism. Logical empiricism, the scientific method, and Neoclassical economics have been criticized for portraying two reductionist tendencies: decomposing topics for analysis into small pieces to identify cause-and-effect relations, and creating broad categories into which dissimilar members are placed. During such processes, the investigator may either lose sight of important problems or mask them. To illustrate, Post-Keynesians reject aggregating consumers and firms into a separate categories. Marxians and Institutionalists prefer to approach matters of academic inquiry by considering all relevant social and political factors affecting a person's status in the economy. Political economy is both reductionist and holist, but some variations of it are probably more holist than others.

A Methodology?

> Methodology . . . does not mean technique or method. [It] refers
> . . . to the logic behind procedure. [H. Leibhafsky, *The Nature of
> Price Theory*, Homewood: Irwin, 1968, pp. 7-8.]

Does political economy constitute a separate school of economic thought (or "brand," as T. W. Hutchison prefers to say)[53] with a distinctive methodology? Each school of economic thought features its own set of unique assumptions and steps for pursuing knowledge. Methodology is often equated with some statistical procedure for evaluating empirical data or testing hypotheses, but more precisely refers to a body of rules and postulates followed by scholars in a discipline. To savor the essence of methodology, the investigator must engage in a conceptual and abstract inquiry. Indeed, methodology is essentially synonymous with "philosophical foundations."[54] Does political economy in its broad dimension contain an identifiable philosophical basis?

Usually, an enduring brand of economic thought has been based on some important philosophical movement of its time. Political economy is not tied to a specific school of philosophy, but is loosely related to different philosophical positions depending on the variation involved. Radicals identify with Marx, Public Choice with Neoclassical economics and logical positivism, Classical economists with Natural Law philosophy, and Institutionalists with evolutionary growth.

Technically, a theory is a set of cause-and-effect relationships, based on certain postulates and assumptions, which serves as a generalized explanation of a subject and has predictive ability. A theory does not necessarily have to be quantitative or stated in mathematical form. Political economy is based on theoretical and methodological qualities within each specific variation. Each of the seven subdivisions discussed is tied to a particular methodology having definite philosophical underpinnings of its own. As a result, there is a methodology of Classical Political Economy, of Marxian Political Economy, of Neoclassical Political Economy, and so on. One might speak of Classical theory, Neoclassical theory, or Marxian theory, but probably not of a theory of political economy. The theoretical qualities of specific variations of political economy can be identified, but until there is some agreement about assumptions, procedure, and world view, it will be difficult to specify the theoretical qualities of political economy in general.

A Kuhnian Paradigm?

A paradigm is what the members of a scientific community share, and conversely, a scientific community consists of men who share a paradigm. [T. Kuhn, *The Structure of Scientific Revolutions*, Chicago: University of Chicago Press, 1970, p. 176.]

In *The Structure of Scientific Revolutions*, T. Kuhn establishes two criteria for an achievement to be a paradigm: (1) "sufficiently unprecedented to attract an enduring group of adherents away from competing modes of scientific activity," and (2) "sufficiently open-ended to leave all sorts of problems for the redefined group of practitioners to resolve."[55] For Stigler, a paradigm contains a body of "analytical and empirical techniques . . . accepted by the dominant members of the science, . . . is open-ended and allows the continuous utilization of its apparatus to deal with an . . . unlimited number of unsolved problems. . ."[56] To Stanfield, a paradigm is "a world view, a set of implicit and explicit guides or examples defining the world and the questions and methods for analyzing the world."[57]

As a term, political economy is not unprecedented. It has been used for more than two centuries to describe a special type of relation between State and market. Present-day scholars of political economy share a common dissatisfaction with orthodox theory dating back to 1898.[58] Not all those who practice political economy react against Neoclassical Economics; but for those who do, reactions vary. Public Choice economists apply the Neoclassical model, giving a central role to subjective utility, whereas Post-Keynesians and Institutionalists seek to reformulate orthodox analysis.

Political economy has attracted a number of proponents, not necessarily to a common approach, but certainly to the term. Whether or not they will endure remains to be seen. Political economy is open-ended, and numerous socio-economic problems have been treated by its broad-based structure. Some problem areas are common to a number of scholars of political economy, but they are not necessarily new. Discrimination, poverty, and poor housing, as examples, have existed and been recognized for some time in most societies. To be a world view, political economy requires a sense of commonality among its proponents. Some common questions may exist, but no common method or procedure for handling them guide analysis and policy. Indeed, each variation of political economy has its own unique agenda for handling those social problems it believes to be most important.

Kuhn formulated three stages of paradigm development: Pre-paradigm, Normal Science, and Crisis. The current status of political economy may be either in Crisis or in Preparadigm. Neoclassical orthodoxy cum logical positivism has been Normal Science more than a half century. Crisis occurs when the prevailing paradigm--accepted as Normal Science--fails to be viable given social problems caused by technological change and institutional adjustment. Dissatisfaction with the state of economic analysis has been accelerating recently because orthodox economics has allegedly failed to provide policy choices for solving crucial problems. In response, alternatives are being proposed, many of them under the banner of political economy. The economics profession, however, has not yet rallied behind any one of these alternatives.

The Crisis stage may be ending so that Pre-Paradigm is in the process of emerging. In Pre-Paradigm, competing views vie to establish an acceptable way of identifying and handling problems. Economists who operate within a variation of political economy appear to be striving for adoption of their own branch by a majority of the profession. The common view, if any, around which the profession might coalesce is not yet known. When an agreed-upon procedure is accepted, the old Normal Science will be replaced by a new paradigm. The new Normal Science may be an existing mutation of the various political economy alternatives, a mixture of some (or all) of them, or something entirely different.

A Distinctive Field?

[With] political economy . . . an attempt is being made to overcome the narrowness of 'pure' economic theory and to accept the inseparability of economics and politics. [B. Frey, *Modern Political Economy*, New York: Wiley, 1978, p. 37.]

It is not yet possible to assert that political economy is a theory or separate school of economic thought with its own methodology which is capable of being called a Kuhnian paradigm. Specific variations of political economy, however, can be identified with a theoretical school having certain methodological features. But is political economy a field? A field is an area of academic specialization--a concentration of knowledge on a particular subject of study. The activity being studied may be approached narrowly or broadly, and treated historically, quantitatively, legally, or through the medium of a school of economic thought. To be a field, an area of academic inquiry requires some unification and agreement on appropriate topics to include (but not necessarily on ways for handling them). International trade is a field, and so are labor economics and regional economics. Microeconomics and macroeconomics undoubtedly qualify as fields. For each, there is substantial agreement as to composition, although one may be approached differently from another--different descriptive and analytical procedures, depending on whether the investigator is Neoclassical, Institutional, Marxian, and so on. Some observers contend that political economy takes a broad social science view whereas economics uses a narrow mathematical-statistical approach. Yet, political economy may involve collecting data, testing hypotheses, and expressing relations in quantitative form, and orthodox economics may treat social, political and other factors of human behavior in order to investigate cause-and-effect relations. Political economy may be in the process of becoming distinct, but general agreement on composition of topics has not yet occurred to establish it as a unified field.

CONCLUDING REMARKS

[P]olitical economy is an art--a somewhat opinionated art . . . with enough conviction or folly, a person may . . . write political economy. [E. Mishan, *What Political Economy Is All About*, London: Cambridge University Press, 1979, p. 14]

It matters little whether political economy is a school of thought with a distinct methodological approach, a Kuhnian paradigm, or even a separate field within economics. It is important that political economy is a concept which relates State and market, stresses a historical approach, and focuses on institutional mechanisms which distribute power. The economic systems out of which capitalism has emerged were all systems of political economy. In reality, political economy, broadly defined, is practiced within an economic system--the way that a nation is organized to answer basic economic questions which all societies must answer. Accordingly, political economy is studied by investigating the historical features of a nation's economic organization over time.

Political economy inquires into the way that political and economic power interact within a nation's institutional structure and how its institutions operate. Four basic economic systems--perhaps "politico-economic" systems, or systems of political economy--can be contrasted with capitalism--namely, feudalism, mercantilism, fascism, and socialism. Modern American capitalism can be treated as a system of political economy in terms of how its historical development and institutional arrangements relate to other situations of as well as to major sectors within the American economy. Important areas of economic activity--education, transportation, medical care, and military hardware--reflect how influence by the market on the State, and vice versa, facilitates and guides economic activity. Such power relations form a basis for political economy, as discussed in the next chapter.

NOTES

1.   P. A. S. Taylor, *A New Dictionary of Economics*, New York: Kelley, 1966, p. 218.

2.   S. T. Lowery, "Recent Literature on Ancient Greek Economic Thought," *Journal of Economic Literature*, March 1979, pp. 65-86.

3.   *Ibid.*, p. 65.

4.   P. Groenewegen, "Political Economy and Economics," in Eatwell, Milgate, and Newman, eds., *The New Palgrave: A Dictionary of Economics*, Vol. 3, London: Macmillan, 1987, pp. 904-07.

5.   *Ibid.*

6.   J. A. Schumpeter, *A History of Economic Analysis*, New York: Oxford University Press, 1954, p. 22.

7.   R. Gilpin, *The Political Economy of International Relations*, Princeton: Princeton University Press, 1987, p. 8.

8.   *Ibid.*, p. 9.

9.   D. R. Fusfeld, *The Age of the Economist*, Glenview: Scott Foresman 1982, p. 159.

10.   E. S. Phelps, *Political Economy An Introductory Text*, New York: Norton, 1985, p. 27.

11. C. Ammer and D. S. Ammer, *Dictionary of Business and Economics*, New York: Macmillan, 1977, p. 320; B. J. Horton, J. Ripley, and M. B. Schnapper, *Dictionary of Modern Economics*, Washington, D.C.: Public Affairs, 1948, p. 110; and H. S. Sloan and A. J. Zurcher, *A Dictionary of Economics*, New York: Barnes & Noble, 1957, p. 245.

12. R. D. C. Black, "The Present Position and Prospects of Political Economy," in A. W. Coats, *Methodological Controversy in Economics*, Greenwich: JAI Press, 1982, pp. 58-62.

13. B. S. Frey, *Modern Political Economy*, New York: Wiley, 1978, p. 35-102.

14. Groenewegen, *op. cit.*, pp. 905-06.

15. L. L. Wade, *Political Economy*, Boston: Kluwer-Nijhoff, 1983, p. 2-22.

16. Gilpin, *op. cit.*, pp. 25-64.

17. K. Diehl, "The Classical School," *Encyclopedia of the Social Sciences*, Vol. 5, New York: Macmillan, 1963, pp. 355-56.

18. T. Sowell, *Classical Economics Reconsidered*, Princeton: Princeton University Press, 1974, pp. 14 and 24.

19. *Ibid.*, p. 30.

20. Black, *op. cit.*, p. 58.

21. *Ibid.*

22. V. I. Lenin, *Collected Works*, Moscow: Foreign Languages Publishing, 1968, p. 62-3.

23. K. Marx, *A Contribution to the Critique of Political Economy*, New York: International Publishers, 1970, p. 205.

24. M. Staniland, *What is Political Economy?*, New Haven: Yale University Press, 1985, p. 149.

25. Wade, *op. cit.*, p. 121.

26. R. L. Heilbroner, *Marxism: For and Against*, New York: Norton, 1980, pp. 15-26.

27. W. G. Samuels, ed., *The Chicago School of Political Economy*, East Lansing: MSU Business Studies, 1976, p. 3.

28. G. Stigler, *op. cit.*, p. 70.

29. D. C. Colander, ed., *Neoclassical Political Economy*, Cambridge: Ballinger Publishing, 1984, p. 2.

30. R. L. Heilbroner, "On the Possibility of a Political Economics," *Journal of Economic Issues*, December 1970, p. 14.

31. J. Elliott, "Institutionalism as an Approach to Political Economy," *Journal of Economic Issues*, March 1978, p. 107.

32. A. Lowe, "Toward of Science of Political Economics," in R. L. Heilbroner, ed., *Economic Means and Social Ends*, Englewood Cliffs: Prentice-Hall, 1969.

33. Frey, *op. cit.*, p. 54.

34. G. C. Harcourt, "Post-Keynesian Economics," in Eatwell, Milgate, and Newman, eds., *The New Palgrave A Dictionary of Economics*, Vol. 3, London: Macmillan, 1987, p. 924.

35. *Ibid.*

36. C. K. Wilber and K. P. Jameson, *An Inquiry Into the Poverty of Economics*, South Bend: Notre Dame Press, 1983, pp. 145-6.

37. P. J. Reynolds, *Political Economy*, New York: St. Martin's, 1987, pp. 37-52.

38. P. M. Lichtenstein, *An Introduction to Post-Keynesian and Marxian Theories of Value and Price*, Armonk: Sharpe, 1983, pp. 11-24.

39. Harcourt, *op. cit.*, p. 924.

40. Black, *op. cit.*, p. 62.

41. J. A. Kegel, *The Reconstruction of Political Economy: An Introduction to Post-Keynesian Economics*, New York: Wiley, 1973, p. xv.

42. A. S. Eichner, ed., *A Guide to Post-Keynesian Economics*, White Plains: Sharpe, 1979, pp. 3-18; and P. Davidson, "Post-Keynesian Economics," in Greenwald, *op. cit.*, pp. 738-42.

43. Frey, *op. cit.*, p. 67.

44. D. Mueller, *Public Choice*, London: Cambridge University Press, 1979, p. 1.

45. G. Tullock, "Public Choice," in Eatwell, Milgate, and Newman, *op. cit.*, pp. 1041.

46. G. B. Christiansen, "James Buchanan and the Revival of Classical Political Economy," *Challenge*, March-April 1988, pp. 12-14.

47. Frey, *op. cit.*, p. 41.

48. "Introduction," *Review of Radical Political Economics*, Vol. 13, No. 1, p. iii.

49. D. Flaherty, "Radical Political Economy," in Eatwell, Milgate, and Newman, *op. cit.*, p. 36.

50. *The Review of Radical Political Economics*, *op. cit.*, p. viii.

51. A. Davis and R. England, "Radical Economics and the New Economists: A Comment," *The Review of Radical Political Economics*, Vol. 7, No. 1, Spring 1975, pp. 79-81.

52. H. J. Sherman, *Foundations of Radical Political Economy*, Armonk: Sharpe, 1987, pp. 5-7.

53. T. W. Hutchison, *Knowledge and Ignorance in Economics*, Chicago: University of Chicago Press, 1977, p. 6.

54. D. Fusfeld, "The Existentialist Economist: A Critique of the Conceptual Framework of Contemporary Economics," paper presented at Midwest Economics Association, Chicago, Illinois, April 8, 1978, p. 7.

55. T. S. Kuhn, *The Structure of Scientific Revolutions*, Chicago: University of Chicago Press, 1970, p. 10.

56. G. J. Stigler, "Does Economics Have a Useful Past?", *History of Political Economy*, Fall 1969, p. 223.

57. J. R. Stanfield, "Kuhnian Scientific Revolutions and the Keynesian Revolution," *Journal of Economic Issues*, March 1978, p. 106.

58. T. B. Veblen, "Why is Economics Not an Evolutionary Science?" *Quarterly Journal of Economics*, July 1898.

3

POWER

INTRODUCTION

[N]o one may be trusted with much power--no person, no faction, no nation, no religious body, no corporation, no labor union, . . . no organization of any kind. [H. Simons, *Economic Policy for a Free Society*, Chicago: University of Chicago Press, 1948, p. 241.]

Power has been a topic of concern for centuries. Several excellent evaluations have appeared recently which analyze power and inquire into problems created by its existence.[1] Whereas economists have identified the nature, sources, and extent of power, other social scientists have focused on its application and impact on people. What is power? How does it operate? Why is it important to political economy? This chapter considers how power characterizes political economy and manifests its presence in modern American capitalism.

Background

Neoclassical economic theory has generally neglected the possession and use of power. Except for brief excursions into topics such as monopoly, price discrimination, inelasticity, and product differentiation, value and distribution theory ordinarily focuses on the competitive market in which power plays a minor role. In a competitive market, compared to production and exchange under mercantilism and fascism, price and output are supposedly determined in a powerless arena. Whenever power is introduced into neoclassical economics, it has been considered as a departure from the normal path.

Basic Definition

Power has a number of synonyms. Its Latin root is from *potis*: in Old French, *poeir*; and in Middle English, *pouer*.[2] All refer to the ability to do something. A recent contemporary dictionary presents a dozen synonyms for power: ability, capacity, capability, strength, force, might, influence, effectiveness, aptitude, faculty, authority, and forcefulness.[3] Considering ordinary usages, a continuum from strong to weak indicates the extent that power-oriented terms characterize our language.

Ubiquity of Power

Why are social scientists interested in power? Is it because a feeling of helplessness occurs whenever an individual confronts business, government, and other organizations in society? Is it because people expect freedom to prevail over authority in a democratic society? Is it because power appears to reside in an increasing number of public and private agencies? Is it because conventional analyses of power fail to capture the essence of recent developments in the world?

For many persons, a resounding "yes" answers each question. Power is perceived to be all around us. Power exists in the domestic economy, on the international scene, in the political arena, in financial sectors, in the neighborhood, city hall, church, family, and countless other locations. Given the perceptions about the pervasiveness of power, it is no wonder that many citizens feel powerless, or even betrayed, by democratic, capitalist society.

POWER IN ACTION

Power, next to sex and love, is perhaps the oldest social phenomenon in human history. [A. Berle, Jr., *Power Without Property*, New York: Harcourt, Brace, and World, 1959, p. 77.]

Not only are there perceptions that power is sought, held, and exercised by an increasing number of groups, but there are misconceptions as to what constitutes power. Some observers overemphasize the requirements for power, while others underestimate its effect on members of society.

What Power Is Not

As noted, the word power is derived from the Old French, *poeir*, meaning "to be able." Power is related to ability and often defined as force and strength. Power, however, does not mean "required" or "must." In some ideological circles, the use of power has been subjected to extension of argument, as in this statement: "Power means that you can *make* someone do something that he/she does not want to do." Such a pronouncement can be met with skepticism in a democratic society, and the net effect is to relegate power to rare occurrences in the American economy. Whenever an extreme position is taken regarding power, an unsuspecting listener might be tricked into believing that power signifies the absolute ability to force someone to act (or not to act) in a certain manner, with resistance being impossible. As such, power becomes a drastic concept against which there is no alternative except to yield. In the limit, refusing to follow the dictates of the holder-user of power would result in immediate calamity. But it is hokum--bunk!--to define power as extreme force in order to try to deny the existence of power. Those who argue this way ought to be ashamed of themselves.

Neither the root nor definition of power is confined to necessity, requirement, or being compelled to do (or not to do) something. Possessing and using power need not require that the victim "has to" respond in a desired way. Indeed, the use and application of power does not always involve physical harm as an alternative, such as a gun to one's head or a knife at the throat. Power does not automatically imply that the victim will be deprived of life, liberty, or property, in either a violent or mild form, unless surrender occurs. In the application of power, the sanction to the victim for not yielding to the holder-user may be the *denial* of something desired which the victim does not now possess. The item being sought need not always a life-saving medicine with an exorbitant price tag.

It is empty rhetoric to assert, "Why the federal government has more power over you than General Motors. GM cannot make you do anything you do not want to do." Statements of this sort miss the point about the nature, exercise, and consequences of economic power. Instead, power must be considered in terms of the economics of market exchanges in which consumers and business firms regularly engage to facilitate commercial transactions.

Operational Power

What does it mean to say that a person or organization has power? In a practical sense, how is power used or applied against a victim? What can the holder-user of power "do" to a victim who fails to surrender to the application of power? To what extent is the victim compelled to do (or not do) something?

Power means the ability of its holder-user to maneuver a victim to an end sought by the former. In a practical, everyday setting the key factor in the power mechanism is a coordination of mutual desires. The desire of the holder-user of power and the desire of the victim need not be inconsistent or incompatible with each other. As it occurs for exchange either in the product or resource market, the status of buyer and seller must be considered as well as the nature of the product.

The seller wants to receive a payment, generally in money terms, from the buyer in exchange for a good or service which the seller is willing to surrender for a certain price. The buyer seeks the benefits from using a good or service, and is willing to part with some of his/her purchasing power in exchange for the item. It is expected that the seller seeks to receive as much as he/she can for the item, just as it is expected that the buyer seeks to pay as little as he/she can for the item. The prevailing party depends for his/her advantage on the relative scarcity of the item, its quality, and the urgency or strength of desire. Not every product is a life-saving or urgently needed service or commodity which the prospective buyer "must" have lest he/she (or some helpless baby) die a violent death.

Corporate consumer-goods advertising brings the existence of an item to the attention of prospective buyers and may stimulate their desire for it by them. In this way, preferences for the branded product of a promoting company are created vis-a-vis the products of other companies. The promoted brand may, due to quality, either technically or perceived, render that company's product a distinctive item in itself. If someone wants it, then he/she may be willing to pay the price to get it. If a price above the competitive level is paid, it is difficult to sustain that the prospective buyer "had to" buy the product "or else". Such a situation is not so much "power over someone" as it is the ability of the company to have manufactured a product possessing characteristics which convince a prospective buyer that a price higher than for alternative goods is justified when purchasing that particular brand. If a person is unwilling to pay the price (and there ordinarily *is* a choice in the matter), then he/she will be denied something which is desired. In these circumstances, life, liberty, and property are not being taken by force. Nevertheless, there is an element of power in the sense that if the price is paid, it can be claimed that the seller had some extent of "ability" to induce the sale by threatening to deprive the consumer of a certain satisfaction if the purchase is not made. But it was not by ultimatum, by force, or by requirement. The absence of compulsion does not deny the presence of power. Instead, power can be acquired, possessed, and exercised in subtle ways as well as by violent means.

SOCIAL SCIENCE CONCEPTS OF POWER

Power may be relatively concentrated or diffused; and the share of power . . . may be relatively great or small. [R. Dahl, *International Encyclopedia of Social Science*, Vol. 12, New York: Macmillan, 1968, p. 405.]

Just as an ordinary dictionary shows nearly a dozen synonyms for power, so do academic disciplines attach various meanings to the word. A difference is especially apparent between the way that power is treated in the natural and social sciences. In physics, for example, power is the rate at which work is done, and is expressed quantitatively as the first derivative of work with respect to time. In mathematics, a power takes the form of an exponent which alters the magnitude of a number; and in statistics, a power is the probability of rejecting the null hypothesis. In all three situations, a transformation of one thing into something else occurs in a positive, rather than a normative, way. Whenever power is contemplated in the social sciences change is involved, but value judgments tend to creep into the discussion. In addition to economics, four disciplines in the social science and humanities treat power extensively: sociology, political science, management science, and jurisprudence. These fields have, among other features, one important attribute in common: they deal with the behavior of people toward one another.

Sociology

Prior to the 1960s, power was not a topic of primary concern for most sociologists. Recently, interest has increased in social organization, which treats the problem of social power. In sociology, power arises through human interaction, and refers to the ability to affect group activities.

Most introductory sociology texts[4] adopt Max Weber's definition of power: "the capacity of an individual or group to control or influence the behavior of others, even in the face of opposition."[5] It is recognized that "power is not a 'thing' possessed by social actors, but rather a dynamic process that occurs in all areas of life."[6] In economic language, power is a flow, not a stock, concept.

Social theorists have identified attributes of power. Etzioni stresses that power is relative, not absolute.[7] To Bierstedt, the sources of power are people who interact with resources.[8] For Dubin, power in a social context depends on the functions that a person performs, and the importance of those functions to members of the group.[9] The belief by sociologists that power is exercised through social institutions--behavioral arrangements established and sanctioned by people to accomplish some purpose--fits well with the assertion that societal organizations (such as unions, churches, corporations) make decisions which often *limit the range of human choice* for some persons. Indeed, such is the essence of possessing and exercising power.

Political Science

Political scientists also understand that power is a human, behavioral *process* by stressing that it relates to who will govern, and how government will be conducted. Most introductory texts of American government follow the notion of power developed by Robert A. Dahl: "the capacity to get people to do something that they would not otherwise do."[10]

It must be noted that Dahl does not use "force" or "required" in his definition. Being interested in achieving representative government, political scientists view power broadly, from the use of persuasion and cajolery to the use of pressure and intimidation. A benefit-cost criterion has even been used to analyze power: "the strengths of A's influence is measured by the 'cost' to B of complying."[11] Yet, power is only a subset of influence; for it is the possibility of sanction which differentiates the former from the latter.[12] An extensive literature in political science considers how power is expressed in a democracy, as will be noted when the subjects of elitism and pluralism are discussed below.

Management Science

A manager seeks to achieve organizational goals by motivating subordinates to accomplish tasks. A question naturally arises as to the locus and extent of power and authority whenever exercising assigned responsibilities. Management scientists have classified several sources of power: (1) *reward power* (managers can praise, give raises, and promote); (2) *coercive power* (managers can reprimand, suspend, and fire); (3) *legitimate power* (managers have a superior position usually recognized by subordinates); (4) *expert power* (managers often have special skills, talent, and abilities); (5) *referent power* (managers may be admired because of age, charisma, and reputation).[13] These facets of power are not mutually exclusive; for any given manager may possess all simultaneously. But power by itself is not sufficient in a management context. To get things done, power needs to be buttressed by *authority*--the warrant given from the organization with a mutual acceptance by those who are managed.

Legal Aspects

Jurisprudence--being the discipline of law--treats power in the context of control over property. Whereas this control[14] may have been derived legally within the framework of constitutional, statutory, and case law, whether it is *legitimate* has been questioned.[15]   Legal scholars have challenged the legitimacy of the corporation's power over property by asking several questions: Whose property is it? Where did it originate? Why does the holder have it? How is the holder able to retain control over property and use it as a basis for power? Has the system been rigged so only a few persons have control over vast amounts of property? Has the rigging mechanism been the corporate form of ownership? Is the corporation a natural capitalist institution (or is it an alien form of organization which is not democratic, competitive, and capitalist at all)? These questions will be considered in the next chapter.

POLITICAL ECONOMY OF POWER

[B]usiness enterprise may obtain power from . . . political privilege, franchises and patents. [C. Edwards, *Big Business and the Policy of Competition*, Westport: Greenwood, 1956, p. 28.]

Two contrasting views on power in political economy are elitism and pluralism. The former holds that a handful of influential persons shape public policy. The latter, in its idealistic form, holds that American democracy allows anyone and everyone to participate equally in political affairs. The cluster hypothesis, a realistic variation of pluralism, holds that power becomes consolidated in the hands of special interest groups. In either situation, elitism or pluralistic cluster, power exists and permeates the economic system.

Elitism

The elitist hypothesis confronts power directly by admitting that it exists, identifying where it resides, and describing how it affects public policy decisions. Elitism in political theory was summarized by G. Mosca in 1939,[16] and popularized by C. Wright Mills in 1956.[17] According to this view, society is divided into two classes: "the few who govern (elites) and the many who are governed (masses)."[18] Elites are tacitly organized through economic institutions; the masses are not.

The elitist hypothesis holds that American institutions are controlled by a small number of persons whose backgrounds, characteristics, and values are similar. Elites come from upper classes of society--the wealthy and educated--and are often white, Anglo-Saxon, and Protestant. Elites form a relatively homogenous body which caters to its members, and who are organized into special-interest groups that become platforms for power in the economic system. As elites wield power and govern, they do so by balancing their own economic interests with the general welfare.

Research results suggest that elites are more tolerant and committed to democratic values than the masses.[19] Some political scientists claim that democracy would not survive if the masses were in control rather than elites. As a result, from the standpoint of preserving American democracy and capitalism, power in the hands of the elites is desirable according to this hypothesis.

Pluralism and Power Clusters[20]

A variation of pluralism holds that public policy decisions are made through a system of semi-autonomous power clusters. Policy specialization occurs within this framework. A power cluster deals with a given group of interrelated social, political, or economic issues, but may be fragmented into subclusters. There are clusters for each primary area of domestic and foreign policy: agriculture, banking, commerce, labor, defense, education, environment, health, welfare, and so on. Each cluster operates apart from others to identify policy issues, design proposals, offer legislation, and execute policy. The political parties, *per se*, are rarely involved in this process. Each power cluster is comprised of administrative agencies, executive review personnel, legislative committees, interest groups, and certain influential citizens. Policy decisions are the product of intensive interaction among the basic components of one or more power clusters. This system provides an effective means to simplify the gigantic and difficult job of accommodating the nation's policy goals. The interest group is at the center of this process.

Interest Groups and Power

In modern American capitalism, most persons receive money income based on the amount and type of physical and human resources they control. As a result, there is an incentive to acquire productive resources and to join with persons of similar circumstances to influence legislation and its execution. If a property-owning group is successful in having laws passed and interpreted which will enhance the value and effectiveness of its property resources, then members can increase their incomes relative to others. An elaborate network of voluntary association--special interest groups--provides representation in the political economy for many individuals. American capitalism is a vast array of these competing groups which are engaged in a continuous process of building alliances, appealing for popular support, bargaining, pressuring, negotiating, and compromising. The outcome is often economic advantage for the victorious group.

As political pressure groups from different segments of the citizenry assemble to negotiate, the result is often a compromise skewed in favor of those who were most successful at using their bargaining strengths. Success is often based on the number of persons a bargainer represents and the property and wealth backing the bargainers. Those with the most political influence are often groups with the most economic advantage. Once both have been acquired, they reciprocate and reinforce each other, especially if property holders are active in the political arena, pressuring to get laws passed for their benefit, or to gain privileges, subsidies, and favors for themselves from the system. All of this is a logical extension of freedom, self-interest, and profit seeking, being constitutional under the first amendment.

ECONOMICS AND POWER

Market power has many sources and outlets, and no single measure yet . . . can fully capture the many nuances of its real or potential exercise . . . [J. Koch, *Industrial Organization and Price*, Englewood Cliffs: Prentice-Hall, 1980, p. 61.]

The maximization hypothesis undergirds Neoclassical economics, and is embodied within its functional relations. Indeed, the cost curve is derived from tangencies of isoquants and isocosts, and the demand curve is derived from tangencies of the budget constraints and preference functions of a consumer. Both sets of tangencies indicate optimizing conditions. Orthodox analyses of market power relations for imperfect competition using elasticity of demand and the height of price above cost necessarily presume optimization--minimization of cost and/or maximization of utility. However, if maximization is being neither pursued nor reached for various reasons, then the efficacy of the different measures of market power may be incomplete.

Concentration and Power

The traditional industrial organization paradigm holds that market structure is directly related to market conduct, and that both interact to determine market performance. This set of interconnections abstracts from the basic biological framework that environment (structure) shapes behavior (conduct), and that both govern outcomes or results (performance).[21] In economics, these relations are expressed within the Neoclassical models of perfect competition and oligopoly. In the former, a large number of relatively small firms producing a homogeneous output are unable to distinguish and promote their respective products. As a result, they accept the going market price, which is competed down to near production costs, and thereupon receive only normal profits. In the latter, a few relatively large firms are able to differentiate and promote their outputs. As a result, each firm has control over its own price (which is set somewhere above production costs), and can receive above-normal profits.

Among the elements of market structure, seller concentration holds a central position. Industrial concentration refers to the extent that some part of economic activity is centralized in the hands of a few companies. The concentration ratio for a monopolist would be equal to 100 percent; but for any single perfect (pure) competitor, it would be near zero. Thus, the higher the one-firm seller concentration ratio, the closer is that market structure to the monopoly side of the economic ledger. Whenever seller concentration is used to infer monopoly power, the analyst implicitly applies a standard based on elasticity of demand, and divergence of marginal revenue from marginal cost.

Industrial power ordinarily has been measured by a concentration ratio.[22] Generally, the higher the ratio, the greater the claim for a the presence of industrial power. Probably the most meaningful and oft-used concentration ratio is one which measures *market* or *industry* concentration. Many economists believe that competition, or the lack of it, occurs among a group of firms which produce substitutable products with similar production processes that are sold to a common group of buyers in a well-defined geographic area. In this way, competition in a relevant product and geographic market occurs on the basis of both price and non-price rivalry among firms which challenge each other for customers. By confining a concentration ratio to an industry or a market, the analyst can identify competitiveness narrowly in a sector of the economy rather than broadly for the entire economy itself.

Industry concentration ratios have been used to compare different industries in the American economy. Whenever concentration is high or increasing, the conclusion is usually drawn that power (or control, or influence, or domination) exists in that particular market. The same conclusion is drawn whenever aggregate concentration indicates that a relatively small portion of the nation's corporations contributes to a relatively large share of the nation's economic activity. Indeed, concentration and power tend to be connected as a cause-and-effect relation, or even equated in the sense that high concentration *is* power, control and dominance. But such an assertion, even if true, fails to identify the effects of power on the individual, or to uncover the pervasiveness of power in society. To do this, some economists abandon Neoclassical economics and turn to Institutional economics.

Institutional Treatment of Power

Power can be analyzed both quantitatively and qualitatively. To measure market power, economists use concentration ratios to indicate whether domination might exist in some part of the economic system. However, quantitative measures may not capture the presence of industrial power. Indeed, merely counting something in absolute or relative terms does not necessarily establish the extent of power. A qualitative framework, based on broad concepts of economic activity, may shed light on where power resides and how its presence impacts society.

Economic activity involves the level, composition, and distribution of national output. This output is created from scarce resources which, by themselves, are not very productive. Economic activity occurs when technology is applied to the resource base. But economic institutions-- coordinating mechanisms for planning, organizing, and directing according to some agenda--are needed to bring technology and resources together productively. A nation's economy presumably tries to satisfy as many of the supposedly unlimited human wants as possible from its scarce resources by striving to be efficient. Unfortunately, the nation often fails to achieve its potential and operates chronically in a state of *un*employment and underemployment: it could produce additional output; it could allocate a different mix of resources to investment and consumption goods; and it could alter the division of output to reduce misery. These objectives are rarely reached because economic institutions are "sticky" (i.e., suffer from inertia) and do not allow technology to be applied to resources as fully and as quickly as possible. Economic institutions are shackled by the rigidities of ceremonial behavior[23] which impede economic progress.

The economic process is plagued by institutional drag and cultural lag. As Alfred Marshall once stated, *Natura non facit saltum*:[24] nature does not make great leaps. Technology continuously advances, albeit sometimes at a faster pace than at others. However, institutional adjustment to technological change takes time and imposes hardships during the adjustment period. But *why* do institutions take so long to adjust? Any society obtains its institutions from its values and its culture. Both are past-binding and resistant to change. New technology is slow to become accepted by society, embodied within its culture, and adjusted to its values. By the time that technological feedback absorbs previous technology into the culture, and subsequently within societal values, so that institutional adjustment applies technology more fully to the resource base for augmenting level, composition and distribution of output, new technology comes on the scene once again. These conditions are pervasive and contribute to a perpetual feedback-and-adjustment process. As it occurs, some resources are wasted, some unmet wants are forestalled, and some members of society continue to be disadvantaged. Moreover, as the process is repeated from period to period, there is the possibility--indeed, a probability--that various persons or groups will influence the feedback mechanism of "institutional adjustment to technological change" for their own benefit to the detriment of others.

The key to understanding power in our economic system is to recognize its role within the institutional framework. Power permeates the entire system, from control over resources, to influence on the direction and pace of technological change, to decisions over what and how much will be produced and distributed (including the allocation mechanism), to the adjustment process wherein values affect institutions and their ability to connect technology to the resource base. Even the feed-back mechanism itself--the way that advancing technology becomes absorbed into culture--is subjected to influence and power.

CONCLUDING REMARKS

[N]either the direct attack on market power nor the control of business conduct on market power criteria will reduce market power to zero. [C. Kaysen and D. Turner, *Antitrust Policy*, Cambridge: Harvard University Press, 1959, p. 90.]

As a political economy *and* a market economy, modern American capitalism contains numerous expressions of power. Indeed, power is not a singular, absolute concept but a condition or quality which resides in most parts of human existence. Whereas the market, contemplated in its competitive, free enterprise form, is supposedly void of power and control, wherever property rights are assigned, resources allocated, and incomes distributed, power in some form or another is inevitably present.

Whenever considering interaction between the political economy and the market, concerns about monopoly power, market power, and economic power are certain to arise. Some observers tend to downplay the existence of monopoly and market power. By denying their presence, other expressions of power might continue to operate but remain ignored if efforts are successful for establishing the belief that power is absent.

The first step in creating a belief that power probably does not reside in the business system is casually to cite *monopoly* and then define it in terms of the textbook model of pure monopoly: only one firm in an industry with no other existing or potential firms producing substitute products. At this point in the conversation, it is necessary to mention that economists consider such a definition of pure monopoly to be proper and accurate. The consequence is to eliminate most of the economic system from the arena of power; for there are few markets with only one firm and there are few products for which no substitutes exist.

The second step is to shorten "pure monopoly" to "monopoly," and then pass the latter off as the former. Thus, whenever monopoly is mentioned, the image is created of a large firm facing no business rivals which could challenge its price and production policies. This maneuver solidifies the connection established in the first step.

The third step is to equate both monopoly and pure monopoly with monopoly power. This quantum leap allows the subterfuge of claiming that a firm with a substantial share of market sales is the only firm in the industry, somewhat of a logical inconsistency. If the intent of mythmaking is to establish that claims of power are empty, this step succeeds in achieving that goal.

The fourth step is to equate monopoly power with both market power and economic power. By contending that all three terms are interchangeable--that each refers basically to the same condition--the stage is now set to draw the ultimate conclusion that neither market power nor economic power exist to any extent in the real world of business.

Based on the above reasoning, a complaint about the evils of monopoly power in some particular situations can be defeated directly on the grounds that the situation does not involve a single firm producing a non-substitutable product (or, in technical language, that no pure monopolist is present). The mischief is furthered by extension of the argument. Whenever someone complains of the presence or exercise of economic (or of market) power, its existence can also be disavowed with the same line of reasoning. But these three forms of power are in fact distinguishable, and a delineation of them is crucial to understand how power operates in the political economy of American industrial capitalism.

Monopoly power refers to a dominant firm in an industry which is able to exercise substantial control over the seller side of the market. Monopoly power exists whenever the dominant firm has the ability to influence significantly, the price, output and/or entry of other firms in the same line of commerce. Monopoly power may go so far as to embody the ability to exclude competitors and to discipline rivals by reducing their sales and profits.

With *market power*, there are a few large firms in an industry rather than just one dominant company. In oligopoly, for example, interdependence among a few large firms may be so tight and strong that one of the oligopolists is able to make decisions which others follow for fear of starting a destructive price war. Such mutual forbearance by the major firms in the industry thwarts rivalry over the incidents of exchange, or terms of trade. The result is a relatively stable price and above normal profits.

Whereas monopoly power is narrow in its applicability to the political economy, *economic power* is a broad concept. A firm does not have to be a monopolist, or even one of a few dominant firms, to possess and exercise economic power. In a negotiation and exchange, if a seller or buyer is able to extract concessions from the party on the other side of a transaction, it probably has some economic power. Economic power is superior bargaining ability based on some attribute of the product, condition of sale, or buyer preference.[25]   Some observers contend that economic power based on uniqueness giving rise to strong buyer preferences, which in turn allows a seller to extract certain concessions from buyers, essentially amounts to monopoly power (albeit over only a narrow range of sale conditions). However, such a conclusion must be rejected because the use of the term monopoly, as already noted, leads to extension of argument and erroneous conclusions.

It is not uncommon to witness the acquisition and exercise of power in the political economy. Such activities are to be expected as a normal part of the operation of the business system. Indeed, one can observe and encounter power in the market economy without the rigid strictures of monopoly-like situations. Economic power, especially, has undoubtedly been experienced from ancient times and into the modern era. In recent years, the corporate form of business organization has been subjected to close scrutiny for the alleged power that it wields in the economy. To investigate this relationship, the concept of *legitimacy* must be examined, the topic to which we turn in the next chapter.

NOTES

1.   Some excellent examples are: (a) A. A. Berle, *Power*, New York: Harcourt, Brace, and World, 1967; (b) A. Cox, P. Furlong, and E. Page, *Power in Capitalist Societies: Theory, Explanations, and Cases*, New York: St. Martin's, 1985; (c) J. K. Galbraith, *The Anatomy of Power*, Boston: Houghton Mifflin, 1983; (d) N. Cousins, *The Pathology of Power*, New York: Norton, 1987; and (e) W. Adams and J. W. Brock, *The Bigness Complex*, New York: Pantheon Books, 1986.

2.   *The American Heritage Dictionary*, Second College Edition, Boston: Houghton Mifflin, 1983, p. 971.

3.   *Ibid.*, pp. 971-72.

4.   As examples: C. H. Persell, *Understanding Society,* New York: Harper and Row, 1987, p. 354; and I. Robertson, *Sociology*, New York: Worth, 1987, p. 596.

5.   M. Weber, *The Theory of Social and Economic Organization*, New York: Free Press, 1957 (as quoted in A. Thio, *Sociology: An Introduction*, New York: Harper and Row, 1986, p. 357).

6.   M. E. Olsen, *Power in Societies*, New York: Macmillan, 1970, p. 3.

7.   A. Etzioni, *The Active Society*, New York: Free Press, 1968, pp. 314-23 and 357-61.

8.   R. Bierstedt, "An Analysis of Social Power," *American Sociological Review*, December 1950, pp. 730-38.

9.   R. Dubin, "Power, Function, and Organization," *Pacific Sociological Review*, Spring 1963, pp. 16-22.

10. R. A. Dahl, "The Concept of Power," *Behavioral Science*, July 1957, p. 202.

11. *Ibid.*, p. 204.

12. H. D. Lasswell and A. Kaplan, *Power and Society*, New Haven: Yale University Press, 1950.

13. D. Hellriegel, J. W. Slocum, and R. W. Woodman, *Organizational Behavior*, St. Paul: West, 1986, pp. 462-64.

14. "Control" in the sense of ability to decide how property can be used subject to statutory and case law.

15. See A. A. Berle, *The American Economic Republic*, New York: Harcourt, Brace, and World, 1963, pp. 24-54; and D. A. Bazelon, *The Paper Economy*, New York: Random House, 1963, pp. 175-90.

16. G. E. Mosca, *The Ruling Class*, New York: McGraw-Hill, 1939.

17. C. W. Mills, *The Power Elite*, New York: Oxford University Press, 1956.

18. T. R. Dye and L. H. Zeigler, *The Irony of Democracy*, North Scituate: Duxbury Press, 1982, pp. 3-18.

19. P. Bachrach, *The Theory of Democratic Elitism*, Boston: Little, Brown, 1967.

20. This section is based on: D. M. Ogden, Jr., "How National Policy is Made," *Increasing Understanding of Public Problems and Policies*, Chicago: Farm Foundation, 1971, pp. 5-9.

21. See R. D. Peterson, "Product Differentiation, Implicit Theorizing, and the Methodology of Industrial Organization," *Nebraska Journal of Economics and Business*, Spring 1980, pp. 22-36.

22. A. P. Lerner, "The Concept of Monopoly and the Measurement of Monopoly Power," *Review of Economic Studies*, June 1934, pp. 157-75, and J. V. Koch, *Industrial Organization and Prices*, 2nd ed., Englewood Cliffs: Prentice-Hall, 1980, pp. 62-3.

23. This point is discussed in C. E. Ayres, *The Theory of Economic Progress*, New York: Schrocken, 1962, pp. 155-76.

24. A. Marshall, *Principles of Economics*, 8th ed., New York: Macmillan, 1948.

25. E. H. Chamberlin, *The Theory of Monopolistic Competition*, 8th ed., Cambridge: Harvard University Press, 1962, pp. 56-7.

4

LEGITIMACY

INTRODUCTION

> If an institution loses its legitimacy it loses everything, for it can no longer continue to function . . . [K. Boulding, "The Legitimation of the Market," *Nebraska Journal of Economics and Business*, Fall, 1967, p. 3.]

Inquiring into the political economy of modern American capitalism invites a consideration of certain mechanisms which guide its operations. One factor is power, a quality which ostensibly permeates all economic systems in one way or another. Power existed in feudalism and in mercantilism. Although the form may have been altered somewhat, power certainly exists under fascism and socialism. Countless observers have pointed out that this attribute is present within American capitalism as well.

The nature and importance of power were introduced broadly in Chapter 3. The focus now shifts to one particular repository of power--the corporation. The status of this form of business organization has not gone unchallenged.[1] The nature and magnitude of corporate power are relevant topics for inquiry into American capitalism. This chapter investigates the corporation in terms of its "legitimacy"--the rightfulness associated with, and the exercise of power derived from, the possession of property.

A primary characteristic of political economy is for a privilege to have been granted to some individual or group. Among other perquisites, such privilege gives rise to an ability to influence property rights, income distribution, and resource allocation. Given the self-interest hypothesis, ostensibly a valid description of human motives and behavior, such influence is ordinarily exerted for the benefit of its holder and user. The scarcity of resources suggests a zero-sum game in which some may benefit but others lose. As a result, the possession and application of power and influence naturally becomes a springboard for inquiry and challenge.

The corporation is not the only holder and user of power. Labor unions, selected professions, the military, churches, foundations, and certain families all come to mind when the topic of power is contemplated. There are obviously others. When power exists, it is not uncommon for citizens of both authoritarian and democratic societies to wonder about its source, who has it, how it was obtained, for what purposes, where and how it will be exercised, who may be affected by it in which ways, and whether it might persist and grow. These concerns constitute the subject matter of legitimacy. But what is "legitimacy"? How does it apply to the corporation? And why question the legitimacy of corporate property and power?

NATURE OF LEGITIMACY

Legitimacy means more than grudging acceptance of the inevitable. The word suggests at least confidence and respect and, at times, even warmth and affection. [J. Rohr, *To Run A Constitution*, Lawrence: University Press of Kansas, 1986, p. x.]

Before considering directly the issue of corporate legitimacy, it is appropriate to examine the meaning of legitimacy itself. Restating its definition and examining three views from the social sciences provides a basis for understanding the relevance of this intriguing concept.

Background

The word legitimacy is derived from the Latin, *legitimus*, meaning "what conforms to ancient custom."[2] Contemporary dictionaries ordinarily define legitimate as "lawful; in accordance with accepted patterns and standards; . . . reasonable; authentic, genuine. . . "[3] However, legitimacy is not mere legality, but the perceived morality of a social relationship which impacts the lives of people. Associated with its use are "legitimated" and "illegitimate." A variety of synonyms have also been offered to identify what legitimate and legitimacy connote: real, true, valid, authorized, supported, reasonable, and possessing title or status.

Social Aspects

Among the relations which affect how people in organized society conduct themselves, the concept of an institution is of prime importance. An economic institution is an arrangement, a way of doing things, a coordinating mechanism between technology and resources which is associated with economic activity. An institution is the product of human interaction which becomes established in response to a need that members of society believe is necessary to enhance their well-being.[4] For an institution to enjoy standing and continue to function, those members must agree that a situation merits the creation of intervening procedures to alleviate tensions. To be operative, a social arrangement must be ratified, or legitimated, for society to approve its administration. If and when this status is attained, the institution then becomes legitimate. To illustrate, marriage is a social institution. It was created to fulfill a need sanctioned by society, enjoys recognized legal status and existence, and has been ratified, approved, and accepted. It has the continued confidence and support of a majority of organized society. As a result, marriage has legitimacy and is a legitimate social institution in our culture.

Politics

Politically, legitimacy refers to the exercise of power by a government which possesses the right to govern that is recognized by the governed. Legitimacy is contrary to usurpation but is a challenge to the divine right of kings. Usurpers try to seize power and establish authority by fiat. Usurpation is distinguished from revolutions which often embody a strong sense of legitimacy. Some religions use the concept of a "god-king" to create an aura of legitimacy through dogma, fear and awe. In modern politics, "civil legitimacy" refers to "a system of government . . . based on agreement between equally autonomous constituents who have combined to cooperate toward some common good."[5] Civil legitimacy requires governmental offices to be "ordered by trust rather than exercised by dominion."[6] Members of society have questioned both the legitimacy of government to grant special privileges, and the privilege itself.

Economic Affairs[7]

Legitimacy can be internal (e.g., acceptance and justification of one's role in life) or external (e.g., acceptance of the environment in which an institution exists). An economic institution is more likely to be recognized, accepted, and justified--legitimated--if it (1) yields positive payoffs, (2) is consistent with willingness to sacrifice, (3) provides mystery and charisma, (4) contains respected rituals and symbols, (5) has endured to become a part of culture, or (6) relates to other legitimate institutions.

Implications

Debates over legitimacy often focus on whether one who holds power over another obtained it "properly." Whereas power may have been acquired lawfully, a question remains as to whether it was morally right to have acquired it. Four crucial questions delineate the problem of legitimacy as it relates to economic power: (1) Is it "right" that society created institutions which allow property to be accumulated so that power might develop? (2) Is it "right" that a particular person or group has amassed and controlled property so that he/she/it possesses power? (3) Is it "right" if a holder of property and power use them to affect others adversely? (4) Is it "right" that holder-users of property and power might answer only to themselves, not to society?

THE CORPORATION

The corporation . . . has group interests distinguishable from the individual interests of its individual members. [H. Henn and J. Alexander, *Laws of Corporations*, St. Paul: West, 1983, p. 14.]

The corporation exists against a backdrop of the proprietorship and partnership forms of business organization. There are other types of firms with diverse ownership, such as joint stock companies and cooperatives, but corporations control more assets, make more sales, and earn more profits than any other form of business. The corporation enjoys special privileges and therefore has been able to operate and become dominant in modern American capitalism.

Definition

"Corporation" stems from the Latin, *corpus*, meaning "body." Indeed, a corporation is a "body of persons granted a charter legally recognizing them as a separate entity having its own rights, privileges and liabilities distinct from those of its members."[8] Legally, a corporation has personality. Chief Justice Marshall's description is classic: "A corporation is an artificial being, invisible, intangible and existing only in contemplation of law. Being the mere creature of law, it possesses only those properties which the charter of its creation confers upon it, either expressly, or coincidental to its very existence."[9]

The corporation is a legally constituted mechanism which can be used by individual property owners to associate, to cooperate, to accumulate property, to carry on commerce, and to grow. Through the corporate mechanism, private property leaves the control of its owner and becomes transferred to managers who mix it with the properties of others. This procedure allows a corporation to become large, to achieve dominance, to gain influence, and to exercise increasing control over its environment. But is such a scenario reasonable and fair? Are corporate directors using property and power responsibly? Are power and influence of the corporation being employed for social ends? In a word, is the corporation legitimate?

History

Although the corporation "is an institution of unknown antiquity,"[10] its original characteristics were somewhat different from business corporations of today. Basic corporate ideas can be traced to ancient times, and a corporate concept was fostered during the Roman Empire.[11] As a means of organization, the corporation was used during the early Norman period in Anglo-Saxon history.[12] The present-day corporation can be traced to the English corporations of the seventeenth and eighteenth centuries.

In America, while drafting the constitution, the subject arose as to whether the federal government should have the power to create corporations. Madison's notes indicate a negative feeling on this matter because of the tendency for incorporation to beget monopoly power, a dangerous potential to be avoided.[13] "So the Federal government was specifically denied the power to create corporations . . . it was assumed that [the states] would not exercise this power or, if they did, would exercise it only as a means of carrying on government."[14]

Characteristics

The typical basic business text stresses several features to differentiate the corporation from proprietorships and partnerships: (1) legal existence granted by government charter; (2) transferable shares of ownership; (3) authority in the hands of a board of directors appointed by stockholders; (4) unlimited life; and (5) limited liability. These are the primary features which give the corporation an advantage over other forms of business ownership, but there are others. Corporate characteristics are presented in the Model Business Corporation Act, adopted by more than 20 states, and a basis for legislation in another 15 states.[15] This Act lists 16 specific corporate powers which, taken together, provide a basis for raising the question of corporate legitimacy: to have perpetual succession; to sue and be sued; to possess a recognized corporate seal; to own and sell property; to lend money; to buy, own, and sell shares of stock of other corporations; to make contracts; to lend money; to conduct business in other states; to elect and appoint officers for itself; to make and alter its own by-laws; to make donations; to transact any lawful business; to pay pensions and bonuses; to be a promoter or partner in other business ventures; and to exercise actions to carry out the aforementioned powers.[16]

INDICATORS OF CORPORATE POWER

The market power which large absolute and relative size gives to the giant corporation is the basis not only of economic power but also of considerable political and social power . . . [C. Kaysen, "The Corporation: How Much Power? What Scope?" in E. Mason, *The Corporation in Modern Society*, Cambridge: Harvard University Press, 1959, p. 99.]

The corporation is involved with countless activities in the political economy to seek, acquire, and perpetuate property and power. Among the manifestations of corporate power examined in recent years are lobbying,[17] investing in foreign markets,[18] infiltrating boards of directors of financial institutions,[19] and influencing community development.[20]   There are others.[21]   In this section, three indicators of corporate power are discussed: domination of business sales, aggregate concentration, and tax avoidance.

Dominant Corporate Sales

As Table 4.1 shows, approximately 16.9 million businesses operated in the American economy during 1985, but 13.6 million of them were proprietorships and partnerships. The remaining 3.3 million firms were incorporated firms, nearly 40 percent of which were small units with less than $100,000 in total sales. The American dream of an economy of many small, independent enterprises appears to have been fulfilled with the corporate form playing a minor part on the business scene. However, when business sales are examined a dramatically different picture emerges.

Figures in Table 4.1 indicate for all forms of business, both the number of firms and their sales receipts have increased significantly over that 40-year period. The proprietorship persists as the preferred form of ownership, but its relative incidence has waned in recent years. Whereas the number of partnerships increased, it is the corporate form of organization which has grown most significantly, especially in the past 20 years.

Data in Table 4.2 show the relative importance of the corporate compared to the non-corporate form according to the percent of the firms, by type of ownership, that receive various percentages of sales. The corporate form is obviously dominant in American capitalism. In 1985,

Table 4.1   Number and Receipts of Business, By Type, United States,
           Selected Years, 1945-1985

TYPE   OF   ORGANIZATION

Year	Proprietorship Number (Thou)	Sales (Bil)	Partnerships Number (Thou)	Sales (Bil)	Corporations Number (Thou)	Sales (Bil)
1945	5689	$ 79	627	$ 47	21	255
1953	7715	144	959	80	698	558
1965	9078	199	914	75	1424	1195
1975	10822	339	1073	146	2024	3199
1985	11929	540	1714	368	3277	8398

Source: *Statistical Abstract of the United States*, Selected Issues.

Table 4.2   Percent of Business Sales Received by Non-Incorporated
           Firms, United States, Selected Years, 1945-1985

Year	Non-Incorporated Firms Cos. (%)	Sales (%)	Incorporated Firms Cos. (%)	Sales (%)
1945	94	33	6	67
1953	93	29	7	71
1965	88	19	12	81
1975	87	12	13	88
1985	81	10	19	90

Source: *Statistical Abstract of the United States*, Selected Issues.

corporations captured 90 percent of national aggregate business
sales. Whereas 81 percent of American business firms were proprietorships
and partnerships, together they received only 10 percent of all market sales.
Indeed, on average during 1985, each of the nearly 3.3 million corporations
received approximately $2,568,000 in sales whereas each of the 13.6 million
unincorporated firms received average sales of only $66,554. The difference
amounts to a factor of 38.5 times greater for corporations compared to
non-corporations.

Table 4.3   Shares   of   Value-Added,   Largest   Manufacturing
Corporations, United States, Selected Years, 1947-1982
(data in percent)

YEAR	TOP 50	TOP 100	TOP 200
1947	17	23	30
1954	23	30	37
1958	23	30	38
1963	25	33	41
1967	25	33	42
1972	25	33	43
1977	24	33	44
1982	24	33	43

Source: "Concentration Ratios in Manufacturing," *1982 Census of
Manufactures*, MC82-S-7, U.S. Department of Commerce,
Bureau of the Census, Washington, D.C.

Concentration

That large industrial corporations dominate the American economy can
be shown by measuring aggregate concentration. Table 4.3 reports total
value-added by the 50, 100 and 200 largest American manufacturing firms.
Comparing the figures for 1947 with those of 1982, aggregate concentration
increased significantly. Most of the growth occurred during the decade
immediately after World War Two with the level having been stabilized in
more recent years.

To summarize, there are nearly 17 million business firms in the United
States, slightly more than 3 million of which are corporations. The 50
largest entities combined produce one-fourth of all value-added in
manufacturing, and the largest 200 produce nearly one-half (43 percent, to
be precise) of this measure of business output. These data attest to the
concentration of power and ability of the corporate form of organization to
dominate economic activity in modern American capitalism.

Declining Corporate Tax Share

Another important indicator of corporate power and influence is its
relative tax burden. Table 4.4 shows revenue receipts of all levels of
government for the period, 1950-1985. Three tax categories are reported:
on individual income, on corporate profits, and for social security. Data
confirm what every citizen knows: governmental revenues from taxation have

Table 4.4   Gross National Product and Governmental Receipts, by Source, United States, Selected Years, 1950-1985 (dollars in billions)

Year	GNP	Personal Income Tax	Corporate Profit Tax	Social Security Contrib.	Total Receipts Collected
1950	$ 288.3	$ 20.6	$17.9	$ 7.4	$ 69.4
1955	405.9	35.4	22.0	12.0	101.6
1960	515.3	50.5	22.7	21.9	140.4
1965	705.1	65.2	30.9	31.6	190.2
1970	1015.5	116.2	34.4	62.0	306.8
1975	1598.4	170.6	50.9	118.5	480.0
1980	2732.0	340.5	84.8	216.5	855.1
1985	3998.1	486.5	91.8	355.7	1265.4

Source: *Economic Report of the President*, 1987.

increased markedly in the Post-War period--nearly 15-fold over 35 years! Moreover, personal income taxes have risen from $20.6 billion in 1950 to $486.5 billion in 1985, or more than 23 times. Corporate profit tax collections have increased only five-fold during the same period. Table 4.5 demonstrates that the corporate profit tax once provided a significant share of all governmental revenues but now plays a diminishing role. In 1950, the portion of governmental revenue derived from the personal income tax was close to that of the corporate profit tax, but the burden has shifted dramatically since then. Indeed, the corporate profit tax contributed more than one quarter of all government receipts in 1950 but by 1985, the corporate share was down to less than 10 percent. The personal income tax, on the other hand, provided less than 30 percent of all government receipts in 1950, but by 1985, its share had risen to nearly 40 percent.

Data in Table 4.5 show a steady decline in corporate profit tax receipts as a percent of GNP for all levels of government: from 6.2 percent in 1950 to 2.3 percent by 1985. Conversely, the share provided by the personal income tax has risen from 7.1 percent to 12.2 percent for the same period.

Corporations--or, persons managing corporations in the American economy--have apparently been successful with lobbying efforts to adjust the American tax structure. Whereas it might be argued that "businesses don't pay taxes, people do," this view misses the point. No doubt that people, eventually, pay taxes. However, a distinction must be made between stockholders and workers. For the corporate profit tax, the incidence

Table 4.5   Personal Income and Corporate Profit Taxes as a Percent
             of GNP and All Governmental Revenues, United States,
             Selected Years, 1950-1985

Year	Pers Tax GNP	Pers Tax Govt Rev	Corp Tax GNP	Corp Tax Govt Rev
1950	.071	.297	.062	.258
1955	.087	.348	.054	.216
1960	.098	.360	.044	.162
1965	.092	.344	.044	.162
1970	.114	.379	.034	.112
1975	.107	.355	.032	.106
1980	.125	.398	.031	.099
1985	.122	.384	.023	.073

Source: *Economic Report of the President*, 1987

involves stockholders of corporations. For the personal income tax, the incidence involves wage-and-salary workers. Corporations are owned by millions of stockholders, but not all of the nearly 100 million wage-and-salary workers in the American labor force are stockholders. For those who do own stock, the dollar value of their security portfolios are ordinarily smaller than those in middle- and upper-management positions in American corporations.

LEGITIMACY OF THE CORPORATION

[W]henever there is a question of power there is question of legitimacy. . . . These instrumentalities of tremendous power have the slenderest claim of legitimacy. [A. Berle, *Economic Power and the Free Society*, Santa Barbara: Center for the Study of Democratic Institutions, 1957, p. 16.]

The corporation has been legitimated because its existence serves a need which has been endorsed by members of society who influence public policy and who perceive themselves as enjoying the fruits of corporate endeavors. But did the corporation rightfully obtain the property it controls? To whom is the corporation responsible? Is it using its power responsibly? Has the confidence of society enjoyed by the corporation been eroded? Such questions of corporate legitimacy have been subjected to serious inquiry.

The following accounts deal with the haunting question, "Is the giant business corporation legitimate?"

Concentrated Corporate Power

Corporate legitimacy has been questioned against the backdrop of concentrated economic power.[22] The corporation brings people together to surrender property and accumulate it in the form of stock certificates; corporate managers then control it as "passive" property.[23] Concentrated corporate power is often justified--legitimized--as being necessary to provide low-cost mass production. However, research indicates that for many industrial processes, such large size is not needed for cost efficiency.[24] That corporate power was misused and needed to be controlled is suggested by three important landmarks of public policy: public utility regulation, antitrust legislation, and the income tax laws.[25] Each was an attempt to reduce the power of great inherited wealth and monopoly activities associated with the corporate form of organization.[26]

Self-Appointed Power

Whereas there are a few million corporations, less than 200 of the largest continue to "embrace nearly two-thirds of all nonagricultural economic activity."[27] As a result, a small number of corporate managers control the majority of national output. But query: "Who selected these men, . . . and to whom are they responsible?"[28] The answer is astounding: they selected themselves, and their line of responsibility to society is not clear! This situation represents a remarkable turn of events. In the corporation of the previous century, "The owner, if not the manager himself, selected the management, and the management was responsible to the owners."[29] Today, the separation of ownership from control has led to a "self-perpetuating oligarchy" and a type of syndicalism. It suggests that certain qualified persons may be denied the chance to be in charge of one of most important societal institutions. This problem is not confined to the corporation. It exists in other bureaucracies as well.

Accountability[30]

Several interrelated criteria are necessary for legitimacy. An institution should be neither an end in itself nor autonomous. Legitimacy is not necessarily achieved through self-perpetuation. Institutions possessing and using power should be responsible and accountable. Responsibility requires usefulness in achieving a social goals. Whether the corporation has legitimacy depends on the extent to which it is doing socially useful activities and reacting positively to societal needs. Legitimacy of the governmental system which created the corporation and continued to grant it increasing power can be questioned as much as the legitimacy of the corporation itself. Expansion of corporate powers has been accepted by a society that places prime importance on ways to promote, develop, and consolidate commercial enterprise. Yet, corporate accountability appears to be lacking.

Disenfranchisement

A legal challenge has been made to the legitimacy of the corporation. Nearly a century ago, Henry C. Adams, then president of the American Economic Association, pointed out that corporations were originally agencies of the State which had been created to serve the social ends of government. The corporation was designed to use private means to achieve public goals. However, its original purpose has been subverted. Whereas corporations contain private property, corporate managers have become "authoritarian private baronies legitimated by nothing more than their existence."[31]   As a result, the ordinary stockholder has given up the franchise to control his/her property.   Although corporations were not provided for in the federal Constitution, the corporate form has been made legal and has appeared to be legitimate. But there is "unlegitimate power of corporate managements without basis in ownership. . ."[32] The state has apparently become an arm of the corporate sector which acts to legitimize and perpetuate the corporate culture.

Relegitimation

Corporations were originally chartered by the State for the public interest and the organization was consequently accountable to it. Legitimation was accomplished in the nineteenth century by the competitive market based on private property and free labor. This "traditional dual" became eroded in the twentieth century so that the flow of accountability passed from the State to legitimating bodies themselves. Today, separation of ownership from control in the modern corporation no longer makes it accountable to the State, only to itself. Relegitimation is critically needed and can be established by creating a structure in which, for example, making charitable contributions is a legal obligation of corporate managers. The profit maximization goal may be consistent with charity; for generosity enhances corporate prestige and adds to revenues and profits in the long run.   Several proposals would accomplish this goal: (1) expand "the corporate constituency beyond shareholders to include employees, franchise dealers, and the general populace"; (2) establish judicial review boards to oversee mergers, prices, patent uses, and international investment; and (3) limit corporate use of pension funds, stock options, and seniority rules.

CONCLUDING REMARKS

[P]ower centered . . . in the hands of administrators and experts . . . to win approval of corporation leaders. Workers, farmers, and small businessmen . . . had less . . . power, even though . . . they had gained recognition as legitimate social forces. [J. Weinstein, *The Corporate Ideal in the Liberal State*, Boston: Beacon Press,1968, p. 252.]

The corporation is a key institution in the political economy of American capitalism. This medium for organizing and accumulating property and power had its status granted by the State, with the sanction of those in society who were able to form public policy. The corporation has been instrumental for influencing key economic activities which help perpetuate property and power: the assignment of property rights, the allocation of resources, and the distribution of income.

Statistical data show that the corporate form of business organization is becoming increasingly dominant in the United States. Unincorporated businesses--mainly proprietorships and partnerships--although large in numbers, contribute a decreasing amount of economic activity to the business system. Indeed, as measured by assets, sales, and profits, corporations and especially the very large corporation, dominate the economy. Corporate power is evident in the volume of sales, the level of concentration, and the ability to reduce direct taxation. The corporate form obtained this ability--power, as it were--legally. Both statutory and case law support the formation and activity of corporations. A well-developed body of corporate law monitors their management and operations. The courts protect corporations in their conduct of economic, political, and social activities.

A number of influential personages have questioned the existence, viability, and efficacy of the corporate form. Large corporations often become aligned with governmental agencies, the military, educational institutions, and even labor unions to achieve their own goals. This is to be expected and has been applauded by proponents of an economic system which stresses self-interest, pragmatism, and self-determination.

But is the corporation legitimate? That no definitive answer has been made to this question should be of minor concern. It is important that the question was raised and its relevance connected to modern American capitalism. The corporation may be legal and even legitimate, but challenging its presence and operations on grounds of legitimacy provides a platform for public policy discussion.

Currently, a majority of economic society recognizes, accepts, approves, and justifies the corporation and the power over property that it enjoys. Whether its structure, privileges, and activities will be altered or readjusted remains to be seen. If changes are to occur, they will occur by the ballot box, either directly or indirectly, to the extent that Congressional representatives and senators reflect the collective wishes of society. Some proposals have already been made which will affect the property and power of large corporations. Among them are tightened legislation toward mergers, divisional reporting, interlocking directorates, and predatory pricing. Other proposals deal with corporate taxation, political contributions (especially by Political Action Committees), consumer representatives on boards of directors, federal chartering of corporations, and restricting the ultra vires ("beyond the scope") section of corporate charters. These changes in corporate policy would hopefully achieve objectives which scholars with democratic values have sought for many decades:

> Where economic power exists in the big collective enterprise, we want it used in such a way that it achieves much the same end results that made classical competition such a valuable institution. . .
> [G. Means, *The Corporate Revolution in America*, Collier: New York, 1962, p. 169.]

NOTES

1.   Several insightful books on the subject of the corporation are: (1) G. Bannock, *The Juggernauts, The Age of the Big Corporation*, Indianapolis: Bobbs Merrill, 1971; (2) P. Drucker, *Concept of the Corporation*, New York: John Day, 1972; (3) J. Munkirs, *The Transformation of American Capitalism*, Armonk: Sharpe, 1985; and (4) A. Toffler, *The Adaptive Corporation*, New York: McGraw-Hill, 1985.

2.   D. Sternberger, "Legitimacy," *Encyclopedia of the Social Sciences*, Vol. IX, New York: Macmillan, 1968, p. 245.

3.   *The American Heritage Dictionary*, second ed., Boston: Houghton Mifflin, 1982, p. 273.

4.   J. Hertzler, "Institution," *Collier's Encyclopedia*, New York: McGraw-Hill, 1960, p. 272.

5.   *Encyclopedia of Social Sciences, op. cit.*, p. 245.

6.   *Ibid.*

7.   See: (1) K. Boulding, "The Legitimacy of Economics," *Western Economic Journal*, September 1967, pp. 299-307 and (2) K. Boulding, "The Legitimation of the Market," *Nebraska Journal of Economics and Business*, Autumn 1967, pp. 3-14.

8.   *American Heritage Dictionary, op. cit.*, p. 326.

9. The Trustees of Dartmouth College v. Woodward, 4 Wheaton 518 (U.S. 1819).

10. E. Mason, "Corporation," *International Encyclopedia of the Social Sciences*, Vol. 3, New York: Macmillan and Free Press, 1968, p. 396.

11. H. Henn and J. Alexander, *Laws of Corporations*, St. Paul: West, 1983, p. 14.

12. *Encyclopedia of Social Science, op. cit.*, p. 414.

13. A. Berle, *Economic Power and the Free Society*, Santa Barbara: Center for the Study of Democratic Institutions, 1957, p. 4.

14. *Ibid.*

15. R. Hamilton, *Statutory Supplement to Corporations*, St. Paul: West, 1981, pp. 57-58.

16. *Ibid.*

17. G. Bramm, *Influence of Business Firms on Government*, New York: Mouton, 1981.

18. J. Hyatt, "Going International: The Partnership Route," *Inc.*, December 1988, p. 145-48.

19. M. Mizruchi and L. Stearns, "A Longitudinal Study of the Formation of Interlocking Directorates," *Administrative Science Quarterly*, June 1988, pp. 194-210.

20. This charge can be traced to the mid-1930s, and the "chain-store" problem. See: J. Bain, *Industrial Organization*, New York: Wiley, 1968, pp. 482-85.

21. See: (1) A. Berle, *Power Without Property*, New York: Harcourt, Brace, and World, 1959 and (2) A. Berle, *The American Economic Republic*, New York: Harcourt, Brace, and World, 1963.

22. *American Economic Republic, Ibid.*, pp. 42-47.

23. F. Scherer, *Industrial Market Structure and Economic Performance*, Boston: Houghton Mifflin, 1980, pp. 96-118.

24. *Power Without Property, op. cit.*, pp. 100-105.

25. *American Economic Republic, op. cit.*, pp. 117-160.

26. E. Mason, *The Corporation in Modern Society*, Cambridge: Harvard University Press, 1959, p. 5.

27. *Ibid.*

28. *Ibid.*

29. J. Hurst, *The Legitimacy of the Business Corporation in the Law of the United States, 1780-1970*, Charlottesville: University Press of Virginia, 1970, pp. 58-111.

30.   D. Bazelon, *The Paper Economy*, New York: Random House, 1959, pp. 184-85.

31.   *Ibid.*, pp. 190-91.

32.   J. Stanfield, "Legitimacy and Value in Corporate Society, *Nebraska Journal of Economics and Business*, Winter 1975, pp. 3-18.

5

FEUDALISM

INTRODUCTION

> Feudalism isn't really . . . [a] . . . "nationwide" economic system.
> There isn't any "nation," . . . just a lot of independent units. . . each
> operating almost entirely on its own.[E. Bowden, *Economic
> Evolution*, Cincinnati: South-Western, 1981, p. 86.]

The American economic system is a product of an extensive historical
background. Its past is rooted in a colonial heritage of mercantilism,
including various political, social, and economic arrangements which gave
rise to that system. The long-standing use of clocks and calendars has
created a false sense of structure, at least for observers of developed areas,
for thinking discretely rather than continuously. But historical periods do
not have distinctive borders. So-called epochs have fuzzy lines of
demarcation which tend to merge over time. Moreover, historical patterns
differ by era as well as area. As a result, generalizing about a particular
experience of political economy is somewhat hazardous.

One way to handle such past events is to reconstruct separate forms of
social (or political, or economic) organization through which humankind has
passed over the centuries and to recognize their overlap. Whereas scholars
have identified and labelled cultural systems--social arrangements--beginning
with prehistoric and ancient times, a convenient place to begin is the fall of
the Roman Empire. The historical period called the Middle Ages gave rise
to feudalism, which was in turn a forerunner to mercantilism and capitalism.
A brief description of important events during that time may shed light on
certain institutional arrangements today.

One feature of this book is to present an evaluation of the nature of
modern American capitalism. This task is accomplished partly through the
mechanism of comparative systems: feudalism, mercantilism, fascism, and
socialism. In recent years, various scholars have compared and contrasted

modern American capitalism with different forms of economic organization. One important connection focuses on the nature of and reasons for the transition from manorialism or feudalism to capitalism. In that spirit, this chapter investigates the organization of feudalism during the medieval period. What was feudalism? Where did it operate? When did it come into existence? Which arrangements identify its structure and functions? How did feudal ideas give rise to mercantilism and then capitalism? Do any vestiges of feudalism linger in American capitalism?

After describing the nature of feudalism, including its background, the topics of medieval economics and the decline of feudalism are considered. The narrative then shifts to the relation between feudal arrangements and present-day activities in the American economic system. The discussion concludes with some implications for understanding modern American capitalism.

NATURE OF FEUDALISM

Many historians, . . . prefer not to offer rigorous definitions of feudalism, but rather to describe feudal society, . . . [D. Herlihy, *The History of Feudalism*, New York: Walker, 1970, p. xix.]

As a social, political, military, and economic system, feudalism existed in Europe, Asia, the Middle East, and other areas. Evidences of feudalism and feudal-like societies can still be found in the world today. The primary concern here is with feudalism in Western Europe, the area from which our laws and institutions were derived. This is not to suggest an America for Europeans, but only to remind that the heritage of American capitalism is the colonial imperialism of England, France, and Spain.

Origin

Feudalism can be traced to events that occurred during the Roman Empire (31 B.C. to A.D. 476), a period which endured for 500 years and eventually encompassed an area from England to Hungary to the Caspian Sea and thence from the northern edges of Africa into Spain. By A.D. 395, this vast area was governed by an Emperor of the East and an Emperor of the West. During that time, the institution of *latifundia* had created social distinctions between landowners and peasants. An increasing shortage of slaves caused landlords to rent their domestic holdings to free tenants and even to slaves for payment either in kind or by money. At the same time, frontier areas to which landlords had laid claim were settled with military personnel for defense purposes.[1] The former relation anticipated the feudal manor; the latter, the mercantilist colony.

When the western part of the Roman Empire disintegrated around the time of A.D. 476, the political network which held it together began to disintegrate. Many of the administrative units became difficult to coordinate and control. In various regions and areas, persons living in separate isolated localities had to resort to self-management. Thousands of small individually governed principalities and estates developed, with a tendency toward ever-smaller units similar to plantations. A general breakdown of law and order occurred as people were forced to look out for themselves.[2]

Feudalism did not exist when the Roman Empire declined, but evolved slowly over several centuries. Feudalist roots took hold in the eighth century, and what is now called feudalism was in full bloom by the eleventh century in Western Europe. With the Norman invasion of England and the subsequent Battle of Hastings in A.D. 1066 by William the Conqueror, feudalism was implanted in Britain.

The fall of the Roman Empire caused political chaos in Western Europe. Stability was largely regained under the rulers of Carolingian dynasty--Charles Martel, Pepin, and Charlemagne--who governed kingdoms in the vicinity of France, Germany, and Italy between A.D. 714-987. When that empire fell in the tenth century, political instability was in the process of being reduced.

Feudalism developed during the political fragmentation of the Carolingian dynasty[3] and "coincided with a profound weakening of the State."[4] Primitive transportation and communications facilities meant limited mobility. Raids, pillage, and plunder by robbers required that protective measures be taken. The continual threat of disease and invasion caused people to organize into small geographic units for defense and survival, so they became self-reliant and self-sufficient.[5] As a resource, land was vital to the existence of feudal society. Economic life revolved around agriculture and handicraft production with barter as an important basis for exchange. In the Middle Ages, two institutions were recognized and accepted: inequality among people resulting in social classes, and authority of the Church with its religious and secular power.[6] These relationships spawned a division between landowners and peasants, and a tendency for the Church to control large tracts of land.

Characteristics

Members of feudal society did not refer to their world as feudalism. A significant observation for the period is that neither feudalism (English) nor *feodalite* (French) "seems to have come into use until the latter eighteenth century."[7] "Feudal" has a Germanic origin from fehu-od from which the English and French term, fief, is derived.[8] Words such as *feos* (Burgundian, meaning moveable property), *fehu* (Frankish, meaning possession), and *fevum* (Latin, meaning grant of land)[9] help define feudalism. By 1100,

"feodum . . . began to prevail [as the] standard Latin term for . . . fief [and]
feudum . . . to connote a concrete object--a piece of land, conveyed not
absolutely but with conditions attached . . ."[10]

Feudalism was a system of social relationships based primarily on land
and personal service: (1) a relation between lord and vassal; (2) local
government; (3) a contractual land-tenure system for the use of land in
return for service; (4) private armies with military obligations, and (5) a lord
who has taxing and locational rights over a peasant.[11] These relations
were characterized by oath, loyalty, obligation, social rank, dependency, and
power.[12] Thus, three complementary concepts help describe the political
economy of feudalism. The first is a social organization in which a free
person obligates himself to work and give military service to a landlord in
return for protection and maintenance. The second is a type of
governmental domination within small diverse political areas controlled by
inherited power. The third focuses on social classes in which peasants are
dominated by landlords and coerced into creating economic rent for the
latter.[13]

Feudal Arrangements[14]

Stability and order in feudal society were based on its institutions. In
the Middle Ages, there was a need for continual protection because of the
constant threat of attack and pillage by invaders. The springboard for
establishing feudal relations began with the act of gaining control over
property, usually land. Peasants ordinarily lived throughout the fertile
tillable land, produced its agricultural output, and existed on a subsistence
basis.[15]

The fundamental institutions of feudalism were the fief and vassalage.
A fief was not land per se, but an estate in land--i.e., certain rights
associated with the use of land. The size of the fief varied from a small farm
to a vast plantation or a small town or village. Nonfeudal population--
chiefly peasants who tilled the soil--lived on the fief, but ordinarily paid rent
in a combination of ways: money, service, or in kind. Serfs and peasants
were technically not a part of the formal feudal ceremony. The vassal was
the lord of his own part of the fief who, by assuming the role of a vassal,
became a part of the feudal (or upper social) class.

A feudal contract was made when a man (e.g., a knight or an artisan)
paid homage to a lord (who was a vassal, or subordinate of someone else)
by pledging his loyalty (fealty) to him. The soon-to-be vassal knelt in front
of the lord, placed his hands between those of the latter, and promised to
serve his lord. The lord, in turn, promised to protect his vassal who owed
him military service, political obligations, and financial payments. The vassal
was expected to be a soldier and defend his lord against aggression or
invasion. When the lord held court, the vassal was expected to provide

counsel or advice if beckoned. The lord reserved partial control over the vassal's fief and could demand monetary payment from him.[16] As feudalism evolved, fiefs could be inherited but the survivor had to renew homage and fealty individually, including the possible payment of "relief" in the form of money, goods, or land. Subinfeudation--the act of one vassal partitioning his fief via homage and fealty to endow and create a vassal of his own--was not uncommon.

Lords wanted to retain control over land and to perpetuate feudal obligations. Vassals wanted their children to be able to manage the lord's estate, enjoy the fruits of the fief, and benefit from the protection of the manor. As a result, complicated procedures for holding, using and transferring land eventually emerged. Conflicts among vassals and serfs were resolved by a court system based on a case-by-case determination of rights and damages. To this end, a system of "common law," flowing from reciprocal responsibilities of feudal land tenure, developed slowly over the centuries from A.D. 1066 to the fifteenth century.

MEDIEVAL ECONOMICS

[T]he special situation in which the parties found themselves, was to be governed by the fundamental idea of the Middle Ages that no one should take advantage of another. [W. Kuhn, *The Evolution of Economic Thought*, Cincinnati: Southwestern, 1970, p. 8.]

The Middle Ages, or medieval era, spanned a thousand years from the fall of Rome in A.D. 476 to the fall of Constantinople in A.D. 1453. Feudalism flourished during the latter part of that period. Medieval economic thinking in feudalism was forged and tempered by the prevailing philosophical view of the time--that of Scholasticism. Notions of equity and justice dominated economic thinking, as reflected in the doctrines of just price, fair wage, avoiding usury, and a clearly defined role for the state.

Scholasticism

As a philosophical doctrine, Scholasticism is associated with St. Augustine (A.D. 354-430) who explained the fall of Rome as a conflict between God and man.[17] It reached its zenith with St. Thomas Aquinas (A.D. 1225-1274), the ultimate scholastic scholar, who argued that "faith and revelation do not contradict reason; they transcend it."[18] Truth based on Christian revelation was more acceptable than truth obtained by reason alone. Scholasticism was influential during the reign of Charlemagne and his progeny over the Carolingian empire. As a philosophical doctrine, it was deeply rooted in Roman Catholicism and natural law philosophy. Most persons who professed to be intellectuals then were churchmen.[19]

Basically, Scholasticism attempted to reconcile faith and reason "by organizing all knowledge under theology, the Supreme Authority."[20] Scholastic writers--the "Schoolmen"--based many of their views on the concept of justice from Plato and Aristotle, and on rules for business conduct from Roman law. Scholastic doctrine established a religious standard by which to gauge the righteousness of economic behavior rather than to analyze economic activity or the economy itself.[21]

Scholasticism was dogmatic and authoritarian; it stressed a deep sense of duty, responsibility, and ethical behavior. Scholastics believed that knowledge was derived from the senses and that rules of logic must be followed whenever searching for truth and wisdom. Although philosophy was subordinated to Christian theology, it did not prevent "scholastic philosophy from developing a rational explanation of reality."[22] Nevertheless, "the Church was not simply an organ of feudal society but an organism distinct from [it] that always remained a power in its own right."[23]

Just Price

The core of medieval economic thought lay in the doctrine of *justum pretium*, the "just price," which focused primarily on exchange value. At the time, little capital equipment existed, so labor and land the basic factors of production. A primary belief was that one person should not take advantage of another or benefit from his/her predicaments. Scholastics questioned whether Christian dogma prevented one from making a profit by selling an item for more than its cost. St. Thomas Aquinas argued that such an act would be sinful and immoral.[24] Thus, a price charged could not be unfair and an item should be sold only for what it was worth--nothing more. To this end, "every commodity has some one true value which is absolute, . . . objective, . . . on the basis of . . . cost of production, [mainly] labor."[25] Cost of production would then be "just," and goods which embodied similar amounts of labor would exchange equally.[26]

A seller had a duty to disclose defects in goods sold if they were known. During the Middle Ages, rules against forestalling, regrating, and engrossing were enforced. Moreover, fixing a maximum price was a common feature of regulation under the guild system in feudalism.[27]

Fair Wage

The doctrine of a fair wage is a corollary to the concept of a just price, a wage being the price of labor (*pretium laboris*). Both ideas are based on concepts of ethics and justice. The fair or just wage was a customary payment, absent of exploitation. St. Antoninus argued that the agreed-on wage must be paid punctually.[28] A person who rendered services was supposed to obtain enough in payment from them to live the status of life destined for him by God. Indeed, the "purpose of wages was to enable the worker to support himself and his dependents on his social level."[29] This view was consistent with the overall goal during the Middle Ages of insuring socio-economic stability.

Usury

Scholastic and contemporary understandings of usury are somewhat different. To the Schoolmen, usury was any amount charged for a loan of anything on which a contract was made, i.e., usury was equivalent to interest. The modern view is that "usury is an exorbitant, oppressive interest rate."[30]

Aristotle considered money to be barren and that taking interest was unnatural.[31] For him, money was to be used as "a means of facilitating legitimate (natural) exchange."[32] Both the Old and New Testament[33] indicate that interest--"profiting from loans"--is wrong. In A.D. 325, at the Council of Nicea, the Catholic Church adopted a position "against usury part of its official doctrine."[34] Charity was a Christian duty and doctrines of equity and justice had to guide the receipt of interest. Above all, one person must not take advantage of another. St. Thomas, like Aristotle, held that money had no value in itself and should not be an object of exchange. He claimed that interest on consumer goods was sinful whereas interest on productive goods was acceptable.[35]

Economic Role of State

A key feature of feudalism was that many separate estates were managed locally without any unified central government. The Roman Catholic Church, however, was under the authority of the Bishop of Rome, i.e., the Pope. Scholastics believed in a philosophy which rested on central authority. These were based on Church dogma and the Roman concept of law and responsibility. Functions of government were to sustain the population, provide for the poor, establish safe and free roads, maintain weights and measures, decrease litigation, and ensure exact and unchanging coinage for purpose of monetary control. These were lofty goals, for conditions were chaotic in feudalism; economic affairs were in turmoil, especially weights, measures, coinage, and transportation.[36]

DECLINE OF FEUDALISM

It was the beginning of a process which in the long run was destined to throw aside medieval internationalism, and to imbue the relations of states with each other. . . [H. Pirenne, *Economic and Social History of Medieval Europe*, New York: Harcourt, Brace & World, 1965, p. 217.]

The Middle Ages began to close during the fifteenth century. A number of interrelated events occurred which ultimately led to a decline in the institution of feudalism.

Organizational

When the Roman and Carolingian empires fell, centralized government also fell. Feudalism developed because local control was necessary to provide stability and order. But internal tensions within feudalism generated a desire to centralize government again, and to bring the diverse individualized units together into larger, more cohesive, manageable units.[37] Conflicts occurred among aggressive barons as they vied to increase the size of their manors. As a result, there was a tendency to centralize power and control over the landed areas.

Intellectual

During the eleventh and twelfth centuries, the Crusades produced a cross-fertilization of values between Europe and the Byzantine, or East Roman, Empire. Ideas from Greece and the Moslem world expanded people's thinking beyond Scholasticism. Toward the end of the Middle Ages, intellectual thought progressed so that "a rational and scientific approach to social problems" began to be taken.[38] Moreover, the spiritual power of Christianity declined somewhat, and so did its central doctrinal authority. The seeds of the Protestant Reformation were being sown. People began to think more for themselves and started to criticize church practices.[39] As the Crusades stimulated trade and commerce, a tendency developed toward creating large, wealthy and powerful nation-states.[40]

Technological

Technological advances brought about changes in agrarian organization as well as in military weaponry and tactics: an improved plow, crop rotation, printing, gunpowder, the cannon, and the gun. Economic activity, productivity, and one's ability to survive in feudalism stemmed from the land. As feudal institutions matured, a powerful incentive developed for vassals and serfs to try to gain control over land. One way to achieve this goal was to have as many heirs as possible. Population growth and expansion of towns increased the demand for food, so trade and commerce diverted some agricultural output from the manor to the city.

As trade and commerce grew, cities and nation-states developed. As technology progressed, the growth of commerce diminished subsistence farming.[41] In addition, the enclosure movement converted arable land into pasture in order to increase wool production for expanding textile markets. The commons was reduced with the effect that subsistence agriculture characterizing feudalism could no longer be sustained at former levels.

Militaristic

The feudal land-tenure system had allowed the feudal lord to "obtain a force of expert cavalry, garrison his castles, and provide for all ordinary needs of government without the expenditure of cash."[42] By the end of the fourteenth century a series of events occurred which changed this manner of conducting military operations.

In the feudal structure, kings, princes, and other nobility controlled vast areas of land, which had been divided into large estates overseen by manorial lords (their vassals) in return for certain services--primarily military. These lords, in turn, vassalized others through feudal investiture. By subinfeudation, the latter vassalized others in return for similar services. Whenever raising an army to conduct military operations became necessary, the nobleman called on the lord of the manor who then called on his vassals. The key figure for raising and directing the army was lord of the manor, but his control did not effectively extend to vassals established by subinfeudation.

As commerce and trade expanded, as transportation and technology improved, and as towns developed and the population grew, trade caravans travelling through a nobleman's area were charged a toll. Judicial adjustments were made on some estates in order to attract cases to their own courts to collect payments for those services. In addition, an increasing number of different taxes were instituted to increase the royal treasury. The nobility, especially kings, began to accumulate cash which allowed the direct hiring of mercenaries whenever an army was needed, thereby no longer having to rely on manorial lord to assemble an army.[43]

A Transition

Feudalism was a system of production for use based on custom and tradition, as well as a system of coercion and exploitation for accumulation of property and profit.[44] The organizational, philosophical, technological, and militaristic changes described above contributed to the decline of feudalism. Perhaps the major economic factor contributing to this decline was a fall in agricultural productivity. Moreover, both the nobility and lords sought additional sources of profit. A class society already existed in feudalism, and it was merely extended as the feudal mode of production gave way to a capitalist mode. Advances in technology fostered ocean navigation, foreign commerce, trade, and colonialism. The late fifteenth century voyages of discovery and import of monetary metals--gold and silver from the New World--had dramatic and far-reaching effects on the old order. A coordination of efforts leading to territorial expansion and control occurred because of the alternating population decline and growth, the rise of towns and urban centers from local markets, and the formation of centralized governments. The ultimate result was a transition from feudalism into mercantilism and pre-capitalism.[45]

VESTIGES OF FEUDAL INSTITUTIONS

[F]eudalism left behind . . . legacies. . . in our methods of behaviour and thought and feeling, in the ways in which we express our ideas.[F. Ganshof, *Feudalism*, New York: Harper & Row, 1961, p. 170.]

Several remnants of feudalism remain in Western nations, including American capitalism. Some are ceremonial but others are operational and functional.

Overview[46]

A few vestiges of feudalism remain in France and other parts of the continent in Western Europe. However, in England and the United States several traces may be observed. The English House of Lords, which descended from the Magna Curia of the twelfth century, is a pattern for the U.S. Senate. There is also the pageantry of the British Court, the royal coronation, and the chivalrous belief that a "gentleman" ought to be from the landed aristocracy. Some persons even yearn for knighthood or titles of courtesy, and aspire to be called "esquire."

Some Important Remnants

Remnants exist in the form of the prestige of the military profession, the binding force of agreements or contracts freely entered into, and refusals to follow an order inconsistent with the dignity of a free person. The fidelity or loyalty in human interaction with neighbor, employer, and supervisor can be related to feudalism. Moreover, many states have usury and sales-below-cost ("fair-trade pricing") statutes as well as minimum-wage-laws (passed in 1938 at the federal level). In addition, the obligations of government for roads, coinage, and other social programs had their origin in the Roman Empire, have persisted through feudalism, and now exist in the modern era.

The vassal owed military service to his lord during times of military conflict. Likewise, the United States has used conscription to insure an adequate army during times of war. Inheritance taxes are a modern form of the "relief" that surviving heirs of a vassal paid to the lord upon assuming feudal obligations. Taxes on land are related to the financial support the vassal paid the lord in exchange for the latter's protection. Even the practice of chivalry, the proper conduct for a man, carries over from feudalism and exhibits "two unique qualities":[47] (1) to be willing to fight, and (2) to act courteously, not only on the battle field but regarding women. Perhaps even the Mafia godfather is a lingering feudal idea?

English Common Law

By the Declaration of Independence and the United States Constitution, America inherited the common law of England, which was in effect at the Norman Conquest. Moreover, representative government, which stems directly from the Magna Carta of A.D. 1215, developed out of the feudal era. One legal case cited for first-year law students is I de S et ux. v. W de S, decided in A.D. 1348 and still the law today, holding that civil assault can occur without actual touching.[48] Several other case-law holdings from the feudal period are often cited. The common law of torts, contracts, and property is directly related to institutional arrangements developed in feudal England. When the medieval period began to close in A.D. 1456, these institutions did not suddenly die. They were adjusted and expanded, but not abandoned.

Land Tenure[49]

The United States derived its real property law from England, the roots of which extend to the Battle of Hastings, in 1066. For centuries, courts have resolved conflicts for such matters as possession, use, inheritance, and acquisition of land. Several feudal land-tenure concepts from the medieval period have counterparts in modern-day legal doctrine.

Escheat: If a tenant died without heirs, land was returned to the lord of the manor. Today, the legal operation of escheat is for "unclaimed" land to revert to the State.

Relief: When a tenant died and left an heir, the latter had to pay the lord for the privilege of succession to rights to use the land. A counterpart is the present-day inheritance tax on property.

Frankalmoin: For gifts of land to the church, the feudal obligations of service or duty did not apply. Today, church property enjoys some taxation privileges.

Socage: Men holding land via socage were obligated to work the lord's land and provide him some of its output. A long-standing practice in rural America has been for a tenant who lives on and uses an owner's land to yield to the landowner between one-third and two-fifths of crops grown.

Alienation: After A.D. 1066, a tenant was unable to transfer his rights to land without the lord's permission and the payment of a fine. This was abolished in A.D. 1290 by the English Statute of Quia Emptores, but the feudal rule of obtaining permission continued to exist. Today, zoning ordinances regulate changes in land use.

Seisen: Seisen is a medieval metaphysical concept which refers to gaining control over land and holding it by peaceful possession. A who person "owned" land had certain rights to it which were recognized and accepted by society as being complete. He/she may or may not have lived on that land by "occupying" it. A tenant living on the land but not holding legally recognized ownership to it did not have seisen. This bifurcation exists today, for the law distinguishes carefully between "possession" and "ownership," and seisen is still used in modern-day court decisions.

Fee Simple: The largest bundle of rights to land in common-law countries has been known as "an estate in fee simple" for many centuries. With it, there are two basic conditions: (1) rights exist ostensibly for a limitless time period; and (2) an owner can transfer these complete, durable rights to others, including one's descendants. The concept of an estate in fee simple was developed between A.D. 1066 and A.D. 1290 (when the Statute Quia Emptores was enacted). Today, in England, Canada, Australia, New Zealand, and the United States, holding an estate in land "in fee simple" still means absolute rights forever (but subject to state action).

Fee Tail: Before A.D. 1285, land could be given to someone "and the heirs of his body." A condition was thereby created: if the donee had no blood children, or the blood children died before the donee, the land would revert to the donor. If blood children existed, then the courts held that the donee could alienate the land in fee simple (even though contrary to donor's intent). In A.D. 1285, the Statute De Donis Conditionalibus was passed, and the concept of "fee tail" was created: land given by a donor to a donee with the words, "and heirs of his body," meant that the land must pass to the blood children if any existed. Today, "fee tail" is still followed in Delaware, Maine, Massachusetts, and Rhode Island. Eight other states adjust the fee tail to give the heirs of the donee a remainder interest in the land (which essentially resembles the original fee-tail concept).

Future Interests: A "future interest" is a planned and committed conveyance of something, usually real property, to a second and/or third party. The law of future interests, followed in United States and other common-law countries, traces to the medieval period. Feudal tenure was abolished by the Statute Quia Emptores in A.D. 1290, but its effect leaves remnants influenced by feudal arrangements. At common law today, the following age-old legal relations exist: "reversion" (land transferred for a limited duration to grantee); "possibility of a reverter" (land transferred on a condition which fails to occur); "right of entry for condition broken" (land transferred on condition that certain events not occur but which, in fact, do occur) and the "remainder" (land transferred for a limited duration to one party but is passed to another party after that).

Courts of Equity[50]

A plaintiff can take legal action against a defendant in both civil law and equity, the former by jury trial for monetary damages and the latter for determining some right without a jury. Courts of equity developed in medieval England as an alternative to the strict rules for relief imposed by courts of law. Originally, the king dispensed justice by deciding cases not heard by courts of law, but eventually a chancellor was appointed to hear special grievances. In A.D. 1258, the Provisions of Oxford restricted the ability of a Chancellor to grant equitable "writs" but in A.D. 1285, the Statute of Westminster II again allowed the hearing of cases in equity.

The United States had separate courts of law and of equity until they were merged in 1938 in most jurisdictions. Today, distinct actions in equity persist--restitution, rescission, partition, injunction, reformation, specific performance--which are heard and decided by a judge with no jury. In addition, "small claims courts" exist to dispense justice in both equity and law without a jury trial (which may include minor claims for monetary damage).

CONCLUDING REMARKS

[W]e have to understand that the time-dimensions of social change are much slower, and the processes more complex, than . . . apocalyptic vision, religious or revolutionary, would have us believe.[D. Bell, *The Cultural Contradictions of Capitalism*, New York: Basic, 1976, p. 8.]

Economic systems ostensibly exist on a continuum, evolving slowly before eventually merging into one another. Feudalism gave rise to capitalism through a transition stage of mercantilism. Just as the latter contained remnants of feudalism, so capitalism contains remnants of both situations. Given the apparent overlap, care must be taken whenever attempting to identify unique elements within each.

Feudalism was a type of social organization out of which developed related political and economic arrangements. Any "political economy" of feudalism, however, would be primitive compared to the elaborate superstructures of today. Political economy refers to coordination by government of the production of goods which realigns property, resources, and income. A status of power emerges somewhere, and class distinctions eventually arise. Obviously, there was a tightly organized society under feudalism which deliberately strove to generate stability. Economic affairs were connected to land. Political aspects related to control over land and obligations based on that control. The economy was labor-intensive with little equipment or machinery. Modern practices of political economy center on a capital-intensive industrial base for begetting economic activity. Political economy involves vying for control over these productive resources. In feudalism, power existed and so did class distinctions. Moreover, property rights were assigned and resource allocation was regulated; both interacted to cause a differential impact on the distribution of income.

Casual observers of social history frequently claim that present-day class distinctions between rich and poor constitute feudalism in modern dress. Complaints concerning the distribution of tax burdens are often associated with a continuation of feudal policies. That lower-income persons may comprise a disproportionate share of the military is alleged to be akin to the feudal practice of serfs supporting landlords in their warfare endeavors. Some persons even contend that the property class currently relegates the working class to a status of serfdom. But such contentions hardly establish that the American economy is feudalistic, or that the citizens live under feudalism. A few remnants of feudalistic institutions can be found in American capitalism, especially certain legal relations (such as the ownership and transfer of real property).

Care must be taken not to draw hasty conclusions about feudalism. Technology was at a low level then, conditions were primitive, and many persons lived at a subsistence level. Harsh economic circumstances meant relatively short lives. Both the Church and the social system were authoritative. However, reciprocal social and economic obligations existed among lords, vassals, and serfs. Despite the presence of a rigid class structure, human existence was not uncivilized and uncultured. Feudalism may have been exploitative--serfs produced (barely) enough to reproduce themselves with a surplus taken by vassals and lords--but a strong sense of mutual concern and social justice apparently characterized everyday affairs. Feelings of duty, honor, and responsibility were widespread. A legacy of feudalism to capitalism therefore might be that both public policy and individual action reflect greater social awareness and concern for basic needs among all citizens. Indeed, recognition of this quality is not a recent idea, but one which has a long and respectable history.

NOTES

1. E. Roll, *A History of Economic Thought*, Englewood Cliffs: Prentice-Hall, 1956, pp. 41-42.

2. A. Ferrill, "Roman Empire," *The Encyclopedia Americana*, Danbury: Grolier, 1989, pp. 738-39.

3. R. Brenner, "Feudalism," *The New Palgrave: A Dictionary of Economics*, Vol. 2, London: Macmillan, 1987, p. 310.

4. M. Bloch, *Feudal Society*, Vol. 2, Chicago: University of Chicago Press, 1964, p. 443.

5. H. Pirenne, *Economic and Social History of Medieval Europe*, New York: Harcourt Brace & World, 1937, pp. 7-8 and 66-70.

6. Roll, *op. cit.*, p. 43.

7. C. Stephenson, *Medieval Feudalism*, Ithaca: Cornell University Press, 1942, p. 1.

8. J. Prawer, and S. Eisenstadt, "Feudalism," *International Encyclopedia of the Social Sciences*, Vol. 5, New York: Macmillan and Freepress, 1968, p. 393.

9. D. Herlihy, *The History of Feudalism*, New York: Harper & Row, 1970, p. xiii.

10. *Ibid.*, p. xiv.

11. R. Coulborn, *Feudalism in History*, Hamden: Archon, 1965.

12. M. Weber, *The Theory of Social and Economic Organization*,Glencoe: Free Press, 1947, pp. 373-81.

13. Brenner, *Palgrave, op. cit.*, p. 309.

14. See Stephenson, *op. cit.*; F. Ganshof, *Feudalism*, New York: Harper Torchbooks, 1964; and J. Critchley, *Feudalism*, London: George Allen & Unwin, 1978, pp. 10-55, for a general description of the institutions of feudalism.

15. G. Duby, *The Early Growth of the European Economy*, Ithaca: Cornell University Press, 1974, pp. 157-210.

16. *Ibid.*, pp. 310-11.

17. I. Rima, *Development of Economic Analysis*, Homewood: Irwin, 1986, p. 7.

18. "Scholasticism," *The Encyclopedia Americana*, Vol. 24, Danbury: Grolier, Inc., 1989, p. 368.

19. J. Schumpeter, *History of Economic Analysis*, New York: Oxford University Press, 1954, p. 75.

20. J. Bell, *A History of Economic Thought*, New York: Ronald, 1967, p. 43.

21. "Medieval Philosophy," *The Encyclopedia of Philosophy*, Vol. 5, New York: Macmillan, pp. 252-54.

22. M. De Wulf, "Scholasticism," *Encyclopedia of the Social Sciences*, Vol. 13, New York: Macmillan, 1963, pp. 578-81.

23. "Scholasticism," *Americana*, p. 368.

24. R. Heilbroner, *The Making of Economic Society*, Englewood Cliffs: Prentice-Hall, 1962, p. 39.

25. L. Haney, L., *History of Economic Thought*, New York: Macmillan, 1954, p. 99.

26. Bell, *op. cit.*, p. 44.

27. Roll, *op. cit.*, pp. 46-47.

28. R. De Roover, "Economic Thought," *International Encyclopedia of the Social Sciences*, Vol. 4, New York: Macmillan and Free Press, 1968, p. 434.

29. *Ibid.*

30. *Ibid.*

31. Roll, *op. cit.*, p. 49.

32. *Ibid.*

33. See Exodus 22:25 and Luke 6:35.

34. R. Eklund, and R. Hebert, *A History of Economic Theory and Method*, New York: McGraw-Hill, 1979, p. 34.

35. M. Landreth, *History of Economic Theory*, Boston: Houghton Mifflin, 1988, p. 18.

36. E. Whittaker, *History of Economic Ideas*, New York: Longmans, 1940, pp. 31-32.

37. Roll, *op. cit.*, pp. 54-55.

38. *Ibid.*, p. 55.

39. Whittaker, *op. cit.*, p. 33.

40. *Ibid.*, p. 32.

41. F. Cazel, "Feudalism," *The Encyclopedia Americana*, Vol. 2, Danbury: Grolier, 1989, p. 142.

42. Stephenson, *op. cit.*, p. 97.

43. Prawer and Eisenstadt, *International Encyclopedia*, *op. cit.*, pp. 398-99.

44. R. Gottleib, "Feudalism and Historical Materialism: A Critique and a Synthesis," *Science and Society*, Spring 1984, pp. 2-7.

45. R. Hilton, ed., *The Transition from Feudalism to Capitalism*, London: Humanities, 1976, pp. 9-30 and 141-158.

46. Stephenson, *op. cit.*, pp. 105-07.

47. Ganshof, *op. cit.*, p. 170. (See also Herlihy, *op. cit.*, pp. 281-82.)

48. W. Prosser, *Law of Torts*, St. Paul: West, 1971, p. 38.

49. C. Moynihan, *Introduction to the Law of Real Property*, St. Paul: West, 1962, p. 22-125.

50. D. Dobbs, *Remedies*, St. Paul: West, 1973, pp. 24-91.

6   MERCANTILISM

INTRODUCTION

[T]he West has, since 1945, passed through a second long boom period of "disguised mercantilism." The leader in self-deception on this occasion would have been, not Britain, but the new Anglo-Saxon superpower, the United States. [J. Knapp, "Economics or Political Economy?" *Lloyds Bank Review*, January 1973, p. 41.]

American capitalism began to relinquish its competitive, free-enterprise, laissez faire, market ideals before the turn of the present century.[1] In their place appear a resurgence of pre-classical economic principles in new guises. British economists identified mercantilist behavior among western developed nations a few decades ago. Joan Robinson delivered a lecture in 1965 at Cambridge University on "the new mercantilism."[2] A few years later, the economics section of the British Association for the Advancement of Science addressed the same subject.[3] During the 1970s, *Business Week* twice suggested that mercantilist tendencies were present in the United States as well.[4]

Foreign investment abroad, a favorable balance of payments, and the enactment of trade barriers have been cited as primary goals of neomercantilism on both sides of the Atlantic. Mercantilist institutions and practices involve much more than international protectionism, however. This chapter describes a broader range of mercantilist features and reviews how they have been identified with modern American capitalism.

THE QUADRUPLE COINCIDENCE

[T]he scope of government must be limited ... [and] ... government power must be dispersed. [In] competitive capitalism--the organization of the bulk of economic activity [is] through private

enterprise operating in a free market--as a system of economic
freedom . . . [M. Friedman, *Capitalism and Freedom*, Chicago:
University of Chicago Press, 1964, pp. 2-4.]

The ideological scene is cluttered with diverse views on the nature of the
American economy. Some observers contend that the system is moving
toward socialism.[5] Others believe it is already fascist.[6] There is little
debate from either conservatives or liberals, however, that ours is a
government-intense economy. The argument centers on whether incursions
by the state into business and private affairs are left-oriented or right-
oriented. The important question concerns the nature of what is called
capitalism. Certainly the mixed capitalism[7] of today is different from the
small-enterprise capitalism of yesterday. The distinction is neither
recognized nor mentioned by some observers who take our system for
granted.[8]

Capitalism in General

In a narrow sense, "capitalism" refers to the large-scale use of machinery
in manufacturing, as opposed to labor-intensive or land-intensive modes of
production.[9] By this criterion, all industrially developed countries are
capitalist, even the 1950-1990 Soviet Union. What is distinctive in western
democracies is that most productive capital is privately owned property.
Although the profit motive, consumer sovereignty, self-interest, and
specialization are also alleged characteristics of western capitalism, the
institution of private ownership of property is in a central position.[10]

Capitalism often is regarded as synonymous with the business system in
the United States. The American business ideology[11] stresses as axiomatic
that business power, if it exists, is legitimate power; that business provides
productive capital so that workers will have jobs and can earn wages to buy
goods and services; that business provides services to consumers; that
business pays taxes to support social programs; that competition is an
expression of natural forces in society; and that government restrictions on
business activities tend to move the economy toward socialism.[12]

The conventional wisdom holds that capitalism is a quadruple
coincidence among free-enterprise, competition, laissez faire, and the
market.[13] There probably is no other system of belief which has become
so ingrained into the American ethos as this. That its indoctrination has
become complete is evidenced by the tendency of both liberals and
conservatives to repeat it.[14] While each element in the quadruple
coincidence is considered to be an integral part of capitalism in the United
States, the business establishment has become schizoid about laissez faire.
An active role for government is touted as being inconsistent with free-
enterprise and competitive-market ideals, but is tacitly relied upon as

necessary for the growth and development of the American economic system. And certainly this is the case with Japan and the recently industrialized countries (RICs) of Asia.

Role of Government

The ethic of statism--the right of government to intervene into social, economic, religious and cultural affairs--remained essentially unchallenged from the time of the empires of the ancient world to the nation states of the seventeenth century in Europe. Historically, the sovereign powers of certain western nations granted special privileges to selected private interests. State and federal governments dispense similar favors in the United States today. They maintain the domestic price of oil and sugar by establishing import quotas and embargoes; they organize crop restriction programs for farmers; they grant franchises for operating television and radio stations to private companies; they enact protective tariffs which shield industries from foreign competition; they make it illegal for foreign ships to engage in coastal shipping; they set minimum as well as maximum freight rates for railroads and for motor carriers; they restrict entry into public utilities; they protect communications companies from competition; they authorize occupational groups to require the licensing of attorneys, dentists, physicians, nurses, cosmetologists, barbers, and taxi drivers.[15]   A special-interest group benefitting from a government-granted privilege condones its existence but resents the enactment of similar benefits for other special interests.

Business executives usually view government with suspicion and consider it unproductive, extravagant, and harmful. New controls that threaten business freedom are denounced, and managers complain that government is meddling in private affairs. Business nevertheless has always been regulated in America and has prospered despite regulation, and often because of it. American government is not an independent entity possessing a will of its own. The governmental system--federal, state, and local--is a creature of the American people and responds to the pressures brought to bear upon it. Most governmental policies and programs exist because business, labor, and other special interests sought them from their elected representatives.[16]

CHARACTERISTICS OF MERCANTILISM

[M]ercantilism cannot be regarded as a system of power ... [and] of welfare. The economic activity of the commonwealth was *mobilized* for international rivalry; but ... was ordered and balanced for the prosperity, employment, and security of its members ... The merchant, the manufacturer, the lender, and the landlord were

subject to state supervision . . . from standardization of goods to
control of prices. [P. W. Buck, *The Politics of Mercantilism*, New
York: Octagon, 1964, pp. 180-181.]

When Adam Smith published his *Wealth of Nations* during the onset of
the American Revolution, both he and the colonists were reacting against
the encumbering bureaucracy of British mercantilism.   Mercantilist
governments collected vast sums of taxes from the people, established state-
sanctioned monopolies, and enacted a myriad of regulations on business and
personal life.   Mercantilists believed that government could enhance its
wealth by restricting competition, but Smith argued that mercantilist
controls ultimately hinder an economy and bring about inefficiency.
Conversely, the pursuit of competition would permit the "invisible hand" of
self-interest to lead the economy toward the most beneficial pattern of
production and distribution.   Ironically, Smith himself suggested that if
people became overly selfish, they might destroy the legal institutions
protecting private property and competition, thereby ushering in a new form
of mercantilism.[17]

Debate Over Mercantilism

What Smith called the "mercantile" system was not called *mercantilism*
until 1888.[18] Between that time and the early 1930s there was renewed
interest in the political and economic policies which had prevailed from the
Middle Ages until the onset of classical laissez-faire economics. Based on
Smith's incisive remarks in Book IV ("Of Systems of Political Economy") of
the *Wealth of Nations*, several related interpretations of mercantilist goals
and policies emerged. The main figures in this late 19th, early 20th century
debate were Gustav Schmoller, William Cunningham, Eli Heckscher, and
Jacob Viner.

Schmoller argued that mercantilism was primarily *state-making*. The vast
changes which took place in the latter half of the sixteen century had acted
as a catalyst for national unification: advances in transportation and the
opening up of world trade; the use of money and banking facilities; the
development of postal and communications services; and the rise of domestic
manufacturing. Schmoller wrote:

These forces all converging impelled society to some large economic
reorganization on a broader basis, and pointed to the creation of
national states with a corresponding policy . . . [19]

Cunningham reasoned that the opportunities afforded by new technology
led mercantilists to seek and consolidate power. To accomplish this goal,
mercantilists had to manage commerce, oversee the flow of specie, regulate

imports and exports, maintain a strong navy, establish navigation acts, foster industry and agriculture, and encourage a healthy and vigorous population. As a rationale for the mercantile system, Cunningham contended that:

> The end in view was Power. This was furthered by attention to Treasure, Shipping and Population . . . [20]

Heckscher argued that in addition to a desire for *unification*, mercantilists sought *power as an end in itself* through protectionism, a favorable trade balance, and the accumulation of national wealth.[21] Essentially he synthesized the viewpoints of several figures who wrote about mercantilism--Smith, Schmoller, and Cunningham--into a cohesive concept of society. Heckscher was a staunch free-trader and wrote his 1931 treatise[22] on mercantilism as a reaction against the twentieth century trend toward protectionism. Heckscher contended that:

> The mercantilist conception of what was to a country's advantage centered on . . . the supply of commodities and money.[23]

Viner agreed that mercantilist states sought unification along with *power and wealth*; he disagreed with Heckscher's interpretation that power was the sole objective of mercantilists. Viner believed that the quest for power and the quest for wealth went hand in hand, each reinforcing the other as inseparable goals.

According to Viner,

> for the mercantilists power and plenty were regarded as coexisting ends of national policy which were fundamentally harmonious . . . [24]

The debate suggests that mercantilism was never a single unified body of interrelated, consistent principles because it existed in several forms, in various countries, and at different times.[25] Mercantilist ideas and policies were practiced in Spain, the Netherlands, England, and France from the sixteenth to the eighteenth centuries. It consisted of policies to enhance power, wealth, and unification, and also featured programs for internal and external development. Mercantilism was a good example of how the political economy operates.

Mercantilist Political Economy

Mercantilist countries were characterized by governmental control over both foreign trade and the domestic economy. Extensive powers were vested in a monarch because centralized authority was considered to be necessary for accomplishing mercantilist goals. Matters of trade were coordinated by a trade council; board members consisted of merchants, manufacturers, and land owners who advised on methods to protect and increase the wealth of the state. Mercantilists erected protective trade barriers designed to benefit native merchants, trading enterprises, and manufacturing industries. To protect domestic interests, mercantilists established strong navies and navigation laws favorable to local traders.[26]

Mercantilist England provides examples of political arrangements to augment the economic system. Through the Corn Laws, production and price of grains were regulated; to protect local farmers imports were restricted; to keep prices stabilized export duties were charged when prices were high, and bounties were offered to exports when prices were low. Agriculture underwent considerable technological change, chiefly by the introduction of new techniques in land cultivation. The Enclosures Acts had been initiated--at the expense of many tenant farmers--for the purpose of increasing output and profit in the wool and woolens industries by making pasture available.

New industries such as the East India Company and the Hudson's Bay Company were granted monopoly franchises in the form of a corporate charter granted by the Crown and affirmed by Parliament. In exchange for this privilege, government retained the right of control and exercised supervision over prices and quality of goods produced. Commercial expansion increased the demand for borrowing and lending money, so Parliament established a national bank to provide low-interest loans to industry and merchants. Labor also was regulated. The Statute of Artificers encouraged production and fixed wages at a relatively low level. The Poor Law obliged all able-bodied members of the community to engage in productive labor. To prevent wage income from being squandered and to limit domestic consumption, Sumptuary Laws were enacted.

Mercantilism therefore was characterized by a maze of laws, codes, and regulations involving government directly in business, labor, and consumer affairs. Private ownership of land and machines existed, but productive resources often were concentrated in the hands of the few favored by government. There was a symbiotic relationship between business and government.

Toward the end of the mercantilist period (c. 1750) private property rights were broadened. Free entry into selected lines of business was encouraged as was competition. Laissez faire began to win favor and government increasingly relied on market forces.[27] As mercantilism evolved into market capitalism, the quadruple coincidence became integrated into economic thought. But the political economy of the earlier era appears to have been replaced by a political economy of a different form.

VIEWS ON MERCANTILISM IN AMERICA

[A] new mercantilism seems to be emerging, on its face very different from the old yet leading to policies and tactics . . . that would meet with hearty approval from . . . the chief architects of the old mercantilism. [J. Cobbs, "The New Mercantilism: Hoarding Jobs," *Business Week*, March 31, 1973, p. 38.]

Political economy in modern American capitalism has been contrasted with the policies and practices of mercantilism. The contention that the economic system of the United States contains mercantilist arrangements is neither new nor unique, and has been suggested several times during recent decades.

Keynes: Notes on Mercantilism

Three important areas of Keynes' thinking reflect mercantilist doctrines: his concepts of money, of government regulation, and of a favorable balance of trade. In the *General Theory*,[28] Keynes considered whether a favorable or an unfavorable balance of trade was most advantageous for a nation. He was particularly sympathetic toward the favorable-balance theory held by mercantilists, and criticized the classicists for having objected to it. To mercantilists, regulation aided economic development. Keynes also called upon the state for protection, suggesting that some kind of central authority may be necessary to achieve efficient resource allocation. Keynes supported direct governmental involvement to promote foreign investment because he believed it would help to reduce unemployment. Indeed, the Keynesian multiplier operates on foreign as well as on domestic investment.

While the ends advocated by mercantilists were power, privilege, and profit for special interests, Keynes was initially concerned with the general welfare. Keynes' economics had a definite mercantilist flavor to it, and to the extent the post-Keynesian macroeconomic policy makers in the United States have adopted the goal of a favorable balance of trade (including tariffs, quotas, and subsidies to achieve it), mercantilist thinking still persisted in modern American capitalism. Keynes' thinking probably influenced some of the social legislation under Franklin D. Roosevelt's (FDR's) second and third administrations.[29]

Golob: American Neomercantilism

According to Eugene Golob, the United States always has been characterized by the political economy of mercantilism: our system has perpetuated English economic traditions from colonial times to the present day.[30] Not only was Alexander Hamilton instrumental in continuing the mercantilist heritage, but the influential economists Henry C. Cary and Simon N. Patton also promulgated this view. Golob also classifies both Theodore Roosevelt and Woodrow Wilson as neomercantilists, and argues that the New Deal was a democratic form of neomercantilism because of the active way in which the administration of Franklin D. Roosevelt was involved in the economy.[31]

FDR's policy objectives and economic programs (Social Security, labor unions, housing, industrial recovery, agricultural development, and taxation) elicited legislation which brought neomercantilism face-to-face with democratic capitalism. In particular, the New Deal:

> . . . was neomercantilism in its insistence on the right and duty of the state to intervene in social and economic affairs . . ., in its maintenance of the role of private property and ownership . . ., of the nation as an economic and social entity, in its use of fiscal and monetary devices.[32]

English mercantilism was characterized by programs of governmental aid and control. New Deal legislation sanctioned price fixing, market sharing, and industry pooling arrangements. In fact, two massive New Deal programs, one for industry (the National Industry Recovery Act) and one for agriculture (the Agricultural Adjustment Act) were declared unconstitutional by the Supreme Court because they were anticompetitive and unreasonably restricted private property rights.

Adams and Gray: Monopoly in America

Just as Adam Smith's *Wealth of Nations* was a critique of eighteenth century English mercantilism, a polemic written by Walter Adams and Horace Gray (*Monopoly in America*) is an attack on mercantilist-like policies of American government.[33] Adams and Gray draw a parallel between the Crown-granted privileges under mercantilism and government promotion of monopoly power under American capitalism. Under mercantilism, special privileges, subsidies, and protection were granted to large-scale business interests. These policies encouraged economic concentration and monopoly power. In a competitive, free market economy such policies represent an abuse of government authority. Published in 1955, their analysis continues to be relevant because it describes accurately the political economy of the American business system.

Adams and Gray suggest examples of modern mercantilist practices in the United States: public utility regulation, tax loopholes, defense procurement, the disposal of surplus war property, government control over atomic energy, and American oil policy. Also cited is

. . . the federal government's activity in foreign trading resale price maintenance, guarantee of private debts, provision of capital and credit, legislative exemptions from the Sherman Act.[34]

Each of these arrangements involves special privileges granted by government which enhances the economic position of large-scale enterprise.

Robinson: The New Mercantilism

One dominant feature of eighteenth century mercantilism was the possession and exploitation of colonies. Joan Robinson contends that modern capitalist countries, especially the United States, continue to practice a form of mercantilist colonialism.[35] The American business sector, backed by strong foreign policy, exerts monopsony power in buying natural resources from developing nations, and exercises monopoly power in selling them manufactured goods. From Adam Smith to John Maynard Keynes, the free-trade doctrine was based on the conditions of orthodox perfect competition. In reality, however, very few traditional competitive conditions exist, so it is not surprising that Keynes and others recommend mercantilist-like policies to stimulate foreign trade for purposes of reducing domestic unemployment. The economic effects of the new mercantilism, according to Robinson, has not been to enhance the general welfare, but like seventeenth century mercantilism, to bestow benefits upon a selected private special interest groups, including workers who might otherwise lose their jobs.

Galbraith: The New Industrial State

John Kenneth Galbraith describes the American economy as dualistic, consisting of a small, subordinate market sector with a large, dominant planning sector.[36] Competition prevails in the former, but the market is dying in the latter. The "new industrial state," a modernized term for the "neomercantilist economy,"[37] consists of a planning sector which produces the majority of industrial output.

As emphasized in Chapter 4, the most important business arrangement in the United States is the corporate form of organization. The corporation was a key institution of seventeenth century English mercantilism because through it the Crown granted exclusive operational charters to selected private interest groups. With its corporate franchise, an English monopoly could establish a commercial beachhead in a foreign land. This exclusive right to carry on commerce in an area was secured and protected by the English navy. Galbraith's new industrial state is mercantilist because of a symbiotic relationship among big corporations, big military, big government, and big unions which dominate the economic system.

Since the industrial revolution the United States has seen accelerated progress in science and technology, especially after World War Two. Galbraith suggests this chain reaction: technology requires complex, large-scale production facilities; the corporation is well-suited for large size; expensive technological equipment increases risk and begets long-range planning; risk and planning require stability and certainty. Seeking and receiving vast amounts of aid from the State helps large corporations achieve these goals. Research and development are sponsored largely by government, scientific manpower is trained mainly by the government (in public schools and universities) aggregate demand is supported and stabilized by the government, failing companies are sometimes subsidized by the government, and foreign investment abroad is protected and insured by the government. In all of these ways, according to Galbraith, there is a striking similarity between economic activity in the planning system of the new industrial state and of pre-19th century mercantilism.

Papandreou: Paternalistic Capitalism[38]

For Andreas G. Papandreou, our type of capitalism is no longer competitive. The market has broken down, and the federal government has assumed many of the tasks previously accomplished by market forces. Welfare programs and defense spending augment aggregate demand, and the corporate managerial capitalist elite are "national security managers" who dominate domestic and foreign economic policies. Papandreou labels modern American capitalism as neomercantilist because of its international business and military policies. He contends that "paternalistic" capitalism fosters a military-industrial complex through which government makes defense contracts with a network of multinational corporations.

The structure and behavior of the multinational corporation . . . its military and intelligence arms, and the resulting nexus between private economic gain and the promotion of the strategic-security interests . . . justify the characterization of the . . . emerging system as neo-mercantilism.[39]

The political economy of these arrangements involves extensive planning. Indeed, political and social control of the economic environment is an inescapable requirement of neomercantilism.

CONCLUDING REMARKS

> For some time in America we have been moving from one
> ideological framework to another; . . . the old structure has been
> disintegrating and a new one is . . . being put in its place. [G. C.
> Lodge, *The New American Ideology*, New York: Knopf, 1975, p. 9.]

The mercantilism of seventeenth century Britain, France, Spain, and the
Netherlands featured deliberate government regulation of private business
activities. Controls over domestic manufactures, commerce, agriculture, and
foreign trade, and the maintenance of colonies characterized the seventeenth
century mercantilist state. Royal franchises, government-sponsored trade
councils, protective tariffs, and laws regulating labor, consumption,
innovation, and prices were enacted and administered by mercantilist
governments.

There is growing recognition that the contemporary American economy
contains mercantilist tendencies. Keynes' *General Theory*, the basis for many
of our contemporary macroeconomic policy tools, provides a justification for
current stabilization policies which exhibit mercantilist trappings.
Roosevelt's New Deal contained several mercantilist-like arrangements.
Governmental programs to regulate and aid industry, commerce, and utilities
have fostered monopoly power, similar to Crown policies under
mercantilism. United States foreign policy is partly designed to support a
subtle form of mercantilist colonialism. Economic dualism in the American
economy--a dominant concentrated corporate sector and a subservient
competitive sector--is akin to the structure of the mercantilist economy. The
symbiotic relationship among big business, big military, big government, big
unions, and big education, as contained in the military-industrial complex,
for example, is suggestive of American neomercantilism.

Amidst contentions that "creeping socialism" pervades America, definite
changes are occurring in the economic system. What commonly is called
capitalism probably is more accurately described as *neomercantilism*. (In
some corners, it may be considered as *neofascism*.) Instead of the quadruple
coincidence of free-enterprise, competition, laissez faire, and the market,
modern American "capitalism" reflects mercantilist arrangements reflecting
the technological changes that have occurred over the past two centuries.
Perhaps the American economic system never really lost its mercantilist
tendencies. Perhaps the polity failed to weave the quadruple coincidence
into the American fabric by underestimating the power of the old ways to
perpetuate themselves.

Business managers often lament that we ought to go back to the days
when the quadruple coincidence reigned supreme. But is there really a
"back when" to which we may go? Are we to go back to the 1920s when
small competitive enterprises were combining with larger firms and
augmenting industrial concentration? Are we to go back to the days of

reconstruction after the Civil War, the days of the trusts and robber barons of the Gilded Age? Are we to go back to the settlement of the western frontier when economic power was concentrated in the hands of the local merchants and government protectionism, subsidy, and control closely guided expansion and development? Are we to go back to the days of the First and Second Banks of the United States and that era of government-sanctioned monopoly power? Direct government expenditure, protection, and encouragement in the economic system, at the urgent request of business interests themselves, are so extensive in American history that only the intellectually dishonest, the ill-informed, or the naive can avoid recognizing their influence.[40]

Technological changes have been an important catalyst in this matter, but the corporation probably is the key institution in the evolution of capitalism *cum* mercantilism. Our legal system is based on English common law which has feudal roots and attained stature under mercantilism. Laws and courts exist to protect private property, and the corporation is a device which permits property to be accumulated and protected. Pilgrims came to America partly to escape the effects of the symbiotic relation between the Crown and corporations. Indeed, most of the colonies *were* Crown corporations! The legitimacy of the corporate form of business ownership was treated in Chapter 4. Yet, consider these relations. Multinational corporations are directly involved in a covert form of colonialism. Corporate conglomerates contribute to aggregate or economy-wide concentration. Large corporations support trade associations, lobbyists, and the symbiotic relations with the federal government. When we examine the military-industrial complex, we focus on large corporate complexes.

Is it worthwhile to debate the capitalism *qua* mercantilism issue? Or, as T. S. Ashton suggests, does

> . . . the whole practice of coining phrases and attaching them to particular periods of time . . . cloud, rather than illumine, our vision of the past?[41]

With budget deficits, adverse balance of payments, maldistribution of income and wealth, and a host of other economic ills bedeviling our country, is it useful to argue labels and ideology, or would our scarce time and effort be better allocated seeking practical solutions for socioeconomic problems? Yet, the ideological framework within which economic decisions are made ultimately does affect economic behavior and performance. Power to influence the allocative and distributive mechanism is often in the hands of special interests rather than widely dispersed according to the Jeffersonian dream.[42] The basic issue in the modern American economic system, be it capitalist or mercantilist, is not ideology *per se*, but the development, distribution, and legitimation of power.

If citizens continue to be inculcated with the idea that capitalism is synonymous with the quadruple coincidence, it may draw our attention away from the source of contemporary problems. Confusion as to the kind of economic system we really have may cause us to treat symptoms rather than causes as we search for corrective stabilization policies. If American capitalism is not the quadruple coincidence, designing economic policy to solve problems based on classical capitalist assumptions may promote instability and waste resources as well as perpetuating inequities. A thorough review and understanding of mercantilist institutions and practices might aid public officials to design appropriate political economy for America in the 21st century.

NOTES

1.   Some writers place the turning point in the first half of the nineteenth century; for example, see R. A. Solo, *The Political Authority of the Market System*, Cincinnati: Southwestern, 1974, pp. 45-64. Other scholars claim that it occurred at the turn of the 20th century; for examples, see J. Weinstein, *The Corporate Ideal in the Liberal State*, Boston: Beacon Press, 1968, and R. H. Wiebe, *The Search for Order*, New York: Hill and Wang, 1967.

2.   J. Robinson, *The New Mercantilism*, London: Cambridge University Press, 1966.

3.   H. G. Johnson, ed., *The New Mercantilism*, New York: St. Martin's, 1974.

4.   J. Cobbs, "The New Mercantilism: Hoarding Jobs," *Business Week*, March 31, 1973, p. 38; and "Neo-Mercantilism in the '80s," *Business Week*, July 9, 1979, pp. 50-54.

5.   Since the days of the New Deal, even before, it has been commonplace for many conservatives to contend that government involvement into private affairs is an indication of "creeping socialism." A good example of this is P. Hawley, "The Economics of Medical Care," *Vital Speeches*, May 1, 1949, pp. 420-425.

6.   There are several recent publications which stress this point. See: (1) C. Twight, *America's Emerging Fascist Economy*, New Rochelle: Arlington, 1975; and (2) B. M. Gross, "Friendly Fascism, A Model for America," *Social Policy*, Nov./Dec. 1970, pp. 44-52. This topic is addressed in the next chapter.

7.   That the United States has "mixed" capitalism means a mixture of government sponsorship and the market. A summary of arrangements for this hybrid form can be found in: (1) E. Mansfield, *Economics*, New York: Norton, 1977, pp. 39-55; and (2) C. R. McConnell, *Economics*, New York: McGraw Hill, 1978, pp. 105-124.

8.   To illustrate, in 1977 the United States Chamber of Commerce engaged in an extensive promotional campaign stressing how our "free-enterprise" economy of market, competitive arrangements is productive, efficient, and fair. However, there was little or no reference to the subsidies, protectionism, and special privileges granted by government to business.

9.   E. E. Nemmers, *Dictionary of Economics and Business*, Totowa, New Jersey: Littlefield, Adams, 1959, p. 57.

10.   See (1) G. L. Bach, *Economics*, Englewood Cliffs: Prentice-Hall, 1977, p. 443; and (2) H. C. Simons, *Economic Policy for a Free Society*, Chicago: University of Chicago Press, 1948, pp. 27-29.

11.   F. X. Sutton, et al., *The American Business Creed*, New York: Schrocken, 1962, pp. 2-12.

12.   *Ibid.*, pp. 274-302. Another more recent description of these same points can be found in *The American Economic System . . . and Your Part In It*, Washington, D.C., The Advertising Council and the U.S. Department of Commerce, 1976.

13.   G. C. Lodge cites five parts to traditional American ideology (Lockean ideology components): (1) individualism, (2) property rights, (3 competition, (4) a limited state, and (5) scientific specialization with fragmentation. [See his *The New American Ideology*, New York: Knopf, 1975, pp. 75-112.]

14.   Spokesmen from academic life, business, and government operate from the preconception that capitalism is synonymous with the quadruple coincidence. See the following sources for confirmation of this tendency: (1) J. A. Schumpeter, *Capitalism, Socialism and Democracy*, 3rd ed., New York: Harper and Row, 1962, pp. 250-268. (2) F. von Hayek, *The Road to Serfdom*, Chicago: University of Chicago Press, 1944, pp. 69-70; (3) P. A. Samuelson, *Economics*, 9th ed., New York: McGraw Hill, 1973, pp. 41-52. Also see: (1) "A Primer on Profits," *Kaiser Aluminum News*, Vol. 21, No. 4, 1976, pp. 11-20; (2) *Today's Economics*, Xerox Educational Publications, Education Center, Columbus, Ohio, 1965, p. 5; and (3) U.S. Department of Commerce, *Do You Know Your Economic ABCs?* Washington, D.C.: U.S. Government Printing Office, 1963 (and also *Profits and the American Economy*, 1965, same series).

15.   By 1969, the number of separate licensed occupations varied from a low of 65 in Alaska to a high of 181 in Illinois. Nineteen states had 100 or more licensed occupations. (*Occupational Licensing and the Supply of Nonprofessional Manpower*, Washington, D.C.: U.S. Department of Labor, Manpower Administration, Manpower Research Monograph No. 11, 1969, p. 17.)

16.   C. Wilcox, *Public Policies Toward Business*, Homewood: Irwin, 1966, pp. 4-13.

17.   A. Smith, *An Inquiry Into the Nature and Causes of the Wealth of Nations*, New York, Modern Library, 1937, p. 423.

18.   In the January, 1888 issue of *Harper's Magazine* (as cited in W. E. Minchinton, *Mercantilism: System of Expediency?*, Lexington: Heath, 1969, p. vii).

19.   G. Schmoller, *The Mercantile System and Its Historical Significance*, New York: Macmillan, 1897.

20.   W. Cunningham, *Growth of English Industry and Commerce*, I, Cambridge: Cambridge University Press, 1905, p. 483.

21.   E. Heckscher, "Mercantilism," *Encyclopedia of the Social Sciences*, New York: Macmillan, 1933, pp. 333-339.

22. The English edition of Heckscher's two-volume treatise on mercantilism was published in 1935, but the original Swedish publication of it was in 1931.

23. Heckscher, *op. cit.*, p. 336.

24. J. Viner, "Power Versus Plenty as Objectives of Foreign Policy in the Seventeenth and Eighteenth Centuries," *World Politics 1948-49*, pp. 10-20.

25. D. C. Coleman, "Eli Heckscher and the Idea of Mercantilism," *Scandinavian Economic History Review*, V (1957), pp. 3-25 (as cited in J. A. Gherity, ed., *Economic Thought: A Historical Anthology*, New York: Random House, 1965).

26. The points made in this paragraph and the next one are based on (1) P. W. Buck, *The Politics of Mercantilism*, New York: Octagon, 1964; and (2) C. H. Wilson, *Mercantilism*, London: Cox and Wyman, 1958.

27. W. D. Grampp, "The Liberal Elements in English Mercantilism," *The Quarterly Journal of Economics*, LXVI, 1952, pp. 456-501.

28. J. M. Keynes, *The General Theory of Employment*, Interest and Money, New York: Harcourt, 1936, pp. 333-371.

29. The influence was probably more toward the end of the 1930s rather than during the beginning of Roosevelt's first term. See R. Lekachman, *The Age of Keynes*, New York: Random House, 1966, pp. 112-130.

30. E. Golob, *The "Isms": A History and Evaluation*, New York: Harpers, 1954, pp. 125-145.

31. *Ibid.*, p. 127-128.

32. *Ibid.*, p. 141.

33. W. Adams and H. M. Gray, *Monopoly in America*, New York: Macmillan, 1955.

34. *Ibid.*, p. 3.

35. Robinson, *op. cit.*

36. J. K. Galbraith, *The New Industrial State*, Boston: Houghton Mifflin, 1967, especially Chapters II and III; and J. K. Galbraith, *Economics and the Public Purpose*, Boston: Houghton Mifflin, 1973, especially Chapters X and XVI.

37. Or perhaps it is a non-threatening term for "neo-fascist economy"?

38. A. G. Papandreou, *Paternalistic Competition*, Minneapolis: University of Minnesota Press, 1972.

39. *Ibid.*, pp. 146-147.

40.   Four excellent illustrations of this point are: (1) S. Bruchey, *The Roots of American Economic Growth, 1607-1861*, New York: Harpers, 1965; (2) J. R. T. Hughs, *The Governmental Habit*, New York: Basic, 1977; (3) G. Kolko, *The Triumph of Conservatism*, Chicago: Quadrangle, 1963; and (4) R. A. Solo, *The Political Authority of the Market System*, Cincinnati: Southwestern, 1974.

41.   T. S. Ashton, *The Relation of Economic History to Economic Theory*, as cited in A. J. Taylor, *Laissez-Faire and State Intervention in Nineteenth-Century Britain*, London: Anchor, 1972, pp. 62-63.

42.   An excellent discussion of Jeffersonian democracy can be found in: (1) J. S. Bain, *Industrial Organization*, New York: Wiley, 1968, pp. 35-38; and in T. R. Dye and L. H. Zeigler, *The Irony of Democracy*, 3rd ed., North Scituate: Duxbury, 1975, pp. 70-74.

7   FASCISM

INTRODUCTION

> [I]ndustrial management has been installed in the federal government . . . to control the nation's largest . . . industrial enterprises . . . [as it] . . . combines peak economic, political, and military decision-making. Hitherto, the combination of powers in the same hands has been a feature of statist societies--communist, fascist, and others . . . [S. Melman, *Pentagon Capitalism*, New York: McGraw-Hill, 1970, p. 1].

American capitalism began to be transformed from classical free enterprise into a Leviathan state near the latter part of the nineteenth century.[1] The Dorr War (1843),[2] the adoption of the fourteenth amendment (1868),[3] and the U.S. Supreme Court decision in Santa Clara versus Southern Pacific (1886)[4] were important events contributing to this transformation. Social scientists regularly treat American capitalism as a system in transition.[5] The question is whether the transition is consistent with democratic ideals of a free society. Whereas some observers contend that American capitalism is moving toward socialism and communism, other students of the situation envision a drift toward mercantilism and fascism.[6] After several decades of the Cold War, when suspicions over leftist conspiracies were popular, the pendulum of concern may be swinging to the right. Recently, several writers have suggested that American capitalism exhibits fascist-like tendencies. One author in particular, Charlotte Twight, contemplates *America's Emerging Fascist Economy*.[7] The purpose of this chapter is to consider the nature of fascism, especially the capitalist-and-fascist analogy.

NATURE OF FASCISM

The Fascist State, then, puts its trust in private initiative and private capitalism, both of which are . . . subject to the control of the state. This "control" will consist of regulating present affairs and of planning future developments in the interest of the nation. [S. B. Clough, "The Evolution of Fascist Economic Theory, 1926-1930," *Harvard Business Review*, April 1932, p. 310.]

The word "fascist" is from the Latin, *fascis*, meaning a "bundle." In Italian, *fascio* signifies "union." Whereas fascism may be studied as an economic system, it is difficult to separate political from economic factors.[8] Fascism is an emotive term because it is commonly perceived as being synonymous with Nazism or Hitlerism. This chapter, however, focuses on *economic* relations rather than the vicious, inhumane aspects of a totalitarian police state.[9]

Scholars of comparative systems place communism on the far left of the politico-economic spectrum, socialism to left of center, capitalism to right of center, and fascism on the far right.[10]   As a movement of the conservative right, the administrative, educational, institutional, and economic arrangements in Italy under Mussolini, for example, were designed to uphold the role of the landed and business elites in the face of the post-World War One advance of liberalism and radicalism in that country.[11] Likewise, traditional conservatives rather than the liberal middle classes played the major role in the formation and operation of the Third Reich in Germany.[12]

Fascism tends to arise in post-democratic, post-industrial societies rather than in pre-democratic, pre-industrial countries.[13]   Fascist economics is based on three principles: (1) the interests of the nation are superior to those of the individual; (2) work is a social obligation because production provides national strength; and (3) society should plan and control national output through governmental agencies.[14]   The economic organization features the use of trade associations and cartels coordinated by bureaus of centralized government.   To illustrate, not only did Germany's fascist economic goals favor the establishment of cartels, but it fostered the development of privately organized and controlled industrial combines.   In addition to bringing separate economic units together under a governmentally sponsored agency, individual large industrialists were encouraged to merge with other economic units to bring the latter under the control of a strong parent company.[15]

Fascism is often called a "corporate state" but not in the sense of a giant, privately owned industrial corporation becoming an arm of government. Rather, "corporate state" refers to the operation of government bureaus which are usually called "corporations" in fascist jargon. This usage is related to the Latin root of the word, *corpus* (meaning "body"), to the separate "bodies" of power which are created by the national fascist government. Fascism is a prime example of a partnership between government and the private sector. Business, labor, the military, and government form a coalition ("bundle themselves together," or "unite") to run the economy. In Italy during the 1930s, two governmental agencies were in a key economic position: (a) the Institute for Industrial Recovery controlled all financial institutions and all heavy industrial production; and (2) the Chamber of Corporations brought labor unions and trade associations under the direction of a central governmental bureau.[16]

A fascist economy may contain several governmental departments of business and labor, one for each major industrial group (e.g., in steel, in clothing, in food). Each office wields monopoly power over allocating resources, supervising production, dividing markets, and setting prices and wages. All of these activities occur under the coordination and sanction of government, but representatives of business and labor help formulate the conditions of production and exchange. Private property continues to exist, but competition is reduced and even eliminated, especially among small firms on the fringe of a market. Economic activity in separate industries eventually becomes consolidated into the hands of a few big business companies in the name of "efficiency." Even though private property and individual initiative are preserved in fascism, they are subject to the goals of national economic planning as carried out by a small group of bureaucrats.[17]

Contrary to popular opinion, neither German, nor Italian, nor Japanese fascism during the World War Two era developed out of *revolution*; each system arose insidiously in an *evolutionary* way.[18] For example, many of the economic controls under German fascism were instituted under the Weimar Republic prior to Hitler's takeover of Germany. By enacting statutes which legalized cartels and other relations among government, business, and unions, lawmakers of Weimar introduced certain arrangements which were ultimately extended and formalized under Nazi fascism.[19]

There is no set of universally accepted characteristics of fascism but some basic political elements which characterize movements of *totalitarian* fascism have been suggested by this harsh description: distrust of reason; denial of basic human equality; a code of behavior based on untruths and violence; government by an elite; racism and imperialism; and opposition to international law and order.[20]

FASCIST PARALLELS

> [T]he alleged analogy between the Weimar crisis and current
> American discontent; it is because of this light which German
> experience between 1919 and 1933 may . . . throw on the situation
> in the United States today. [The] analogy . . . hangs . . . upon the
> construction of a theoretical concept of fascism . . . as a product of
> technology and what is called "mass society." . . . [G. Barraclough,
> "The Social Dimensions of Crisis, *Social Research*, Summer 1972, p.
> 341]

The Weimar analogy is the hypothesis that the United States may be
evolving into fascism as Germany did in the 1920s. Fascism arises out of
classical capitalism through the medium of government's involvement in the
economic system. Some observers believe that "state capitalism" may be an
early phase of fascism, as in these stages of the German experience: (1)
private capitalism before and during World War I; (2) *state capitalism* under
the Weimar Republic, 1919 to 1933; and (3) *fascism* under the Third Reich,
1933 to 1944.[21] The term, "state capitalism," has been used to describe
fascism itself, of how "big business, the army, the party and the bureaucracy
share the power of the state, and . . . represent a quantitatively new order
. . .[22] The term is also used to describe events which usher in fascist
arrangements.

> . . . state capitalism, first established in the fascist states of Europe,
> was an anticipation of a general tendency of capitalist development
> toward the elimination of the market in favor of planning, state
> control and manipulation. State capitalism represented a new
> historical stage marked by the termination of the economic character
> of earlier forms of capitalism.[23]

The fascist parallel places the United States today in the middle-to-latter
1920s of the Weimar Republic. Compare Germany in the 1920s with the
United States in the 1970s and 1980s: both had lost a war (Germany, World
War One; the United States, Vietnam); both experienced inflation and
unemployment; both witnessed political parties in severe turmoil and flux;
both perceived ethnic or racial problems; both contained youth who were
alienated from democratic society; in both, there was a tendency to look for
simple solutions to complex problems. The fascist parallel can be examined

by considering fascism as modernization, and the New Deal as an early stage of fascism.

The Modernization Hypothesis

The Weimar analogy is not confined to the United States now and Germany then; it has been extended to industrialized capitalist economies in general. The tendency for right-wing, authoritarian movements to develop in advanced industrialized nations has been explained by an argument bordering on technological determinism which is embodied in a theory of modernization.

According to this theory, the one underlying development of recent history is the displacement of societies by an unprecedentedly thorough and rapid process of change, basically similar everywhere, involving industrialization, urbanization, and rationalization.[24]

In modernization, political coalitions have been ostensibly formed by pulling together diverse groups which perceive that industrial society has neglected them socially, politically and economically. With modernization, there is a tendency for a cultural dichotomy to occur which splinters the citizenry. Modernist confronts traditionalist.[25] Technological advance begets institutional adjustment and, in turn, social change. Those who were secure in the former folk culture become insecure during this process. Traditionalists are receptive to charismatic leadership which will identify with their alienated nature. For example, both Mussolini and Hitler appealed to the masses by promising to control the processes and institutions of modernization for the general welfare.

During the onset of modernization, polarization in society occurs on several fronts. Intellectuals become isolated and held in disdain; progress leads to cultural tensions and conflicts; the values of modernists clash with those of traditionalists; a communications crisis develops as the popular culture offers new forms of expressionism; there is experimentation with new ideas, institutions, and arrangements which are contrary to established beliefs.[26]

The New Deal

Whereas Charlotte Twight writes about America's *emerging* fascist economy,[27] some contemporaries contend that fascism was attempted in the United States while it was being practiced in Europe. The governor of Louisiana, Huey ("Kingfish") Long, allegedly set up a fascist-like dictatorship in that state, and "once jokingly said that if fascism ever came to the United

States, it would be under the slogan of 100 percent Americanism."[28]   On
a larger scale, America's first flirtation with fascism may have been with the
New Deal.   Some observers contend that President Roosevelt was the
architect of American socialism, but others have used the terms
"mercantilism" and "fascism" to describe his economic policies.[29]   As one
observer stated:

> . . . Fascism and the New Deal were attempts to salvage a capitalist
> economy in crisis by the creation of a dirigiste state. But they were
> different solutions, not the same one at different stages of
> development.[30]

When the New Deal was first organized, observers outside the United States
suggested that it was fascist in character. The communists, bitter foes of
fascists, said it forcefully:

> It is now necessary to point out that the Roosevelt "new deal"
> program represents not only the strengthening of the open fascist
> tendencies in America, but also that it is quite consciously and
> systematically supporting and developing social-fascist ideals,
> organizations, and leaders.[31]

The Indian scholar, Rajani Palme Dutt, stated bluntly that the New Deal
constituted "near fascism of [a] prefascist state on the road to full
fascism."[32]

The ill-fated National Industrial Recovery Act (NIRA) has been singled
out as being a fascist arrangement. Although this plan for dealing with the
Great Depression was declared unconstitutional by the Supreme Court,
subsequent New Deal programs embodied provisions which were similar to
those contained in the NIRA.[33]

The United States was in a crisis situation when the New Deal programs
were placed into effect. There was little opposition to this alleged fascist
arrangement:

> The National Industrial Recovery Act was passed by Congress by
> large majorities, and . . . the basic idea of corporatism had been
> accepted . . . the organization of economic functions of society into
> groupings of labor and management for each industry, was one of
> the features of European fascism . . . there was no theoretical reason
> why corporations should be incompatible with democracy.[34]

These arrangements contained some fascist-like elements because the NIRA gave vast economic powers to trade associations and industrial organizations [which] were to regulate wages and prices in their specific product markets.[35]

RECENT VIEWS

In Germany in the 1920s, some leading social democrats advocated supporting, rather than resisting, the trend toward increasing monopolization of industry. They argued that greater concentration of industry would make it easier to run the economy when they came to power. Their argument turned out to be accurate, but the benefits accrued to Hitler. [S. M. Miller, "Planning: Can It Make A Difference in Capitalist America?" *Social Policy*, September-October 1975, p. 16]

The capitalism-*cum*-fascism hypothesis is not new. In addition to the contention that it originated in the early stages of President Roosevelt's New Deal, several political historians and social scientists have examined the hypothesis.

Techno-Urban Fascism?

Bertram Gross shows how modern American capitalism might be developing into an imperialistic garrison state. The stage may already have been set--not necessarily deliberately--for a faceless brand of totalitarianism which would engulf the individual into bureaucratic structures.[36] He focuses on social, political, and economic arrangements--the institutional adjustments that our society has made to technology and to urbanization since the end of World War Two. The result has been complex forms of organization, a decentralized but managed economy of planning and controls, increasing inequality of income and social power, plagued by loneliness, alienation, apathy, and hopelessness. It is only a short step for the installation of "friendly fascism":

Pluralistic in nature, techno-urban fascism would need no charismatic dictator, no one party rule, no mass fascist party, no glorification of the state, no dissolution of legislatures, no discontinuation of elections, no distrust of reason.[37]

Techno-urban fascism is more extensive than the conventional military-industrial complex. Whereas the warfare-business establishment would be sizeable and of central importance under techno-urban fascism, a symbiotic relationship would exist among many branches of the federal government.

Existing institutions would play vital roles in this system. Computerized knowledge in the hands of population monitoring and police organizations (CIA, FBI, IRS, INS) provides the basis for monitor and control. The welfare establishment makes a large part of the citizenry dependent while placating them. The communications establishment keeps virtually every household and office in the economy in continuous contact and vulnerable to indoctrination. Indeed,

> . . . the warfare-welfare-industrial-communication-police complex would be a supramodern fascist form of . . . "oligopolist state capitalism" [with] (1) increasingly differentiated armaments . . .; (2) increasingly specialized . . . welfare programs . . .; (3) industrial products to serve warfare-welfare purposes and provide . . . for acceptance of the system; (4) communications services . . . as instruments [of] surveillance . . .; and (5) police activities designed to cope with the new 'crime' of opposing the system. . .[38]

A Corporate State?

In his 1971 presidential address to the American Association for Evolutionary Economics, Daniel Fusfeld declared "that the United States has moved well down the path toward a corporate state."[39] His perspective aims at the connection among business, government, labor, education and the military as it affects the operation of the American economy in the world market. For Fusfeld, the

> . . . corporate state in America rests on a complex political economy. Its power base is the supercorporation and the executive branch of the positive state. Its goals are strongly oriented toward national power . . . [40]

Moreover, several merger movements have created an economy of big enterprise, the largest being several multinational corporations based in the United States. Supercorporations have become private governments in which management is self-selecting and wields authoritarian control. The federal government has assumed primary responsibility for stabilizing the economy. Risk associated with resource allocation (e.g., in the agricultural sector) has been socialized through a vast network of government programs, many of which were established during the New Deal. A power center lies in the military-industrial complex which, along with American foreign policy, sponsors international business undertakings.

In the corporate state, big business and big government need each other for several reasons. Fiscal policy supports aggregate demand and high employment; government programs underwrite many risks; the public sector educates technical manpower to staff large enterprises. In addition, there is a "subtle mutuality of interest between big business and big unions" as well as a reliance on higher education to provide "much of the basic and applied research on development of new weapons, and . . . experts in overseas areas required by the nation's expanded developments.[41] Finally, managerial elites in business, in government, and in the military cross-coordinate goals, priorities, programs, and resource utilization to formulate national policy. As a result of all this, the

> . . . American corporate state is torn by conflict . . . We face the classic dilemma of the industrial society of the twentieth century . . . Down the path lies the continuing development of our emerging corporate state into a full-blown fascism, the Leviathan of the future.[42]

A Positive State?

Arthur Selwyn Miller, a legal scholar, offers a working definition of the *corporate state*: evidence of a merger between political and economic power that is legally present; existence of a corporal body which magnifies political and economic power; and a reduction in the roles of the individual.[43] Moreover,

> . . . the corporate state, to borrow a term from Otto von Gierke, is a . . . *group-person*; perhaps . . . the ultimate group-person in a given social order.[44]

Miller challenges the legitimacy of the power of the corporation, of its ". . . ability . . . to make or influence decisions of national importance."[45] This situation arises because the courts have treated the corporation as a person under the Fourteenth Amendment. As it exists today,

> . . . the corporate state, American style, is both the culmination of historical legal and economic situations and a milestone on the road to some other type of social order.[46]

The social order which Professor Miller has in mind is a "positive state" whereby government assumes the responsibility for enhancing the well-being of the citizenry and also participates in managing the economy.[47] There are five key features of the positive state as it might characterize American capitalism: (1) "The change from a Constitution of limitations to one of powers"; (2) "The advent of a system of overt economic planning"; (3) "The alteration of governmental framework of separation of powers"; (4) "The politicization of law and the legal process"; (5) "The progressive blurring of

the line between public and private government-business relationships."[48]
An example of the transition from the corporate state *cum* positive state can
be noted by the 1971 wage-and-price controls:

> . . . a fifteen-person Pay Board . . . composed of management, labor,
> and public members, [and] only one person . . . be a full-time
> public employee. The others are private citizens. When the board
> acts, it has delegated power from the state--from Congress to Nixon
> to George Meany . . . that institutionalizes the corporate state.[49]

Fascism by 2000?

Canadians are serious observers of the American scene, particularly of
its political and economic affairs. A Canadian, Robert Alan Cook, presents
a futuristic allegory about the day when "Fascism Comes to the United
States."[50] The paper is presented as though written on April 20, 1989 (the
Centennial of Adolph Hitler's birth date). The author suggests that it may
be a struggle over food which creates a political system that invokes rigorous
economic controls. The scenario involves a collision between increasing
population and limited food supplies: the energy crisis will ultimately cause
such serious shortages to develop that the rate of economic growth will slow
down. Eventually, three categories of countries will be recognized by the
United States: (1) advanced developed manufacturing countries; (2)
developing nations that supply raw materials; and (3) Fourth World
countries with little or nothing to offer. A Triage System[51] will be applied
as modern American capitalism turns toward fascism: food will be traded
only with those nations that have productive potential or that can contribute
something of like pecuniary value in return for food.[52] Cook suggests that
only a fascist political-economic system will be able to rationalize production
and distribution, to protect the rights of property owners, and to maintain
law and order.

Many responsible persons are concerned about what is happening to
modern American capitalism, and this concern is not confined inside the
borders of the United States. Thus, Cook's speculation is ominous:

> [A] stationary American economy could survive only by taking one
> of two routes: either a general redistribution of wealth (. . . all-out
> socialism) or totalitarian fascist repression.[53]

CONCLUDING REMARKS

> [W]e have very few *empirical or theoretical generalizations* about
> "fascism" . . . To say that we understand "fascism" is to say that we

know something of the causes that "gave rise" to "fascism" . . .
Unhappily there is no agreement about which political movements
and political regimes should be included in the class. [A. J. Gregor,
"Fascism: The Contemporary Interpretations," *University Program
Modular Studies*, Morristown: General Learning, 1973, p. 2.)

Are the Weimar analogy and modernization hypothesis plausible? What
direction is the capitalist transition taking?

Some Caveats

A modest body of literature exists as support for the fascist analogy, but
counter arguments have been made. For example, in an investigation of this
relationship, Theodore Draper finds more differences than similarities
between the Germany of the 1920s and America in the 1970s. Professor
Draper admits that "the analogy between the Weimar crisis and the
American crisis is tempting . . .," but his examination leads him to contend
that "none of these views needs to be taken seriously."[54] He attributes the
imperfection of the analogy to misinterpretation, exaggeration, and
uncertainty about the future. Moreover, it is certainly a *non sequitur* to
suggest that whatever conditions actually exist, they necessarily involve
fascism. Yet Draper admits that the connection may have merit:

> A little of the Weimarian analogy may do us some good, to remind
> us that democracy can commit suicide at the same time that it is
> being murdered. But too much of that analogy can only confuse and
> disarm us in a time of trouble. Wherever America is heading, it is
> probably going to get there largely in its own way.[55]

Arnold Beichman argues in the opposite direction about the contention
that the United States is in a stage of fascism. He resents the use of fascism
to describe the transition of modern American capitalism because of its
emotive implication:

> No rational person would suggest that there is fascism in America
> or that we are on the road to fascism in the face of all the obvious
> substantial evidence to the contrary.[56]

Much of Beichman's denial of fascism is based on his observation that
totalitarian activities are largely absent in America; little of his discussion is
devoted to economic affairs. He stresses how freedom is prevalent in the
United States because concentration camps, secret police, and wanton
violations of due process do not exist.

Not only is there no fascism in America but by any empirical standard, but the likelihood of its coming to America is real only to those ... who look upon democracy as a regressive form of government.[57]

Michael Reagan believes that government, labor, corporate enterprise, and the military interact to decide the bulk of the resource allocation and production in the system. Reagan's description of a "managed economy" takes on some of the trappings of the corporate state and of the positive state, but he does not envision the United States to be heading toward fascism.

American ideology is . . . egalitarian as well as respectful of money as a sign of success. . . . when privately held social power is seen to be abusive, we have not hesitated to use government power to control it; and our political process remains open to popular use.[58]

Even the activist left is wary of the fascism hypothesis. Marxists have commonly labeled industrial nations as practicing "monopoly capitalism," as an early stage of fascism. Alan Wolfe does not accept this connection and warns the radical community of its falsity because the

. . . fascist hypothesis, wrenched from its historical context, is bad theory and worse tactics.[59]

Wolfe argues that liberalism has "worked best only when the class which was in power received its benefits."[60] He contends that when lower income classes make claims for equality and freedom, they are repressed. To achieve social, political, and economic change, it does little good to employ namecalling and scare tactics against the opposition to generate a following for one's side. Americans ought not wait for fascism to become established before working for change, but begin to organize a counter-movement against corporations.

. . . those who see fascism emerging are in reality saying that a movement exists which has to be put down. But a movement exists when it accomplishes things, not when it makes empty rhetoric.[61]

The hypothesis that modernization *is* fascism also needs to be examined. Historical interpretations giving rise to this contention focus on the clash between modernists and traditionalists. The former allegedly benefit from technological change and identify with it whereas the latter feel displaced by it socially, politically, economically, spiritually. Traditionalists seek greater control over technology than they perceive they have at present in order to become its beneficiaries. As social discord develops between modernists and traditionalists, the latter tend to rally behind a popular but strong political leader who will pursue their goals. In this way, it is argued, modernization tends to lead to centralized control over the economic system. Yet, in the United States, it has been left-wing activists and reform liberals who have attempted to divert technology away from the military-industrial complex toward social purpose. These are not traditionalists. Small shopkeepers, farmers, blue-collar workers, and members of the professions who are powerless tend to be traditionalists. These groups have not sought to rebel against technological progress as have the minorities, the counter-culture, and certain segments of the liberal left. Therefore, in America, modernization may not give rise to a fascist movement as it did during the latter days of the Weimar Republic.

Capitalist Transition

Capitalism does not stand still. Dialectically, it contains within itself the capability of becoming successively transformed into something different than it is. The structure and organization of the American economy is quite distinctive from that in the 1920s and certainly from the 1820s. After all, technology is continually changing and it would be surprising to find a politico-economic system which remained static for long periods of time under such conditions. That it will remain as it was or is today is improbable. Modern American capitalism is unable to return to the heyday of the small entrepreneur and the minuscule competitive unit.

There is more than a common thread running through the fabric of the alleged fascist tendencies arising out of modern American capitalism. It is doubtful that the United States must inevitably go the way of Weimar (i.e., make a transition from mixed capitalism to warlike totalitarian fascism). It is also doubtful that modernization is synonymous with fascism (i.e., advanced technology and institutional adjustments irreversibly create centralized control over resource allocation, production, and distribution).

An entire pattern is woven into the tapestry of our economics system, and the design suggests a situation in which free-enterprise, competition, and the market are not very prominent. Indeed, definite political and economic arrangements have imprinted a unique set of features on modern American capitalism: a political economy in which large well-organized special interests (of both business *and* labor) are able to garner privileges, subsidies, and favors for themselves via pluralist democracy; a dualistic economy in which a few hundred large corporations make nearly half of all sales but 13 million unincorporated firms receive only 10 percent of all business receipts; a business economy in which organized labor is losing its influence; an interventionist economy in which a strong central government makes expenditures of nearly one-fourth the Gross National Product; an international economy in which American foreign policy, increasingly emulating Japan, is designed to encourage and foster big-business activity abroad. Whether all this is "fascist" or not is uncertain. As Hans Morgenthau reflected on the matter:

> Fifty years from now, historians will point either to the similarities or to the dissimilarities and prove that what happened was bound to happen . . . We must be satisfied with pointing out the similarities and dissimilarities and leave the rest to fate.[62]

NOTES

1.   Some writers place the turning point in the first half of the nineteenth century; for example, see R. A. Solo, *The Political Authority of the Market System*, Cincinnati: Southwestern, 1974, pp. 45-64. Other scholars claim that it occurred at the turn of the twentieth century; for examples, see J. Weinstein, *The Corporate Ideal in the Liberal State*, Boston: Beacon, 1968, and R. H. Wiebe, *The Search for Order*, New York: Hill and Wang, 1967.

2.   A people's convention in Rhode Island in 1842, representing a majority of the citizens, drafted a new constitution, held a referendum, and elected officials but the established minority government refused recognition. Thomas Wilson Dorr, a key leader of the reform, and the elected peoples' governor, sought to establish himself in office. His "attack" was suppressed, and he was tried for treason and jailed. The Dorr War is used by many constitutional scholars as evidence that the courts began then to sustain the established power rather than the majority will of the people. See G. M. Dennison, *The Dorr War*, Lexington: University Press of Kentucky, 1976.

3.   The Fourteenth Amendment declares that states cannot deny the life, liberty, or property of any person without due process of law. Part of the debate as the wording of the amendment was being written centered on whether "citizen" or "person" should be used. The latter word was chosen, and it is a matter of historical record that "person" would hopefully include corporations, which had been considered as "artificial beings" in the eyes of the common law. See J. W. Hurst, *The Legitimacy of the Business Corporation in the Law of the United States, 1780-1970*, Charlottesville: University Press of Virginia, 1970, pp. 64-69.

4.   In this case (Santa Clara County V. Southern Pacific Railroad Co., 118 U.S. 394, 396, 1886) the Supreme Court held that a corporation was a "person" under the Fourteenth Amendment.

5.   A large number of books and articles have been published since the 1960s which investigate the structural changes in our economic system. The writings of Peter Drucker, Robert Heilbroner, and John Kenneth Galbraith contain popular as well as scholarly insights into this matter.

6.   For one view see "The New Mercantilism: Hoarding Jobs," *Business Week*, March 31, 1973, p. 38.

7.   C. Twight, *America's Emerging Fascist Economy*, New Rochelle: Arlington, 1975.

8. B. Nossiter, *The Mythmakers*, Boston: Houghton Mifflin, 1964, pp. 1-2.

9. For an objective treatment of the economic arrangements under fascism, see W. G. Welk, *Fascist Economic Policy*, New York: Russell & Russell, 1968, pp. 23-39 and 134-179.

10. See (1) K. M. Dolbeare and P. Dolbeare, *American Ideologies*, Chicago: Rand McNally, 1973; and (2) L. T. Sargent, *Contemporary Political Ideologies*, Homewood: Dorsey, 1975.

11. H. Finer, *Mussolini's Italy*, Hamden: Archron, 1964, pp. 85-86 and 129-146.

12. J. Weiss, *The Fascist Tradition*, New York: Harper & Row, 1967, pp. 2-6.

13. W. Ebenstein, *Today's Isms*, Englewood Cliffs: Prentice-Hall, 1970, pp. 121-122.

14. H. Kohn, "Fascism," *Encyclopedia Brittanica*, Chicago: Encyclopedia Brittanica Corporation, 1960, pp. 104-106.

15. F. Neumann, *Behemoth*, New York: Harper & Row, 1963, pp. 163-16

16. M. Einaudi, "Fascism," *International Encyclopedia of the Social Sciences*, New York: Macmillan, 1968, p. 337.

17. An excellent discussion of fascist economics in Nazi Germany can be found in A. Schweitzer, "Plans and Markets: Nazi Style," *Kyklos*, Vol. 30, 1977, pp. 88-115.

18. An excellent discussion of the popularity of Hitler and Mussolini and the evolution of fascism in Germany and Italy, can be found in: G. Allardyce, *The Place of Fascism in European History*, Englewood Cliffs: Prentice-Hall, 1971, pp. 2-12.

19. S. W. Halperin, *Mussolini and Italian Fascism*, Princeton: Van Nostrand, 1964, p. 162.

20. W. Ebenstein, *op. cit.*, p. 132.

21. See R. Milibrand, *The State in Capitalist Society*, London: Quartet, 1973; and P. M. Sweezy, *The Theory of Capitalist Development*, New York: Monthly Review, 1956.

22. F. Pollak, "Is National Socialism a New Order?" *Studies in Philosophy and Social Science*, 9 (1941), p. 223.

23. A. G. Rabinbach, "Toward a Marxist Theory of Fascism . . .," *New German Critique*, Fall 1974, pp. 133-4.

24. H. A. Turner, Jr., "Fascism and Modernization," *World Politics*, July 1972, p. 548.

25. D. Bell, *The Cultural Contradictions of Capitalism*, New York: Basic, 1976, p. 79.

26. W. Sauer, "Weimar Culture: Experiments in Modernization," *Social Research*, Summer 1972, pp. 281-283.

27. Twight, *op cit.*

28. W. Ebenstein, *op. cit.*, p. 153.

29. E. Golob, *The "Isms"*, New York: Harpers, 1954, pp. 134-135 and 150-151.

30. Q. Hoare, "What is Fascism?" *New Left Review*, Vol. 20, 1963, p. 100.

31. *The Communist*, August 1933, p. 734.

32. R. P. Dutt, *Fascism and Social Revolution*, New York: International, 1934.

33. A. M. Schlesinger, Jr., *The Politics of Upheaval*, Boston: Houghton Mifflin, 1960, pp. 263-290.

34. E. Golob, *op. cit.*, pp. 134-135.

35. B. Bellush, *The Failure of the NIRA*, New York: Norton, 1975, p. 176.

36. B. M. Gross, "Friendly Fascism, A Model for America," *Social Policy*, November/December 1970, pp. 44-45.

37. *Ibid.*, p. 46.

38. *Ibid.*, p. 48.

39. D. R. Fusfeld, "The Rise of the Corporate State in America," *Journal of Economic Issues*, March 1972, p. 2.

40. *Ibid.*, p. 16.

41. *Ibid.*, pp. 11 and 12.

42. *Ibid.*, p. 18.

43. A. S. Miller, "Legal Foundations of the Corporate State," *Journal of Economic Issues*, March 1972, pp. 60-61.

44. *Ibid.*, p. 61.

45. *Ibid.*, p. 61.

46. *Ibid.*, p. 67.

47. A. S. Miller, "The Rise of the Techno-Corporate State in America," *Bulletin of the Atomic Scientists*, January 1968, pp. 146-7.

48. A. S. Miller, "Legal Foundations . . .," *op. cit.*, 68-71.

49. *Ibid.*, p. 76.

50. R. A. Cook, "April 20, 1989, Fascism Comes to the United States," *Commonweal*, January 2, 1976, pp. 11-19.

51. The Triage System was used in World War I to classify wounded soldiers to determine which persons would be given medical aid. Only those needing aid *and* likely to recover with it were treated.

52. R. A. Cook, *op. cit.*, pp. 13-14.

53. *Ibid.*, p. 75.

54. T. Draper, "The Specter of Weimar," *Social Research*, Summer 1972, pp. 325 and 332.

55. *Ibid.*, p. 340.

56. A. Beichman, *Nine Lies About America*, New York: The Library Press, 1972, p. 41.

57. *Ibid.*, p. 38.

58. M. D. Reagan, *The Managed Economy*, New York: Oxford University Press, 1963, pp. 236-7.

59. A. Wolfe, "Waiting for Right: A Critique of the 'Fascism' Hypothesis," *The Review of Radical Political Economics*, Fall 1973, p. 47.

60. *Ibid.*, p. 52.

61. *Ibid.*, p. 47.

62. H. Morgenthau, "Remarks on the Validity of Historical Analogies," *Social Research*, Summer 1972, p. 364.

8   SOCIALISM

INTRODUCTION

> The socialist movement in the United States was part of . . . a
> broader politico-economic upheaval originating in the latter part of
> the nineteenth century. [E. Ader, *Socialism*, Woodbury: Barron's,
> 1966, p. 94]

Socialism and capitalism have emerged in scholarly discourse, both
written and oral, as the two primary, competing economic systems in the
world today. Concern about socialism as a serious alternative to capitalism
began shortly after Engels assembled the works of Marx for publication
during the latter part of the nineteenth century. This concern matured into
worry, misconception, fear, and then strong rhetoric after the turn of the
century. For more than five decades charges have been made from various
corners of society that the American economy is becoming socialist. Cries
of "creeping socialism," of "moving to the left," of "collectivist regime" and
other accusations have been heard, not only in the New Deal days of the
1930s, but during the war years of the early 1940s, the Cold War of the
1950s and 1960s, and into the present era. A variety of factors are
responsible for these contentions: Government programs, especially for
welfare, progressive taxation, laws controlling private actions, health and
safety, environmental regulations, and general bureaucracy. Whether such
events truly amount to socialism merit inquiry and evaluation.

This chapter addresses the question of whether the American economy
is travelling down the road to socialism, as the well-worn cliche is stated.
First, the concept of socialism is defined and described, and then some
popular beliefs about that system are considered, especially the suggestion
that it already has a foothold on American soil. Next, information on
allegations of socialism in America is presented, including a brief discussion
of the "convergence hypothesis." Finally, socialism as an institution of
political economy is treated by appraising its prospects for becoming
established in the United States.

ELEMENTS OF SOCIALISM

[I]n socialism, the means of production are owned by society, or the state representing society [with] certain centralization of decision-making [and] planning as the mechanism for steering the economy. [E. Neuberger and W. Duffy, *Comparative Economic Systems*, Boston: Allyn and Bacon, 1976, pp. 116-17.]

Socialism means many things to many people. It is a word of ridicule, of hope, of fear, of fairness, of tyranny. It has also become a pejorative term for distasteful events which occur in the political economy. It depends on the attitude of the speaker as to whether the word is used as opprobrium or approval. Whereas the historical development of socialism as a system of political economy indicates a variety of usages, the textbook definition provides a relevant framework for appraising recent developments in the United States.

Background

Socialist thought can be traced to Plato's *The Republic* around 370 B.C., T. More's *Utopia* in 1516, and T. Campanella's *City of the Sun* in 1623. What is now called "modern socialism" developed in Europe after the turn of the nineteenth century.[1] As a word, socialism was initially used in the 1820-30 period by Saint-Simon and Robert Owen.[2] In America, although Edward Bellamy "vehemently denied that he preached socialism," his *Looking Backward* criticized laissez faire capitalism, advocated a "collectivist alternative," and attempted to make socialism respectable.[3] Recently, Michael Harrington's vision of "socialist capitalism" suggests that a program of socialism in America could be consistent with its democratic heritage.[4]

Close inspection of economics textbooks on the history of thought and comparative systems reveals several varieties of socialism. Socialism can be evolutionary or revolutionary; scientific or agrarian; transitional or permanent; democratic or totalitarian; centralized or decentralized; Utopian, Fabian, or Marxian. Additional variations exist. For one observer of the scene, "the meaning of socialism, both logically and sociologically, can only be understood as a contrast to individualism."[5] Apparently, there is no generic socialism; rather, it exists on a continuum exhibiting different characteristics and intensities.

Marxian Socialism

For many persons, socialism is directly associated with the writings of Karl Marx and Frederick Engels. Marx synthesized much of the history of socialist ideas from Plato through Fourier, although his contributions transcend those writers.[6] He not only reacted against capitalism and predicted that socialism would replace it, but he rejected the idealism of Utopian visions as appealing "to the moral and rational consciousness of men [which] . . . lacked an understanding of the actual principles that govern historic, social, and economic processes."[7] Marx proposed a scientific socialism which examined the laws of capitalist production and predicted its consequences. There is no single model of Marxian socialism for it has been preached and practiced in different ways in various countries. Socialism, however, need not be based solely on the ideas of Marx.[8]

The Marxian model of socialism begins with a developed capitalist economy that relies on privately owned capital-intensive production. The working class, by revolution, gains power over the means of production. With worker control and central economic planning, resources become allocated by plan; there would be no income from private ownership of land or capital and increasing equality in the distribution of income and wealth.[9] Labor would be motivated by the satisfaction that workers obtained from creative work.

Marxian socialism is viewed both as a process by which that status can be achieved and as the necessary arrangements for maintaining it. For the former, a democratic revolution would replace feudal institutions with capitalist production; for the latter, a social revolution would result in worker control over those means of production.[10]

Basic Characteristics

To examine whether America is becoming socialist requires establishing a set of criteria to describe the concept. What minimum and inescapable elements must be present for socialism to exist? Which characteristics are involved whenever socialism is cited as a basis for comparison?

Millions of Americans have been influenced about socialism from high school and university social science courses, and by comments appearing in the media about socialism. Leading economics textbooks ordinarily present a brief description and analysis of comparative systems, especially of capitalism, socialism, and communism. In them, socialist economies are said to feature four common characteristics: government ownership of certain productive resources, economic planning, redistribution of income, and peaceful, democratic evolution. Communism, on the other hand, is ordinarily described as an extreme totalitarian variety of socialism in which both the means of production and distribution are managed. A socialist economy ordinarily relies on public (rather than private) ownership and control of the basic means of production. Such ownership may be by an organized government (such as federal or state), in the hands of workers (such as cooperatives), or vested in society itself by some non-governmental mechanism (such as political parties). Areas socialized (or "nationalized") may be confined to primary manufacturing (such as steel) or extend to natural resources, transportation, communications, and finance. Nevertheless, a major characteristic is for some basic productive resources to be non-privately owned and operated.

Another key feature logically flows from the first: publicly owned productive resources must be marshalled into use--allocated, as it were. Allocation, in turn, requires executing a plan, directing activities, and arranging details. As a result, formal economic planning generally characterizes a socialist economy. To facilitate this activity, a governmental agency is usually commissioned to set goals, oversee allocation, and issue orders to translate plans into action. Indeed, for socialism to work, there is a need for some form of "centralized decision making authority."[11]

Socialism seeks to further three ideals, among others: equality, brotherhood, and cooperation.[12] These qualities give rise to a mechanism for redistributing income, and for peaceful or evolutionary change "by the ballot box rather than by the bullet."[13] In most democratic socialist countries (e.g., Sweden), welfare programs supported by taxation and governmental ownership provide for human basic needs, among them medical care, education, and housing. These programs must be planned, and some authority and direction must be exercised over them.

SOME POPULAR BELIEFS

> When we legislate for any part of a planned economy, or to care for the physical wants of our citizens, we are favoring socialized controls. [C. Marvin, "The Pitfalls of a Socialized State," *Vital Speeches*, July 1, 1949, p. 553.]

Whereas Principles and Comparative systems textbooks have instructed millions of Americans over the years about the basic characteristics of socialism, additional millions have been influenced by popular writers and lecturers. Daily newspapers, periodical magazines, and speakers at various functions have presented views on the nature and consequences of socialism. Both the conservative right and liberal left have offered their viewpoints, the former being more active than the latter for criticizing and condemning socialism.

Background

Views of Karl Marx began to attract serious attention in the latter part of the 19th century when his writings were published. The American Socialist Movement was active before the turn of this century, but widespread public awareness of socialism arose prior to 1920 when the Russian Revolution occurred and efforts were being made in the United States to organize workers into labor unions. Both lay and academic circles discussed how and why socialism might be inferior as an alternative to capitalism.[14] An inquiry also occurred into whether Christianity contained any socialist tendencies.[15]

Prior to 1932, only a few articles about socialism in America appeared in the media. After Franklin D. Roosevelt was elected president and began designing legislation to nurse an ailing economy back to health, the New Deal (and even the Democratic party) were associated with socialism by certain groups. From 1932 to 1935, cautious statements were made about how Roosevelt's New Deal exhibited socialist overtones. During the latter 1930s and early 1940s, vicious attacks appeared claiming that Roosevelt and his New Deal advisers were regularly applying socialist policies.

One connection involved an alleged "secret alliance with the communists";[16] another concerned the ill-fated National Recovery Administration as a type of "socialist tyranny."[17] Likewise, social welfare programs were labeled as direct evidence of socialism;[18] centralized power in Washington, D.C. constituted a "dictatorship";[19] and Roosevelt had promoted creeping socialism with New Deal policies dependent on economic planning.[20] When the President ordered the operation of certain strike-bound defense plants just prior to the Pearl Harbor attack, Roosevelt along with the Federal Labor Relations Board and the Mediation Board were accused of "socialist meddling."[21] Early in World War Two, America was going "down the road to state socialism" because Roosevelt issued nearly 500 executive orders.[22] In the late 1940s, fear of socialism grew into fear of communism,[23] culminating in the investigations of Senator Joseph McCarthy.

Diverse Connections

The contention that socialism had invaded America can be traced to conservative reactions against policies of the Roosevelt administration during the Great Depression and World War Two. Throughout these periods, a series of interconnected conditions set the stage for accusations of creeping socialism. Democrats were in power and their ideology of reform liberalism was considered to be a forerunner to socialism.[24] The philosophy of collective responsibility for one another was also an important contributor.[25] Governmental programs ordinarily involve regulation, and any resulting control over private property was equated with socialist practices.[26] These programs raised taxes, which amounted to "confiscation of property"[27] and "encroachment on property rights' by reducing incentives, both said to lead to state socialism.[28] Indeed, bureaucracy was believed to constitute socialism,[29] as did any scheme for the redistributing income and wealth.[30]

The rhetoric intensified in the early 1950s when the political left and socialism were linked to communism.[31] Communists were said to be in the schools--both public school teachers and university students[32]--and in the trade unions.[33] Moreover, neither socialists nor communists could be trusted because they broke their treaties.[34]

During this time, socialism as a system of political economy was severely criticized: it was allegedly inefficient, wasteful[35] and had to be subsidized;[36] it was a failure in Great Britain by testimony of its citizens;[37] it was antithetical to liberty;[38] it was associated with Hitler;[39] its planning led to disaster;[40] and its welfare-state programs were borrowed from totalitarian regimes.[41]

Some relief from supposed creeping socialism was felt when Dwight D. Eisenhower won the presidency in 1952 and ended 20 years of Democratic rule.[42] The conservative press expected that his "policies will lean to the right, away from socialism, toward freer enterprise."[43] Specifically, some persons wanted him to eliminate "socialist" programs already in place: post offices, water projects (e.g, Hoover Dam and the Tennessee Valley Authority), national parks, public lands, and military commissaries.[44] In addition, he was expected to reduce welfare spending and keep union leaders under control.[45] Yet, eight years later this same leader, upon relinquishing the presidency, warned the nation not about the dangers of "creeping socialism" but of business excesses within the powerful military-industrial complex.[46] During President Eisenhower's administration, total governmental expenditures fell by 21 percent in real terms. At the same time, state-local governments increased their real spending by nearly 58 percent! Two recessions occurred while he was in office and the federal government added another $15.8 billion to the national debt under his presidency, 1953-1961.

AMERICAN CAPITALISM CUM SOCIALISM?

> Socialists face . . . an uphill fight in America, for while "socialism"
> is a good word in most of the world, the term carries a powerful
> negative connotation in America. [G. Dorrien, *The Democratic
> Socialist Vision*, Totowa: Littlefield, Adams, 1986, p.160.)

Given a basic definition of socialism and the claim that it exists in America, consider two brief inquiries into socialism and capitalism. The first focuses on the extent of governmental spending in the economy; the second on a suspected tendency for capitalism to move toward socialism.

Governmental Activity

Government's role is primal in socialism: direct ownership and operation of some basic industrial production, and creation of programs for redistribution of income (with unified economic planning for each). Several requirements exist for discerning socialism in America: governmental spending to own and operate output-creating units of production; provision of social welfare programs; and centralized organization and decision-making for administering each. Expenditures for these activities are reported in governmental budget statements. What is the relation between government spending and GNP? How much spending occurs at the federal versus state and local levels? Which expenditure categories are most significant at each level of government?

Table 8.1 shows GNP and governmental spending for the 40-year period following World War Two. Both measures increased sharply during that span. Three tendencies can be noted. First, overall governmental spending since 1950 increased markedly as a percent of GNP. Second, between 1955 and 1970 state-local spending rose steadily not only in absolute terms but also relative to the federal level. Third, over the 15-year period, 1970-85, the ratio of federal spending to GNP rose from 14 percent to 25 percent. When national defense expenditures of $253 billion are removed from $986 billion in federal spending, that ratio falls to 18 percent. Thus, governmental spending does not appear to be dominating the American economic system. Moreover, governmental activity is decentralized because spending is done by hundreds--even thousands--of separate state-local entities (such as school districts). Based on the proportion of economic activity accounted for by the governmental sector, it is inaccurate on this basis to conclude that the American economy is becoming socialist.

Next, consider federal budget outlays shown in Table 8.2. The greatest share of expenditures in 1987 (36 percent) was for welfare, with a combined 15 percent allocated to health and education. If all three categories were considered as a comprehensive "welfare" program, it might be concluded that the federal government has installed a socialist scheme of income redistribution. However, these programs are not centrally unified and directed, and for some (e.g., Medicare), the federal government contracts with private enterprise (viz., Blue Cross/Blue Shield) to facilitate the transfer of payments.

Slightly more than 28 percent of the federal budget is spent for defense. Yet, the federal government owns few, if any, defense production and procurement facilities. Rather, private companies in the so-called military-industrial complex are the entities that produce, monitor, and repair

Table 8.1   Selected Expenditures in Relation to Gross National
                   Product, United States, 1945-1985 (dollars in billions)

Year	GNP	Gov't Spend.	Fed Spend.	S-L Gov't Spend.	Gov/GNP	Fed/GNP
1945	$213	$ 93	$ 85	$ 9	.44	.40
1950	288	61	41	23	.21	.14
1955	406	99	69	33	.24	.17
1960	515	137	94	50	.27	.18
1965	705	190	125	76	.27	.18
1970	1016	317	208	134	.31	.20
1975	1598	545	364	235	.34	.23
1980	2731	890	615	363	.33	.23
1985	4010	1403	986	517	.35	.25

Source: *Economic Report of the President*, 1989.

Table 8.2   Federal Budget Outlays, United States, 1987 (dollars
                   in billions)

Category	Amount	Percent
Defense	$ 282.0	28.1
Welfare	358.4	35.6
Health	115.1	11.5
Education	33.7	3.4
Transportation	26.2	2.6
Interest	136.6	13.6
Other	52.6	5.2
Total:	1,000.6	100.0

Source: *Statistical Abstract of the United States*, 1989.

various kinds of military hardware. The nearly $300 billion budgeted for
defense is contracted with private enterprise, capitalistic corporations.
     The federal government "owns" the federal highways, such as the
interstate system, but construction and maintenance amounts to much less
than the nearly 3 percent of the federal budget spent on all transportation
annually. Nevertheless, highway construction and maintenance at the federal
level, like defense, are contracted to privately owned companies. State and
local governments usually employ their own highway repair crews, but even
at those levels, highway construction is accomplished by private firms.

Table 8.3   State and Local Governmental Expenditures, by
                   Category, United States, 1989 (dollars in billions)

Category	Amount	Percent
Public Schools	$145.1	24.0
Higher Education	56.5	9.4
Highways	49.4	8.8
Health/Hospitals	53.7	8.9
Police/Fire	32.3	5.4
Welfare	73.9	12.2
Recreation	10.2	1.7
Housing	11.3	1.9
Sanitation	19.1	3.2
Administr./Interest	60.7	10.1
Other	91.5	15.2
Total	603.7	100.0

Source: *Statistical Abstract of the United States*, 1989.

Table 8.3 contains data on state-local budget expenditure categories. Many different governmental units at these levels allocate the largest amount of their expenditures--more than one-third--to public school and college/university programs. These entities manage land, buildings, and equipment owned and operated by a level of government. America therefore has state or local "socialism" in the area of education! But the $201 billion spent at the state-local levels for education is only 33 percent of all state-local spending (and a mere 5 percent of GNP). One-fifth of state-local spending is for social programs such as health, hospitals, sanitation, housing, and welfare. Less than 9 percent is spent for highways, typically managed by individual state and local governments.

It is difficult to argue realistically, based on statistical evidence of spending, that additional dollars allocated by government causes the American economy to become increasingly socialist. A sizeable amount of welfare spending exists, but there is minimum governmental ownership, operation, and planning for the basic means of production, especially on a centralized basis. The federal government supports significant, centrally funded income redistribution schemes, such as Social Security old-age pensions. But such programs involve many separate plans, agencies, offices, and requirements. For education, thousands of separate units of state-local governments each own and operate productive resources to create human capital in schools and on college campuses--through broadly structured state plans, but with some federal guidelines. Yet, each is decentralized within individual local school districts or separate governing boards.

For the necessary and sufficient conditions of socialism to be met, all elements are needed, not just one or two isolated requirements. Evidence on levels and patterns of governmental spending would seem to suggest that conditions have not been met, and therefore we do not have socialism in the United States.

Convergence Hypothesis

By the late 1950s, it was apparent that some market economies were using techniques of economic planning or centralized management, and that certain command economies were experimenting with market institutions and decentralization. In 1961, the "convergence hypothesis" was raised by Professor Jan Tinbergen.[47] It was suggested that capitalism and socialism may be travelling down separate paths toward something similar and compatible. For example, did the use of monetary incentives in the Soviet Union indicate it was deserting socialist tendencies and embracing capitalism? Likewise, did the fact that the United States had increased its welfare programs each year indicate abandoning rugged capitalist individualism and accepting a socialist pattern of income distribution? The convergence hypothesis, however, is more complicated than showing that the economies of certain countries "exhibit a growing similarity in their 'essential features'."[48]

Since Tinbergen's classic paper in 1961, the convergence hypothesis has been the subject of debate. Dialectically, an opposing view arose--namely, that there are more signs of divergence than convergence between the two systems.[49] In addition, co-existence was shown to be quite different from convergence.[50] Whereas American economic planning aims at stabilization to control inflation and achieve high employment economic growth, the goal of Eastern-bloc countries was to allocate labor and capital resources directly for the sake of efficiency per se.[51] The convergence hypothesis has not been proven and therefore does not lend much support to the proposition that America is becoming socialist.

In the late 1960s, a popularized version of the convergence hypothesis was presented in John Kenneth Galbraith's *The New Industrial State*.[52] For him, seven tendencies characterize the large American firm: increasing amounts of time, capital, inflexibility, technology, specialized manpower, organization, and planning.[53] Galbraith argued that these requirements guide not only industrial corporations in the United States, but also the productive units of such socialist countries as the Soviet Union. An automobile manufacturing plant in each country faces similar problems and needs because the power of technology affects capitalism and socialism alike. Indeed, "the enemy of the market is not ideology, but the engineer."[54]

However, it is insufficient to claim convergence by showing that socialist firms practicing decentralization may have adopted certain market arrangements. Rather, "decentralization in the Soviet-type economies involves not a return to the market but a shift of some planning functions from the state to the firm."[55]

Convergence is not a model of the future for socialism in the United States. Both systems have acquired and adopted advanced technology, and are trapped in the seven-phase sequence cited above. Both systems are probably heading down similar paths but toward something altogether different than currently characterizes each. Ironically, convergence is something Marx neglected when he prepared his critique of capitalism.[56] If convergence is occurring, it does not necessarily mean that America is heading toward socialism. Our economic system is slowly but steadily evolving toward a structure which is difficult to predict and describe. As technology changes, institutional adjustments to it are continuously made. These conditions alter the handling of property rights, resource allocation, and income distribution, the basic ingredients of any economic system.

Events beginning in 1989 in Eastern Europe and the Soviet Union have lead some observers to suggest that rather than convergence, victory has been achieved over socialism and communism.[57] The tendency for totalitarian communism to be replaced in Poland, Hungary, and Czechoslovakia is used as evidence that these countries will soon develop capitalist institutions. It is too early to tell what will happen, but the model of democratic socialism in certain Scandinavian countries is a possible direction those nations might head.

CONCLUDING REMARKS

Socialists . . . find themselves bewildered and uncertain of the future.. . . the welfare state no longer requires a separate political party. [W. Ebenstein, *Today's Isms*, Englewood Cliffs, Prentice-Hall, 1970, pp. 284 and 287.]

Claims that American capitalism is moving to the left toward socialism are generally based on growing governmental welfare programs financed by supposedly progressive taxation. Spending and taxing both involve hundreds of categories, bureaucracy, regulations, and controls. While giving something to certain groups, something else is taken away from other private citizens. Because requirements or restrictions characterize these actions, the conclusion is drawn that government is interfering with life, liberty, and property. This is what totalitarian communist governments do, so it has become associated with socialism. When these events occur in capitalism, America is said to be moving toward socialism.

Historically, "socialism was brought across the Atlantic by German immigrants who established the first socialist party in 1876."[58] Has anything of significance occurred in the American economy since then to meet the necessary and sufficient conditions of scientific socialism? Where in the United States are governmental ownership and operation of the basic means of production?   Of any means of production?   Is there comprehensive, coordinated, central direction by government for such ownership and operation? Does resource allocation occur for planning, monitoring, and executing investment by an agency of government? Is there substantial redistribution of income through comprehensive but cohesive social welfare programs? Affirmative answers can hardly be given to all of these questions, although for welfare, an argument might be made for a some positive response.

Some occurrences might suggest appearances of socialism in the American economy, but they do not exist where critics say. Levels of government--federal, state, local--play a large role in our economic system. Nearly $1,500 billion in governmental expenditures are not insignificant; yet that constitutes only one-third of the nation's GNP. One makes a huge jump in logic to conclude that 33 percent of the GNP accounted for all levels of government causes a country to be 33 percent socialist!

Primary industrial production units--such as for steel, aluminum, rubber, machine tools--are obviously not owned and operated by government in this country. On the other hand, education--the process of developing human capital--is indeed created largely by government. The basic productive resources used to produce human capital--our schools and universities--are owned and operated mainly by state and local governmental units. However, education is not ordinarily claimed to be socialist by its critics, and those working for and attending these "socialist bureaus" ordinarily do not consider them as such. But this pattern of ownership and operation has existed for some time and is not primarily a program of the left.

Despite fears of the far right and hopes from the far left, socialism is not an appropriate description of the American economic system. There is no substantial movement for nationalization of basic industries or financial institutions. It is doubtful that our primary industries, such as steel or automobile manufacturing, will become socialist bureaus. Some minor nationalization may occur--railroad trackage, for example--but it would probably be in the nature of a bailout with approval of the industry. Such a socialist program would not benefit so much travellers, shippers, and workers as it would owners of railroad capital.

Although public utility regulation is widespread, these entities are primarily private corporations whose stock is owned by numerous citizens and other firms. Whereas some state and local ownership exists for certain utilities, it only forms a minor part of all activity in this regard.

There is some minor interest in worker cooperatives, and a few companies, such as Avis, Inc., are owned by their employees. However, workers as a category receive nearly 75 percent of the national income, and those belonging to labor organizations--less than 17 percent of the work force--receive nearly 30 percent of that share.[59] It seems likely, therefore, that organized labor would have little pecuniary incentive to socialize parts of the economy.

An argument is often made that American welfare policies establish socialist tendencies. However, by the standards of other socialist countries, the welfare system and progressive tax incidence in the United States are not substantial. Even Canada and New Zealand provide Family Allowances and Comprehensive Medical Care to their citizens, social programs which are not imminent in America.

Perhaps the American economy is heading along a path toward socialism. But if it is, it has a long way to go. There are other systems of political economy--such as fascism and mercantilism--which may share more basic elements in common with modern American capitalism than socialism.

NOTES

1. O. Jaszi, "Socialism," *Encyclopedia of the Social Sciences*, Vol. XIII-XIV, New York: Macmillan, 1963, p. 188.

2. D. Bell, "Socialism," *International Encyclopedia of Social Science*, Vol. 14, New York: Macmillan and Free Press, 1968, p. 506.

3. A. Lipow, *Authoritarian Socialism in America*, Berkeley: University of California Press, 1982, pp. 16-17.

4. M. Harrington, *Socialism*, New York: Saturday Review, 1970, pp. 187-215 and 344-73.

5. Bell, *op. cit.*, p. 506.

6. Jaszi, *op. cit.*, p. 197.

7. W. Odajnyk, "Socialism," *Encyclopedia Americana*, Vol. 25, p. 148.

8. J. Elliott, *Comparative Economic Systems*, Englewood Cliffs: Prentice-Hall, 1973, p. 30.

9. *Ibid.*, p. 223.

10. Bell, *op. cit.*, p. 508.

11. See V. Holesovsky, *Economic Systems*, New York: McGraw-Hill, 1977, pp. 21-25.

12. D. Fusfeld, *Economics*, Glenview: Scott, Foresman, 1985, p. 648.

13. P. Samuelson, *Economics*, New York: McGraw-Hill, 1984, p. 872.

14. For examples, see: "American-ism and Socialism," *Outlook*, June 13, 1917, pp. 245-46; G. Watkins, "Present Status of Socialism in the U.S.," *Atlantic*, December 1919, pp. 821-390; and "Has Capitalism Outlived Its Usefulness?" *Current Opinion*, June 1923, pp. 674-76.

15. C. Semple, "Case of Socialism v. Catholic Church in the United States," *Catholic World*, February 1918, pp. 646-53; J. Burke, "Socialism and Catholic Activity," *Commonweal*, October 19, 1932, p. 59; and "Christianity and Socialism," *Nation's Republic*, June 1931, p. 44.

16. R. McCormick, "Our Republic is at Stake," *Vital Speeches*, March 15, 1940, p. 332.

17. *Ibid.*, p. 327.

18. M. Hart, "Did You Say Democracy?" *Vital Speeches*, March 1, 1940, p. 307.

19. *Ibid.*, p. 308.

20. M. Muir, "Shadows of State Socialism," *Vital Speeches*, October 1, 1941, p. 763.

21. D. Robbins, "Slowdown of Defense," *Vital Speeches*, December 1, 1941, p. 126.

22. J. O'Mahoney, "The Declining Power of the States," *Vital Speeches*, February 1, 1943, p. 226.

23. S. Bridges, "American Foreign Policy and Communism," *Vital Speeches*, April 15, 1948, pp. 391-94.

24. W. Carleton, "What of Free Enterprise?" *Vital Speeches of the Day*, April 15, 1944, pp. 401-08; and D. Lawrence, "So-Called 'Liberalism'," *U.S. News & World Report*, December 3, 1954, p. 140.

25. M. Eastman, "The False Promise of Socialism," *Reader's Digest*, November 1955, p. 160.

26. D. Lawrence, "Controlled Capitalism," *U.S. News & World Report*, October 13, 1950, p. 121.

27. "How Socialists Tax Corporations," *U.S. News & World Report*, December 1, 1950, pp. 18-19; and "Truth About Profits," *U.S. News & World Report*, April 25, 1952, pp. 64-66.

28. D. Lawrence, "Conservative Liberalism vs. Radical Liberalism," *U.S. News & World Report*, December 4, 1953, pp. 117-18.

29. Eastman, *op. cit.*, p. 158.

30. D. Lawrence, "The Battle Goes On," *U.S. News & World Report*, November 5, 1954, p. 108.

31. C. de Kieweit, "Communism Sets a Trap," *Vital Speeches*, August 1, 1948, pp. 628-30.

32. J. Hoover, "Communism and Schools . . . ," *U.S. News & World Report*, November 26, 1954, pp. 130-31; and "Communism in the Schools," *Time*, September 22, 1952, p. 69.

33. "Communists in Key Unions: Danger to War Industries," *U.S. News & World Report*, December 22, 1950, p. 22.

34. "What a 'Treaty' Means to Russia," *U.S. News & World Report*, December 4, 1953, p. 118.

35. L. Fertig, "What Price Socialism?" *Reader's Digest*, August 1947, pp. 55-56.

36. H. Hazlitt, "Subsidizing Socialism," *Newsweek*, September 30, 1957, p. 111.

37. "Socialists Sour on Socialism," *U.S. News & World Report*, July 8, 1955, pp. 48-49; and H. Hazlitt, "To a Mitigated Socialism," *Newsweek*, October 15, 1951, p. 77.

38. D. Lawrence, "Educating the 'Educated'," *U.S. News & World Report*, October 27, 1950, p. 82.

39. Fertig, *op. cit.*, p. 55.

40. *Ibid*.

41. H. Hoover, "U.S. is Infected with Marxist Poison," *U.S. News & World Report*, August 20, 1954, p. 104.

42. "'Eisenhower's First 90 Days," *U.S. News & World Report*, April 24, 1953, pp. 15-17; and "What Kind of Change?" *Newsweek*, November 16, 1953, p. 30.

43. "What Eisenhower Will Do," *U.S. News & World Report*, November 14, 1952, p. 13.

44. "President's Plan to Check Socialism in the U.S.," *U.S. News & World Report*, July 23, 1954, pp. 19-21.

45. "What Eisenhower Will Do," *op. cit.*, pp. 14-15.

46. "Eisenhower's Farewell--A Prayer and A Warning," *U.S. News & World Report*, January 30, 1961, p. 69.

47. J. Tinbergen, "Do Communist and Free Countries Show a Converging Pattern?" *Soviet Studies*, April 1961, pp. 333-41.

48. E. Neuberger and W. Duffy, *Comparative Economic Systems*, Boston: Allyn and Bacon, 1976, p. 122.

49. J. Millar, "On the Merits of the Convergence Hypothesis," *Journal of Economic Issues*, March 1968, pp. 63-66.

50. J. Prybyla, "The Convergence of Market-Oriented and Command-Oriented Systems: A Critical Estimate," *Comparative Economic Systems*, New York: Appleton-Century Crofts, 1969, p. 468.

51. R. Eidem and S. Viotti, *Economic Systems*, New York: Wiley, 1978, p. 81.

52. J. Galbraith, *The New Industrial State*, Boston: Houghton Mifflin, 1967.

53. *Ibid.*, pp. 11-21.

54. *Ibid.*, p. 33.

55. *Ibid.*, p. 108.

56. *Ibid.*, p. 391.

57. For example, consider that Associated Press article in the Gannett newspapers, "Soviets May Consider Capitalism," *Coloradoan*, February 20, 1990, p. 2.

58. A. Gruchy, *Comparative Economic Systems*, Boston: Houghton Mifflin, 1966, p. 271.

59. *Statistical Abstract of the United States*, 1982-83, Washington, D.C.: G.P.O., 1982, p. 405.

9   MODERN AMERICAN CAPITALISM

INTRODUCTION

[T]he main sources of the resistance to change . . . are to be found
in the structure of privilege inherent in all societies. [R. Heilbroner,
The Limits of American Capitalism, New York: Harper & Row, 1965,
p. 70.]

The economic system of the United States evolved from the legacy of
Europe's feudal structure and contains more than mere traces of mercantilist
arrangements from its own colonial past. Some observers fear that fascist
and socialist tendencies may soon dominate modern American capitalism.
Others fear that they have already taken control. But the economy will
surely continue to develop into something uniquely American as it always
has. Its features will probably be based on the market, some form of
democracy, and related institutions that have characterized our country for
more than two centuries. It would be inappropriate to attach a historical
label to the impending status of the American economy. Nevertheless, it is
possible to provide a glimpse of how capitalism in the United States
operates as a system of political economy. Unfortunately, this view must be
limited, for it cannot encompass all of the connections and intricacies woven
into the national economic tapestry.

As a concept, political economy has been used several ways. Both words
can be part of a total collective proper noun to signify a distinct approach
or method. *Political* may also be used as an adjective describing the noun,
economy, to distinguish between a "market" economy and a "political"
economy. These usages would be different from "politics and economics" or
"political economics." This chapter appraises the political economy of the
United States by considering how political action helps define property
rights, allocate resources, and distribute income. In this regard, the matter

of being able to deliberately influence legislation so that goals of special interests can be achieved is also faced.

BACKGROUND

> We speak of the United States economy as a free enterprise system, and there is a very general conviction among us that this form of economic organization is both highly productive and particularly desirable. [M. Copeland, *Our Free Enterprise Economy*, New York: Macmillan, 1965, p. 1.]

Modern American capitalism has a rich heritage resting in the archives of historical experience. Behind the traditional institutions of capitalism stand several important connections which bear on how and why our economic system functions the way it does. In this regard, some instruction from Adam Smith and Alfred Marshall help to highlight certain fundamental relations among property, individualism, the market, and economic activity.

Basic Ingredients

Modern American capitalism transforms resources into hopeful consumer satisfaction through a mechanism which diverges somewhat from the Marshallian tradition in neoclassical economics. When Alfred Marshall re-formulated the brand of economics which has been much-used in the West, he quickly declared that consumer demand was the ultimate regulator of all economic activity.[1] Indeed, people need a certain amount of food, clothing, and shelter for their survival, and want other goods and services for their personal enjoyment. Unfortunately, most necessary and desired things do not exist in a form which yields immediate satisfaction. Commodities have to be created out of scarce economic resources, and during the process which transforms resources into goods which will satisfy human desires hard choices must be made. Which resources shall be used? How many of them? What mode of production will transform resources into commodities? Which particular goods will be made? In what quantities? For whom will they be made? On which basis will they be distributed? Any society must organize itself to answer these--and other-- basic economic questions. In the United States, the answers are made in a way which is unique to its economic and political heritage. Interaction between the economic and political spheres is what gives definition to modern American capitalism.

There are 250 million people in the United States. Their combined needs and desires are all but endless. There are surely not enough resources to satisfy the myriad wants for goods and services for these persons. In order to meet some of those wants, scarce economic resources must be allocated among competing uses. In the process, some economists believe that at least three objectives should be met. First, it is to society's benefit for as many of the most urgent wants as possible to be satisfied. Second, because of the limited-resources/unlimited-wants dilemma, our scarce resources should not be wasted. Third, some basis for making choices must be established to facilitate resource allocation. Whatever the criteria for choice happen to be, the same resource cannot be used for more than one purpose: when we choose one thing, we automatically choose not to have something else.

Modern American capitalism is often described as a free-enterprise, competitive, market economy. However, the institutional arrangements which make our economic system work feature a mixture of governmental involvement with private property. These two spheres interact within a democratic structure to allocate scarce economic resources into the production of goods and services that people who have money to spend are willing to purchase for their own personal enjoyment.

Individualism

Capitalism in the United States developed largely out of the British experience. It is no coincidence that the American Revolution and Adam Smith's *Wealth of Nations* both came on the scene in 1776. Smith's treatise was a reaction against the State, and so was the revolution. The "mercantile system" (as Smith called it) consisted of vast governmental involvement in nearly every aspect of British economic life. Parliament and the Crown granted special favors to selected private interests in the form of subsidies, monopoly licenses, and class legislation. Numerous codes, laws, and regulations monitored business activity so extensively that productivity was hampered.[2] Smith proposed a system of economic and political freedoms which featured a limited role for government. He argued that a policy of laissez faire--noninterference with the market--would increase the "wealth of nations" if everyone were left alone to pursue his/her own affairs. Self-interest is probably as old as the human race itself. If it's between "me and thee," most persons will pick "me" every time! The "me," of course, would necessarily include close family members. Selfishness is widely thought to be such an integral part of human nature and behavior that when we observe the pursuit of one's own interests, we say that it is "rational." Smith suggested harnessing it for the common good.

The notion of allowing for individual economic freedom in resource allocation, in production, and in consumption was somewhat different from the system of mercantilism against which Adam Smith had railed. Governmental involvement in the mercantilist world had created a system of *political economy*.[3] Whenever private affairs and the operation of the economy are nurtured through politics and government, the connection is

one of political economy. Smith reacted against political economy because
he believed that its existence reduced freedom, led to waste in the use of
scarce resources, and diminished the general welfare. He proposed an
economic system of free enterprise and of competitive markets which
contained only a minimum but strategically crucial role for government: to
provide for the common defense, to operate the courts, and to *maintain the
free market* as the area for economic activity.

The logic of the institutional arrangements suggested by Adam Smith
featured several interrelated parts. Property was to be owned by private
individuals, and no one should be denied the access to acquiring and using
property. People were to be granted the right to enter into voluntary
agreements--to make contracts and to join organizations--so they could
participate in economic activity for their own self-gain. The courts were
supposed to uphold contracts and to protect private property. Government
was to engage only in those activities which private-property owners could
not and would not do. In essence, if people were guaranteed the right of
enjoying the fruits of their own efforts--of keeping the earnings from their
property and labor when they undertook economic activity--then there would
be an incentive for free people not only to acquire private property, but to
direct its use into those activities where the monetary payoffs were the
largest. Profit would be most in lines of economic activity wherein people
with free consumer choice were willing to pay the highest prices for the
goods and services created by that activity. This connection would optimize
the benefits to society because if consumers were free to spend their incomes
wherever they wanted to, then self-interest would lead them to spend it on
those goods and services which yielded them the most satisfaction. Self-
interest and the profit motive would lead business firms to produce these
same goods. The interaction of the three basic economic groups--resource
owners, business firms, and consumers--each seeking their own respective
objectives of self-interest, would transform society's resources into the goods
and services which satisfied society's most preferred wants. It would be an
automatic mechanism because no government overseer would have to
manage the system. Instead of central direction, argued Smith, an invisible
hand of the private interest operating on private property would guide the
economy toward serving the public interest.

PRIVATE PROPERTY AND INCENTIVES

> Ownership . . . consists essentially of the combination of the rights
> of *control* and of *usufruct*. [F. Knight, *Risk, Uncertainty, and Profit*,
> New York: Harper & Row, 1921, p. 352.]

Many persons appear to be self-righteous and idealistic in their
expectations as to what is fair and proper in terms of how the economic

system of the United States ought to allocate scarce resources. Strong opinions about justice and freedom are often based on a belief that political, social, and economic equality involve an inalienable right to material goods and services based on one's position as a human being rather than say, on the nature of one's contribution to economic activity or inherited wealth and privilege. However, a unique interaction between incentives and property form the basis for production and distribution in the United States.

Under modern American capitalism, most persons receive money income based on the value of their labor services and/or the amount and type of property they own. A piece of property serves as a scarce economic resource which has productive ability. There are essentially two kinds of property resources: physical resources (such as land and machines), and human capital (such as labor skills and managerial abilities embodied in members of the work force). These resources--if used to produce the goods and services that people are willing and able to pay for--generate income for their owners. Our economy has developed into a system in which a person must possess some income-generating property in order to obtain the wherewithal for satisfying his/her needs and desires for goods and services. As a result, there is an incentive in modern American capitalism to try to acquire property resources, either physical or human, or both. For some persons, there is also an incentive to try to get laws passed, interpreted, and applied so that one's property resources will be endowed with special privileges which will enhance their value and income-generating ability.

The incentive to acquire property resources is manifest in several activities: going to school, creating productive physical capital, and joining voluntary associations. First, there is an incentive for a person to invest in his/her own human capital via education and training in order to develop useful and saleable skills. Statistical data show that the more education and training a person has, the higher will be that person's income (assuming that the investment in human capital is in those skills needed to produce the goods and services that people with money to spend are willing and able to pay for).[4] Second, there is an incentive to try to acquire or bring into existence income-earning assets (such as a machine, some land, an apartment house, a stock, or a bond). The acquisition of physical-property resources provides their owner a basis for receiving income in addition to the income earned from working with one's own labor power enhanced by acquired knowledge and skills. Third, there is an incentive to join with persons of similar circumstances to try to influence legislation, which will hopefully promote one's private interest. If a human or physical property-owning group can cause laws to be passed (and administered) which will enhance the value of its property resources, or cause its property resources to be more productive than before, then the members of one group may be able to receive higher incomes than others.

One capitalist institution--inheritance--often transfers physical property to selected individuals. In addition, an inheritance-like mechanism may also transfer human capital to some individuals but not to others. To illustrate, the child of an educated and successful property-owning business executive may not only inherit the physical property of the family, but may also inherit good health, social contacts, a good education, initiative, ambition, organizational skills, and opportunity-identifying-and-seizing acumen from the parents. In addition, the recognition by society that one is a financial success may become reinforced into a positive self-image. The child of a poor, uneducated, propertyless family may be inculcated with a sense of failure, pessimism, insecurity, and despair. Society's treatment of these persons gives them a low self-esteem and a sense of worthlessness. Such intergenerational effects have a direct bearing on the ability to acquire both physical and human capital as well as on the probabilities for enhancing their income-yielding abilities.

PLURALISM AND AMERICAN CAPITALISM

Any society, even one employing the simplest and most primitive techniques, is a mosaic of overlapping groups of various specialized sorts. [D. Truman, *The Governmental Process*, New York: Knopf, 1951, p. 43.]

Two mechanisms for power in the political economy are elitism and pluralism. The pluralist hypothesis holds that in America, the political system is rather open, that a majority of citizens have an opportunity to influence legislation and do so regularly with success. The elitist hypothesis holds that a handful of highly influential persons, some of wealth, some of aristocratic backgrounds, some with intellectual abilities, essentially set the national agenda and make public policy. These hypotheses are not mutually exclusive[5] for both tendencies may interact to reinforce each other. The way that pluralism operates in the political economy is fundamental in American capitalism.

Interest Groups

Under the constitutional guarantees of freedom of assembly, belief, and expression, persons are able to join voluntary associations for purposes of fostering their common interests. Accordingly, American pluralist democracy contains three basic institutional arrangements which allow adjustments to be made in the operation of the economic system. The first provides an opportunity for individuals to voice their demands through the civil rights of freedoms of speech, of the press, and of association. In the second, competing political parties offer to the voters certain (albeit somewhat limited) choices which represent the alternatives that a potential majority of the populace hopefully will vote for in the regular elections. For a third, an elaborate network of voluntary associations--special interest groups--provides supplementary representation for many individuals.[6] These groups reflect a diversity of ethnic, religious, occupational, economic, and regional interests throughout the nation. The political arena is a vast array of these competing groups which are engaged in a continuous process of building alliances, appealing for popular support, bargaining, pressuring, and negotiating.

The interaction among pluralism, property, and political economy is the key to understanding how resources are allocated and income distributed in modern American capitalism. The fundamental connection is manifest in an incentive to try to have legislation enacted and interpreted in one's favor. Special privileges granted by law can increase the income-generating ability of property by reducing the risks involved in using those resources in profit-making ventures. The tendency to elect and/or to influence lawmakers and administrators to enact and interpret special-interest legislation is an expression of American pluralist democracy. Indeed, interest groups, and their lobbying and seeking favors, are attributes of political economy. These features were present in mercantilist England, and their use has continued through the present under modern American capitalism.

Interest groups are constitutional voluntary associations which perform several vital purposes for their members and for society. They provide a link between the individual and government, they help the individual to overcome a feeling of helplessness, and they may even help to reduce conflict.[7] Interest groups are beneficial because they allow citizens to have a voice in the allocation of resources. Organized group activity is a means by which individuals who desire special status from government can pool their resources to get it. Interest groups serve pluralist democracy by assisting government decision makers to respond to the demands of various publics.

There are 535 representatives in the national legislature, numerous representatives in the state legislatures, and countless representatives in the county, city, and town councils across the nation. In addition there are hundreds--indeed, thousands--of administrative agencies at all three levels of government which carry out existing legislation. In the process of issuing administrative rulings these agencies often in effect make policy. Finally, several jurisdictions of courts staffed by judges explain and interpret the laws, and in that course, assign property rights, allocate resources, and distribute income. All these persons at the national, state, and local levels are a part of the system of pluralist democracy and political economy in modern American capitalism. These representatives are from many walks of life, and from every section of the country. They represent different points of view, and respond to various interest groups. When laws are passed, administered, and interpreted resource allocation and economic choices become affected in the arena of pluralism and the political economy.

As political pressure groups from different segments of the citizenry assemble for purposes of bargaining, negotiating, and pressuring, the end result is often a compromise skewed in favor of those who were most successful in using their bargaining power and skill. Outcomes are often based on the (a) number of people a bargainer represents, (2) number of supporters representing an interest group, and (3) the amount of property and wealth which backs the bargainer(s).[8] Those with the most political influence are usually groups with the most economic power. As Jefferson warned, if political power can be acquired, chances are that economic power will not be too difficult to secure.[9] Once both have been acquired, they reciprocate and reinforce each other so that each continues to grow, especially if property holders are active in the political arena, pressuring to get laws passed for their benefit, or to gain privileges, subsidies, and favors for themselves from the system. Those with little or no politico-economic power often bear a greater share of the burden in relation to their income and/or wealth than those who do possess a significant amount of politico-economic power.[10] Yet, all of this is seen as a logical extension of freedom, of self-interest, and of profit seeking. It is not unconstitutional. It is an expected expression and result of pluralist democracy, under conditions of substantial inequality of income, wealth, and power.

Operational Aspects

It is to be expected that pluralism and political economy would develop in our democratic system. After all, it would be an abridgment of our constitutional rights of freedom of assembly and expression if citizens could not provide legislators, governmental officials, and bureaucratic administrators with information, points of view, and requests. If the political system is to be of the people, for the people, and by the people, then the people must be free to communicate their problems, needs, and desires to their elected representatives. Politicians respond to these soundings, and then pass laws to be administered for purposes of satisfying those demands. Given that resources are scarce, the goals of one interest group are not always consistent with the goals of other interest groups. A piece of legislation and its administration may not serve all members of society in a beneficial way. Moreover, not all interest groups are able to influence legislation in direct proportion to the number of members each has. Generally, the larger the membership of an interest group, the less the tendency for its members to contribute to the success of the group, and the less able it is to be successful in the pluralist political arena.[11]

Interest groups can be classified in several ways. One scheme is on the basis of their relation to the three basic economic classes--households, resource owners, and business firms. Consider an interest group from each class: consumer organizations, labor unions, and trade associations. How effective have they been? There are 250 million consumers, and no interest group has ever represented all of them. And of the consumer groups which exist, few have been very successful at bringing about significant consumer legislation. Labor unions account for less than 20 percent of the labor force and have been somewhat successful in their legislative programs. Many trade associations have nearly complete membership of firms in a line of commerce, and have lobbied quite successfully to shape legislation in their favor.[12]

The question often arises as to whether the American capitalism system and its administration is open to influence and change--whether all persons and groups have equal access to the political economy. Occasionally, a victory for the goals sought by Ralph Nader, Cesar Chavez, or the Sierra Club occurs, and is used as evidence that pluralist democracy and the political economy works smoothly by allowing all groups equal opportunity to participate. Whereas the system may be permeable, some political scientists doubt whether it is as porous as the conventional wisdom often contends.[13]

Private and Public Interests

Adam Smith's plan for a politico-economic system merged self-interest with the general welfare. If people were free to pursue their own private interests, the effect would be to serve the public interest at the same time. What constitutes the "general welfare" and the "public interest," however, has not been well-established. It is not surprising that special interests attempt to merge the two notions.

Pluralism within the democratic polity virtually assures that selfishness will characterize interest-group activities. There is a tendency for interest groups to pursue their own goals with little concern for the impact of programs, statutes, and administrative rulings on other groups within the economy. Most interest groups desire government to respond to their own needs, but at the same time they try to identify their objectives with benefits to the country at large. Widespread public awareness of action-group efforts leads each cluster to justify its actions, not always with crass expediency or purely selfish motives but in terms of moral imperatives concerning the entire nation. Interest and morality may become so beclouded that it is difficult to separate them. But they will probably be exposed, for in an open society it is not difficult to challenge what appears to be a violation of accepted beliefs.

Members of pressure groups may even convince themselves that their cause promotes the public interest while it serves their own interests. Indeed, the belief in this rationalization may be so sincere that a large part of the public becomes convinced of its legitimacy. To illustrate, while seeking legislation for occupational licensing, which would ultimately limit supply and raise prices, a profession may base its arguments on reasons of safety and protection of the general welfare. Legislatures, the press, and the public may eventually accept the idea that practicing the profession must legally be limited only to persons who can pass qualification requirements because nonqualified practitioners may do serious harm to the public. Whether harm will be done is subject to interpretation, depending on the private interest group to which the observer belongs.

Many interest groups often act cooperatively rather than competitively. Such cooperative behavior is not always consistent with free-market ideals. Business rivals used to be able to cooperate and still promote competition. Back on the farm at the turn of the century one farmer did not consider the farmer down the road to be a competitor, only a neighbor. Farmers rivaled each other silently and unknowingly in a competitive, free-enterprise market situation, but they still cooperated by helping one another with threshing, quilting bees, and barn raisings. Today competition is often openly rivalrous, but cooperation occurs when business firms join together in a trade association to lobby for special favors and privileges. It is not uncommon for one occupational group or labor union to join with others of a like genre to transform pluralism into action thereby participating in the political economy.

A special-interest group engages in "rent-seeking behavior" when it successfully induces government to pass legislation in its favor.[14] The net effect is to transfer wealth from other persons in society to members of the group. Special interests can often achieve their goals when group size is small and each member will receive a large gain at the expense of a large number of citizens who each incur a relatively small loss. Members of small special-interest groups tend to be knowledgeable and aggressive about lobbying legislators to approve their programs. Those who will ultimately be required to subsidize a program tend to be unorganized and ineffective at resisting such legislation. Legislators support special-interest program to gain the members' election support. The prospect of losing votes from those who will pay is negligible because each member of a large group contemplates losing very little once the program is enacted. Instead, other issues vitally important to large-group members are the basis for judging the performance of the politicians.

Role of Government

Political economy refers to the exercise of power in the economic system. Economic power is the ability to influence price, supply, demand, and terms of trade in the product and resource markets. The government wields economic power; labor unions wield economic power; trade associations (such as those in agriculture, transportation, finance, and manufacturing) wield economic power; and many large corporations wield economic power. Often, when these groups form an organization in the mode of pluralist democracy, they tend to cooperate and compromise rather than to compete. This ironic turn of events raises serious questions about the prevalence of a competitive market economy in the United States. It is the relation between interest groups and government which has caused this skepticism.

In the political economy of modern American capitalism, government is significantly involved in the process of economic decision making. Its involvement affects the choices made in the allocation of resources, the production of output, the distribution of income, the consumption of goods and services, and the productivity and ownership of property. While yielding to the allocation-production-distribution-consumption process, government involvement in the economic system interferes with the functioning of a competitive market.

Some persons naively question and attack government involvement in the political economy. There is often a misunderstanding about the reasons why Congress (state legislatures, county commissions, city councils, school districts) passes so many laws to control, regulate, and supervise private economic activity. Bodies of government usually do not act on their own to pass laws to affect private property (or to control private actions with that property). Generally, laws are passed in response to the will of some of the people as represented by interest groups. It is the mechanism of pluralistic democracy wherein various private groups assemble to get laws passed to foster their own interests. Voluntary associations representing big business, small business, labor, agriculture, education, and a host of other special interests formulate laws and national policy by meeting, debating, and seeking political compromise.[15] The agreement reached affects the allocation of society's scarce resources, and grants one or more special interest groups a legal privilege, favor, or subsidy which often requires the expenditure of public funds to be paid for largely by low- and middle-income taxpayers.[16] The mechanism through which political economy cum pluralist democracy occurs involves the symbiotic relations between government and several private-interest spheres of influence. As Eric Sevareid has said, "We might call these spheres of influence the military-industrial-union-education complex."[17] President Eisenhower simply called it the military-industrial complex, a subject confronted in the next chapter.

CONCLUDING REMARKS

The public bureaucracy . . . can be effectively and durably influenced only by another organization. And between public and private organizations there can be a deeply symbiotic relationship. [J. Galbraith, *Economics and the Public Purpose*, Boston: Houghton Mifflin, 1973, p. 50.]

Pluralism in the political economy is increasing because the need for planning and risk-reduction is a by-product of technological change.[18] The application of scientific knowledge to practical tasks has increased in recent years. Advancing technology has created large-size productive processes, not only in manufacturing, but in agriculture, energy, transportation, and distribution. Specialized, high-speed machinery is complex and expensive. Mass production requires large-size business plants, and the dollar value of the assets of such business firms is relatively high. In order for the large organization with high-cost, specialized equipment to function effectively, planning is necessary. Planning takes time and requires organization. The loss of time in the planning process can cause a significant monetary loss. In the face of the risk of loss of vast amounts of funds committed to expensive, specialized equipment, the large organization pursues a policy of reducing risk, of ensuring its security and survival, and of attempting to control its environment.

We should expect an organism to seek security, to look after its own self-interest, and to try to adapt to its environment in order to optimize its benefits. Big corporations with billions of dollars worth of assets perceive a need to reduce hazards, to plan, and to organize to reduce the risk of loss. Unions perceive similar hazards under advancing technology and large size: workers may become technologically unemployed and this possibility must be contemplated and accommodated. In addition, the sheer size of giant corporations which unions face in collective bargaining tends to lead them to seek to influence legislation in their favor to try to equalize the power relations among them. Each of the major productive segments of the economy has adopted high-technology facilities and adapted business practices to them. As a result, the need for planning, organizing, and protecting is the basic rationale for the direct involvement of pluralism in the political economy.

Whereas some economists contend that the United States has a "mixed economy" of socialism and capitalism, others call it a system of "modified capitalism" with direct governmental intervention into private economic affairs. A few economists and corporate executives even suggest that the United States does not have a market economy at all. The American economy does not operate according to the textbook description of pure competition in which many small sellers and buyers exist, participating in industries where entry is easy, products are standardized, and prices are the result of auction-like bargaining. The market operates in an imperfect way, not only because there are a few large firms in certain industries of partly blocked entry, differentiated products, and administered prices, but also, among other reasons, because there are some resources being allocated and incomes being received as a result of pluralism interacting within the political economy. A type of competition exists among private interest groups largely representing business and labor which operate behind the scenes of the city halls, school districts, the county commissions, state legislatures, and subcommittee rooms in Washington, D. C. Government does not take a passive role in economic affairs and confine its activities to maintaining courts, providing defense, and fostering competition. It takes an active role and the action takes place in an arena that fosters the operation of pluralism and political economy.

It is commonplace for the naive and the intellectually suspect to bemoan the interference of government with business. Critics have only begun to admit that government intrusion into the economic system has become a way of life because business and other interests have petitioned government to do things for them. A main catalyst for this scenario in modern American capitalism has been technology. As technology has advanced, institutional arrangements have arisen as adjustments to it, and so has the fervor with which pluralism interacts with the political economy. Technology has been exploding on many fronts, and there is little reason to expect that its pace will diminish in the future. Even if a movement developed to persuade special interests to cease lobbying governments for subsidies, favors, and privileges--to cease and desist those practices which are undermining the competitive, free-enterprise market system--its success would be doubtful. As with most institutional arrangements which have become a way of life, only the most idealistic could believe that the practice of pluralism in the political economy will ever be discontinued in modern American capitalism.

NOTES

1.   A. Marshall, *Principles of Economics*, 8th Ed., London: Macmillan, 1923, p. 92.

2.   For a good description of mercantilist controls, see P. W. Buck, *The Politics of Mercantilism*, New York: Octagon, 1964.

3.   Diverse papers on the subject of political economy have been published. Among them are: (1) P. W. Barkley, "A Contemporary Political Economy of Family Farming," *American Journal of Agricultural Economics*, December 1976, pp. 812-819; (2) G. P. Shultz, "Reflections on Political Economy," *Challenge*, March-April 1974, p. 6-11; and (3) O. L. Graham, Jr., "The Future of the U. S. Political Economy," *Increasing Understanding of Public Problems and Policies*, Chicago: Farm Foundation, 1976, pp. 1-13.

4.   For example, in 1987 the median income for someone with less than eight years of schooling was $18,718, but $50,908 with more than four years of college. (*Statistical Abstract of the U.S.*, 1989, p. 447.)

5.   See D. Garson, *Group Theories of Politics*, Beverly Hills: Sage, 1978, p. 207.

6.   K. M. Dolbeare and P. Dolbeare, *American Ideologies*, Chicago: Markham, 1974, pp. 53-4.

7.   T. R. Dye and L. H. Zeigler, *The Irony of Democracy*, 3rd Ed., North Scituate: Duxbury, 1975, pp. 255-257.

8.   L. H. Zeigler and W. Peak, *Interest Groups in American Society*, 2nd ed., New York: Prentice-Hall, 1972, pp. 133-155.

9.   For an excellent discussion of the "Jeffersonian ideal," see: J. S. Bain, *Industrial Organization*, New York: Wiley, 1968, pp. 35-38.

10.   The share of all income taxes (and of all government receipts) paid by corporations has been decreasing steadily since 1950.

11.   M. Olson, *The Logic of Collective Action*, Cambridge: Harvard University Press, 1965. [An interesting example of this principle has been discussed by M. Friedman, "The Public Be Damned," *Newsweek*, August 5, 1968.]

12.   Dye and Zeigler, *op. cit.*

13.   See M. Parenti, *Democracy for the Few*, New York: St. Martin's, 1974; and Dye and Zeigler, *op. cit.*

14.   See C. R. McConnell and S. L. Brue, *Microeconomics*, New York: McGraw-Hill, 1990, pp. 356-57.

15.   Two excellent accounts of deliberate, formal, calculated political influence by both business and labor can be found in: (1) D. M. Ogden, Jr., "How National Policy is Made," *Increasing Understanding of Public Problems, Mode and Policies*, Chicago: Farm Foundation, 1971, pp. 5-10, and (2) C. Wilcox, *Public Policies Toward Business*, Homewood: Irwin, 1966, pp. 7-12.

16.   In 1970, families with incomes less than $8,000 paid higher composite tax rates as a percent of income than families receiving between $10,000 and $25,000 income. See R. A. Herriot and H. P. Miller, "The Taxes We Pay," *Conference Board Record*, May 1971, p. 40. This general relation still exits today. See E. K. Browning and W. R. Johnson, *The Distribution of the Tax Burden*, Washington, D.C.: American Enterprise Institute; and J. A. Peckman, *Who Paid the Taxes: 1966-1985*, Washington, D.C.: Brookings, 1985.

17.   CBS Nightly News, April 1977.

18.   This connection was well-elucidated by J. K. Galbraith. See his *The New Industrial State*, Boston: Houghton Mifflin, 1968, pp. 13-17.

10   MILITARY-INDUSTRIAL COMPLEX

INTRODUCTION

> In the councils of government, we must guard against the acquisition of unwarranted influence, whether sought or not sought, by the military-industrial complex. [D. Eisenhower, *U.S. News & World Report*, January 17, 1961, p. 69.]

The claim that modern American capitalism is a "mixed economy" was popularized in Paul Samuelson's classic principles of economics textbook in the 1950s and 1960s.[1] The idea of being "mixed" meant, of course, that the United States does not have a pure market system but contains a substantial amount of governmental involvement which permeates the entire economy. The "mixing" would include not only the federal level but state and local entities as well. In some cases, the extent of connection in the mixed economy is significant; in other areas it is only modest. Nevertheless, the State and the market have been and are intertwined through mutual cross-coordination of programs, transactions, and subsidies. Here, the ingredients for effective political economy are present: a historical pattern of granting privileges, transmitting power, institutionalizing advantages, protecting status, and begetting disparities.

Procurement of arms for the military services demonstrates a thorough mixture of public and private sectors. Not only is the United States Department of Defense involved, but so are various members of the Congress, business executives, and labor leaders. This chapter discusses the evolution and structure of the so-called military-industrial complex. There is probably no better example of political economy in modern American capitalism than the activities of this sector. A number of excellent articles and books have been written on the subject,[2] but the many insights and conclusions contained in them need not be repeated here. Instead, after identifying participants and their activities, a brief history is provided on the development and operation of the military-industrial complex. The presentation closes by discussing some features of political economy guiding this sector of the economic system.

ORGANIZATIONAL DIMENSIONS

> [T]he Army as one of the main agencies responsible for the defense of the nation has the duty to take the initiative in promoting closer relation between civilian and military interests. [D. Eisenhower, Memorandum, Chief of Staff, U. S. Army, April 27, 1946.]

Whereas President Eisenhower called it the "military-industrial" complex, TV news commentator Eric Sevareid called it the "military-industrial-union-education" complex,[3] and so did Professor John Kenneth Galbraith.[4] In order to appreciate how political economy is practiced in this arena, consider the players in the game and the rules by which they play.

Participants

Participants in the military-industrial complex are from various walks of life and wear many hats. In the political economy, representatives from the Department of Defense and the world of business are involved, but relations and interactions encompass somewhat more than that.

The military-industrial complex is an informal, loose but effective coalition of vested-interest groups who derive political power, social status, and economic benefits from the fear of communism, the Cold War, and extensive military preparedness both offensively and defensively. This coalition takes a fundamentalist position with respect to freedom, democracy, and protecting the American way of life--namely, that capitalism in the United States is "good," or "best," and ought to be preserved and even expanded around the globe.

The military-industrial complex consists primarily of executives from leading U.S. manufacturing firms which produce military armaments, high-ranking military officers in the Pentagon who coordinate the nation's defense, and senators and representatives from districts containing defense bases and businesses that produce military equipment and supplies. Also included are members and leaders of labor unions having collective bargaining contracts with companies supplying military equipment; governors, mayors, and city council members of states and communities in which defense items are manufactured; and local retailers who operate firms selling goods both to military personnel and civilian employees (often union members) and defense-industry manufacturers located in their communities. In addition, officials and investigators of research laboratories in the scientific areas conducting basic and applied analyses in chemistry, physics, engineering, and related technical areas belong to this group. Many of these participants are represented by agents who lobby the Congress on behalf of the interests of their principals. These agents ordinarily are members of well-organized and highly effective trade associations.[5]

Activities

The players of the military-industrial complex operate and carry out their mission not only from the boardrooms of private corporations and the briefing rooms of military Chiefs of Staff, but also from labor-union offices, city halls, state capitols, the floors of the Senate and the House, and in hotels, cafes, and restaurants where lobbying efforts are conducted under the guise of "education" and "information."

Members of the military-industrial complex present a broad, unified front to communicate the threat and fear of communism, to perpetuate the Cold War, and to lobby the Congress to increase military spending. Their goal is to prepare the United States to be strategically and tactically ready to carry on both nuclear and conventional war in offensive and defensive contexts. Members urge not only heavy expenditures on military personnel and weaponry, especially with nuclear capability, but on research and development for new ships, tanks, aircraft, armaments, and other military hardware. At this level, intense rivalry among various members takes place. They compete over which specific "weapons delivery system" ought to be designed, funded, built, and maintained.

Basic Framework

The military-industrial complex operates within a structure based on "agenda-set."[6] This condition occurs when a person or group, the perpetrator, seeks to establish a power position for its own benefit, and creates a well-orchestrated belief system backed by an ominous threat of fear. These twin mechanisms are designed and executed so victims are maneuvered into accepting the agenda designed by the perpetrator, which allegedly will save them from dreadful consequences posed by the threat. If successful, then the perpetrator of belief-and-threat can attain its goals of privilege and power. This power, in turn, provides positive payoffs for both parties--perceived relief for the victims and profit, prestige, and additional power for the perpetrator.

In Meredith Wilson's *The Music Man*, Harold Hill practiced "agenda-set" when he raised the haunting spectre of a pool hall in River City. The billiard parlor was portrayed as a threat to the values and well-being of the children. Parents could avoid the dreadful consequences if a boy's band

were established. Mr. Hill, of course, was available to become the savior of
River City by organizing and leading such a group. In the play, had Hill not
been exposed for his fakery, band practice would have kept the boys out of
the alleged trouble so that Hill could receive income from selling
instruments and sheet music.

In America, the military-industrial complex has practiced agenda-set
successfully for several decades. Its main agenda was a Cold War fired by
a fear of communism. These items are based on crisis-oriented thinking to
gain majority support among the citizens to arm the nation heavily. This
strategy created international tensions which further exacerbated and
justified military preparedness for possible hostilities.

EVOLUTIONARY ASPECTS

Since the early days of the republic, the armed forces of the United
States have actively participated in domestic economic affairs.[M.
Smith, in *War, Business and American Society*, London: Kennikat,
1977, p. 24.]

That the military-industrial complex is a product of concern for possible
hostile threats and peacetime defense after World War Two may be true, but
the situation is far more intricate than that. The historical development of
linkages between public and private sectors for providing war materiel can
be traced to industrialization in this country and to similar events in Europe.
Four events are interrelated: the development of American industry;
concerns for economic growth and development; connections between
government and business for procuring war materiel; and the cultivation of
fears about socialism and communism.

Early Background

Great Britain became a colonial, imperialist empire during the 17th
century, and its status as such flourished throughout the 18th century.
During that period, private enterprise companies provided Her Majesty's
Navy with significant amounts of ordnance, food, and supplies.[7] It was, in
fact, the common practice of many European countries to purchase military
requirements from private, profit-seeking businesses during wartime.

Whereas the process of industrialization began in England after 1750,
rapid industrialization did not occur in the United States until just after the
Civil War. Countries such as Great Britain, Germany, and France had a
significant head-start over the United States for investing in factories and
perfecting their productive capacities. As the Industrial Revolution was
occurring in America, Karl Marx was busy setting out the requirements for

socialism and communism as he studied and wrote in the basement of the British Museum in London. The United States experienced the pangs of unbridled market capitalism (such as trusts, concentration of wealth, and industrial combination by so-called Robber Barons)[8], but dialectical challenges arose to counter that consolidation (such as Grangers and populists).[9] Fears were raised about socialism replacing capitalism and of prospects for Marxism in America when Edward Bellamy published *Looking Backward* (1888) and the Sherman Antitrust Act was passed (1890).[10]

Later Developments

By the eve of World War One, the United States had developed into a leading world power. By its balance of payments, America's position changed from being a fledgling debtor nation to one whose integrated machine-tool base was nearly on equal footing to that of Great Britain and Germany.[11] At the time, the United States was still importing human and physical capital as well as continuing to expand its geographical frontier from the mid-west all the way to the Pacific Ocean. The country's demand for equipment and supplies was sufficient to absorb not only its own domestic productive capacity, but also some of Europe's.

During World War One, the War Department wrote a large number of contracts with American private business firms to provide armaments and other items for the front in Europe.[12] When the United States entered the World War, the Russian Revolution was taking place. This objective there was to replace oligarchy and feudalism with a crude form of socialism and communism. Fears accelerated that in America, Marxism might begin to replace democratic, market capitalism.[13] In fact, unions (such as Industrial Workers of the World) were crushed, and the Alien and Sedition Acts were passed.

The United States emerged from World War One as a strong creditor nation.[14] Both its industrial and resource bases had been sufficient to sustain a greater volume of real output of heavy war machines than European belligerents could produce. During the 1920s, investment in social overhead capital, in heavy and light industry, and in commercial enterprise flourished in the United States.[15] By 1929, on the eve of the Great Depression, America had increased its lead as a leading industrial power in the world.

Economic Problems

During the depression years of 1929-41, concerns continued to be expressed about the failure of capitalism and how socialism might be a viable alternative for America.[16] Trade unions were legalized in the early

1930s after a long struggle which had commenced in the late 19th century. Supporters of the absolute right of private property had been tagging unions with labels of socialism and communism for several years. Seeds of suspicion were sown for fearing the far left and they eventually bore fruit in the late 1940s.

To deal with the depression, economists at Cambridge on both sides of the Atlantic, notably John Maynard Keynes in England and Harvard's Alvin Harvey Hansen, argued that government borrowing-and-spending policies could salvage private enterprise and market capitalism. The Keynes-Hansen-Klein model[17] and Roosevelt's New Deal provided theoretical and public-policy justification for explaining and providing solutions to the dire effects of stagnation in a maturing industrialized economy. It is no accident that both Keynesian economics and the New Deal were charged with being socialist endeavors by those who feared that Marxian ideas were becoming irreversibly woven into the American fabric.

Whereas some writers have given credit to the New Deal, and the Keynesian model, for overcoming the Great Depression, World War Two was the primary factor responsible for ending that economic downturn.[18] By 1940, American industry was producing for the war effort in Europe; the Lend Lease program to aid Great Britain was operative in early 1941; and by 1942, war production was in high gear. During World War Two cries of socialism were heard when governmental war production agencies clashed with private property interests. In Europe, the war was a campaign against the NAZIs, an acronym for German National Socialism. Here was another reason to fear socialism and be concerned about it gaining a foothold in America. Both the naive and intellectually dishonest neglected to point out that the last word of National Socialism was a subterfuge for fascism. Indeed, socialism is a movement of the left whereas German fascism was a movement of the right.

Wartime Events

During World War Two, countless agreements were made between the military and private enterprise, chiefly with major American oligopolistic corporations which had collective bargaining contracts with large industrial and craft unions. The War Production Board converted the nation from civilian to military output by requisitioning strategic resources, primary metals, and industrial products. The manufacture of many civilian items was curtailed, and for others, output was drastically reduced. Rationing and materials allocation were imposed. It was virtually impossible to purchase new autos, tires, farm implements, appliances, and sufficient amounts of gasoline. To carry on the war effort, the federal government built, owned, and operated dozens of defense plants, and oversaw production and distribution in hundreds of other already existing private enterprise firms.

When World War Two ended the United States possessed an extensive industrial capacity, although it was somewhat worn out because replacement investment had been delayed.[19] Yet, no bombs had destroyed American factories. Public and private policy makers understood clearly how war had exerted an expansionary effect on the economy. With the demand for military goods now reduced so sharply, there was concern about replacing that part of aggregate demand which had raised the levels of real income and employment so dramatically during the war.

After World War Two, the country invested heavily to generate productive capacity needed to satisfy domestic and foreign demand for American goods. New technology was available from military research conducted during the war years, both for new products and processes. Reconversion to civilian production allowed the manufacture of vehicles, petroleum products, and other items the American people so desperately sought because of wartime shortages. America then provided foreign aid to Europe through the Marshall Plan which was instituted in 1947 and continued for several years after that. The rebuilding of Europe, and to some extent, Japan, augmented domestic aggregate demand modestly by stimulating exports of capital and consumer goods.[20]

After the Marshall Plan had been operative for about three years, conflict developed again in the Far East. Thereupon, the Korean War absorbed some productive capability and raised domestic levels of income and employment. Despite defense expenditures during the Korean affair, the incidents of active war were unable to absorb sufficient productive capacity to continue to increase real income and employment. A suitable replacement had already been found by converting fear of Marxism and communism into a "cold war."

Many Americans had been suspicious of Marxism and socialism since the turn of the century. These fears continued with the expansion of unionism, Rooseveltian governmental agencies, and German National Socialism. When the Soviet Union erected the Iron Curtain after World War Two, both socialism and world communism were perceived as a mounting threat. A strong sense of patriotism and allegiance to fight for American freedom still lingered from the war years. A victorious World War Two general was elected president. He appointed a Secretary of State, John Foster Dulles, who continued a foreign policy of containing communism at its borders, and then called for a policy of massive retaliation. This latter goal was not relaxed until the Soviet Union acquired a nuclear weapons capability and developed a successful space program.

The Cold War probably reached its zenith during the 1950s,[21] but it continued for almost three decades after that. Indeed, the Berlin Wall, the Cuban Missile Crisis, and the War in Southeast Asia also justified military preparedness.

ECONOMIC RATIONALE

[E]ven totally wasteful employment has the result of increasing
useful output and useful labor. [R. Lekachman, *The Age of Keynes*,
New York: Random House, 1966, p. 104.]

The sprouts of the military-industrial complex were germinating during
World War Two, but its seeds had been sown earlier in several ways. In
retrospect, the pieces of a giant jig-saw puzzle fell neatly into place to create
the Cold War and parlay it into economic advantage for the business sector.

Investment Frontiers

The distinguished American economist, Alvin Harvey Hansen, offered
the secular stagnation hypothesis to explain why the Great Depression of the
1930s had developed. A key part of this hypothesis was the notion of an
"investment frontier."[22]   His explanation began with the tremendous
immigration from Europe between 1880 and 1920, and the associated
settlement of land acquired a century earlier by the Louisiana Purchase.

The economic development of the western half of the United States
caused the real economic growth of the nation to rise substantially. Hansen
explained that increases in population provided favorable expectations and
opportunities to the business economy in the form of various investment
outlets or "frontiers." An investment frontier is a large-scale construction
project which occurs over a long period of time, permeates every nook and
cranny of the economy, involves vast expenditures, relies on heavy industry
to supply equipment, and requires sizeable amounts of skilled and unskilled
labor.   Consider the following investment frontiers which have been
associated with the enormous growth and development of the American
economy: The building of farms, ranches, towns, and cities as the west was
being settled; constructing the railroads with their rolling stock and trackage;
introducing the motor car and the resulting ribbons of highways; providing
the nation with electricity and telephones involved installation of poles,
lines, and appliances.   But a decline in the previous rate of population
growth combined with a lack of territorial expansion or major technological
impetus caused economic stagnation because incentives and expectations
supporting the prior expansion were lacking in the late 1920s and early
1930s. The nation had temporarily run out of investment frontiers! Hansen
suggested that government borrowing and spending on public programs
could replace the amounts otherwise spent on previous these outlets for
business expansion.

War As An Investment Frontier

After the depression and the war, America possessed a respectable industrial sector capable of producing heavy equipment. Hansen qua Keynesian convinced public policy makers that continued large-scale government spending was needed to utilize excess productive capacity and to augment aggregate demand. For Hansen, the spending should be on a variety of crucial social programs--parks, recreation, libraries, education.[23] However, once the concept of using fiscal policy to manage the business cycle became acceptable, it was not difficult to apply it to military preparedness.

The Cold War therefore became a convenient political instrument to accommodate a vexing economic problem. It was natural for the bugbear of a Marxist-Communist threat to be a basis for absorbing some of the nation's productive capacity by creating a defensive deterrence and an offensive response. It would keep America safe from the same type of threat the military confronted so victoriously just a few years earlier, and at the same time increase the nation's income and employment to boost the rate of economic growth. It was consistent with certain New Deal and Keynes-Hansen economic policies to forestall the dire effects of secular stagnation. It kept big business and members of big unions employed. It gave the people something to rally behind and feel good about. Above all, it was an acceptable "war" because very few persons would be killed. In short, it was a "Win-Win" situation.[24] The Cold War would be waged by a military-industrial complex. Its components stretched from main street through the corporate board rooms to the briefing chambers of generals. It would be supported by a vast constituency of worried citizens thankful freedom was being safeguarded and jobs were being created for an expanding labor force.

REALITY AND RECOGNITION

Merely because our huge responsibilities necessitate the existence of a military-industrial complex does not automatically make that complex something we must fear or feel ashamed of. [B. Goldwater, "Civilian Complex," U.S Senate Floor, April 15, 1969.]

Does "military-industrial complex" refer to a real-world entity or is the term merely an artificial concept? If it is real, does it have a deliberate structure or did it simply "grow," like Topsy? If it does exist and exhibit both form and structure, is it inevitable for such an institution to develop in an advanced technological society?

Existence?

Coinage of the term, "military-industrial complex" has perhaps been unfortunate. Such a phenomenon could be expected to involve more than military and industry participants, and the word "complex" may suggest something intangible. A number of political observers have argued that the military-industrial complex does not exist. Yet, the *Business Periodicals Index* began listing the term as a separate sub-category in the early 1970s. Some writers use words such as "warfare state," "garrison state," "pentagon capitalism," and "permanent war economy" to clarify its meaning.[25] Ironically, a moderate conservative, Dwight D. Eisenhower, legitimized the concept in 1961,[26] thereby fulfilling the prophesy of a "power elite" by C. W. Mills.[27] And both elitists and pluralists seem to admit that the military-industrial complex does exist.[28]

The presence of a military-industrial complex has been discounted for being based on casual inference, and for amounting to a crude form of economic determinism.[29] One observer recommends "that the concept of the military-industrial complex be discarded as imprecise and colored by ideology."[30] Another scholar prefers the term, "the economics of peacetime defense."[31] Still another suggests that even if the phenomenon does exist, it is nothing to fear.[32]

The existence of a military-industrial complex is difficult to ignore. Arms procured by the United States Department of Defense for various branches of the military services absorbed around 25 percent of the federal budget for several decades. American industrial firms received hundreds of billions of dollars in revenue annually under government contracts from manufacturing and distributing equipment and supplies to the military. Millions of blue- and white-collar workers, and thousands of offices, agencies, and institutions throughout the United States, have been deeply dependent for their livelihoods on this production and distribution of military materiel.

The military-industrial complex hypothesis has been subjected to several empirical tests. Military contracting firms were found to have characteristics distinct from civilian firms.[33] Specific differences can be noted in staffing, pricing, product mix, record keeping, control, and influence.[34] Focusing on taxpayer dollars going to defense corporations, the federal government was found two decades ago to be "a growing factor in the national economy, and . . . its expenditures for the military are of increasing importance in the business world."[35] In similar terms, one analyst contends that "military spending is favored by capitalists and is likely to be defended with considerable vigor . . ."[36] The existence of the military-industrial complex is also established by the frantic maneuvering of defense contractors and military offices in the Pentagon as they respond to the reduction in probable need for arms given the events in the Soviet Union and Eastern Europe in 1989 and 1990.[37]

Conspiratorial?

The existence of a military-industrial complex is difficult to deny. But is its genesis and continued operation a matter of deliberate design and action? The Left suggests that the following sequence of events has led to opportunism capitalized on by industrialists and governmental officials: The communist scare, the policy of containment, the quest to protect American business interests abroad, the desire to utilize excess capacity, and the need to be strong.

The military-industrial complex is probably not a conspiracy in the sense of a formalized, secretive, malignant plot. Rather, it is ostensibly "a subtle interplay of interests and perceptions."[38] As such, it is a predictable response to a fortuitous sequence of events. Its presence involves many people and organizations pursuing their own short-run economic self interests.

Deterministic?

It seems naive to register surprise that a connection between public and private sectors would result in a coalition called the military-industrial complex. But is it inevitable that such an arrangement should exist? Defense is not only a perceived national problem but also a public good. Elected officials of a country's government are responsible for securing the national defense. It appears somewhat inconsistent for the national government of a democratic, market economy to operate its own productive capital to produce and distribute military supplies (at least during times other than an active war).

Consider the contention that fascism is technology gone awry, that modernization is fascism. When useful discoveries are made in chemistry, biology, and physics, the technological improvements based on them result in new processes, products, and procedures. As new machines are introduced, additional expenditures on capital equipment necessarily occur. These, in turn, provide rising income and employment whenever investment funds are spent. As a result, increasing amounts of real assets exist for a nation to protect. There may be a "natural" tendency for militancy, authoritarianism, aggression, belligerency, and a perceived God-given right to power and control to develop. The outcome is a foreign policy of wariness toward those who might be covetous and hostile coupled with a domestic policy of a state of military readiness. Is it inevitable, whenever a large country becomes industrialized, for a nexus to develop among government, the military, and the technological, industrial base to produce arms to protect that industrial base? The argument of technological determinism is that there is no alternative, that there is an irreversible path of military aggression and protection down which a nation necessarily travels

when technology advances rapidly.   But this argument shortchanges
diplomacy, statesmanship, and rationality. It also neglects communication,
negotiation, and cooperation in the pursuit of mutual interests.

CONCLUDING REMARKS

> Our concept is not that American society contains a ruling
> military-industrial complex.   Our concept is more nearly that
> American society is a military-industrial complex. [M. Pilisuk and
> T. Hayden, "Is There a Military Industrial Complex Which Prevents
> Peace?" *Journal of Social Issues*, July 1965, pp. 67-117.]

The military-industrial complex is a prime example of how a market
economy is dependent on the political economy. The connection suggests
that the Neoclassical model incompletely describes how American capitalism
operates.   Even a public-choice argument to justify that heavy defense
spending reflects democratic wishes of the people must somehow recognize
the practice of agenda-set.   And whether elected representatives weigh
equally the views of all citizens also needs to be scrutinized in this regard.
     In the latter 1980s and early 1990s, many of the fears which fed the
military-industrial complex began to diminish. Events in the Soviet Union
and Eastern Europe suggested to many informed citizens and public policy
makers that the Cold War may have come to an end. If it has, is the
military-industrial complex outmoded? Is there room for this phenomenon
in the American economy? Can it survive?
     Some observers of the foreign scene suggest that recent occurrences are
irreversible: German re-unification (e.g., dismantling the Berlin Wall and
exchanging West and East German currencies); independence of Soviet Bloc
countries (e.g., Czechoslovakia, Poland, and Hungary); challenges by Soviet
republics to disassociate from the U.S.S.R. (e.g., Lithuania and Armenia);
the rise of vocal and effective opposition party leaders inside the Soviet
Union (e.g., Boris Yeltsin). Likewise, the words and deeds of the Soviet
leader, Mikhail Gorbachev, were accepted as sincere by many Western
politicians. Quickly, liberals and members of certain special interests began
calling for the "peace dividend" to reallocate funds from defense to social
programs. Given these events, what are prospects for the military-industrial
complex?
     Can we reasonably expect that this nation's defense budget will be
reduced drastically and that meaningful programs for housing, job retraining,
mass transportation, environmental cleanup, and other social benefits will
be instituted? To do so would be to deny the power of vested interests,
especially those which are as well-organized and entrenched in strategic
places, both inside and outside the American economy, as those of the
military-industrial complex.   Past events[39] suggest that the Central

Intelligence Agency, the Trilateral Commission, labor leaders, executives of multinational corporations, and other influential persons can be expected to maneuver both openly and secretively to solidify their status, and to perpetuate their power, privilege, position, and prospects for profits. They can also be expected to develop new threat systems to rationalize the continued existence of the military-industrial complex.

Several arguments suggest continuation of military preparedness and other uses of the resources of the military-industrial complex. Space exploration (and exploitation), being endless, is the ultimate investment frontier on which massive funds could be spent. A substantial amount of both space and military equipment is produced by the productive capital controlled by the military-industrial complex. In addition, situations in several parts of the world potentially pose serious ideological problems for the United States: Africa; the Middle East; and the Philippines. There is even the unfortunate but increasing rhetoric about a "trade war" with Japan developing into something more serious. Moreover, ethnic factionalism in some of the newly independent Soviet Bloc countries (such as in Romania) could threaten the security of American interests in Europe. And perhaps the nation's military posture ought not to be reduced too sharply because it might be needed to counteract the drug war and international terrorism? There are probably other reasons which will be offered to forestall hasty decisions about dismantling the military-industrial complex. Whatever they are, they will undoubtedly be a continuation of the historical pattern of practicing political economy in American capitalism.

NOTES

1.   P. H. Samuelson, *Economics*, 3d edition, New York: McGraw-Hill, 1955.

2.   As examples, see G. Adams, *The Politics of Defense Contracting*, New Brunswick: Transaction, 1982; J. K. Galbraith, *How to Control the Military*, New York: Signet, 1969; S. Melman, *The War Economy of the United States*, New York: St. Martin's, 1971; B. Russett, *The Prisoners of Insecurity*, San Francisco: W. H. Freeman, 1983.

3.   As reported on the CBS Nightly News, April 1977.

4.   J. K. Galbraith, *The New Industrial State*, Boston: Houghton-Mifflin, 1968.

5.   The National Trade Association Directory reports that more than 50,000 trade associations in the United States operated during 1989.

6.   I am indebted to Dr. Robert M. Lawrence, Professor of Political Science, Colorado State University for calling this term to my attention.

7.   T. Robb, "Nineteenth Century European Military-Industrial Complexes," in B. F. Cooling, *War, Business and American Society*, Port Washington: Kennikat, 1977, pp. 10-23.

8.   See R. L. Heilbroner, *The Making of Economic Society*, Englewood Cliffs: Prentice-Hall, 1962, pp. 115-30.

9.   See B. W. Poulson, *Economic History of the United States*, New York: Macmillan, 1981, pp. 294-7.

10.   M. J. Sklar, *The Corporate Reconstruction of American Capitalism, 1890-1916*, Cambridge: Cambridge University Press, 1988, pp. 89-91 and 401-12.

11.   R. M. Robertson, *History of the American Economy*, New York: Harcourt, Brace & World, 1964, pp. 368-75.

12.   D. R. Beaver, "The Problem of American Military Supply, 1890-1920," in Cooling, *op. cit.*, 73-92; and M. Parenti, *The Sword and the Dollar*, New York: St. Martin's, 1989, pp. 135-51.

13.   As examples, see: (1) F. Griffin, "Rising Tide of Socialism," *Outlook*, February 24, 1912, pp. 438-438; (2) F. Grendon, "In Defense of Socialism," *The New Republic*, April 7, 1917, pp. 297-98; and (3) A. Benson, "What the War Has Done to Socialism in America," *Current Opinion*, August 1918, pp. 82-85.

14.   See G. C. Fite and J. E. Reese, *An Economic History of the United States*, Boston: Houghton Mifflin, 1973, pp. 259-62.

15.   R. K. Vedder, *The American Economy in Historical Perspective*, Belmont: Wadsworth, 1976, pp. 344-63.

16.   Some representative samples are: (1) B. Stolberg, "Communist Wreckers in American Labor," *Saturday Evening Post*, September 29, 1939, pp. 5-7; and (2) M. Dies, "Challenge to Democracy: Foreign Isms Threaten Us," *Vital Speeches*, October 1, 1939, pp. 762-65.

17.   As based on: J. M. Keynes, *The General Theory of Employment Interest and Money*, London: Macmillan, 1936; A. H. Hansen, *Fiscal Policy and Business Cycles*, New York: Norton, 1941; and L. R. Klein, *The Keynesian Revolution*, New York: Macmillan, 1947.

18.   In constant dollars (1982=100), in 1929, real GNP was $710 billion and by 1939 it was only $717 billion! In 1942, real GNP was $1,080, augmented mostly by a burst of defense spending in 1941. *Economic Report of the President*, 1989, pp. 310-11.

19.   From 1942 through 1945, total disinvestment amounted to approximately $80 billion in real terms (1982=100). *Ibid.*, p. 327.

20.   However, the Marshall Plan was no panacea because federal expenditures continued to fall between 1945 and 1950. See J. Hughes, *American Economic History*, Glenview: Scott, Foresman, 1987, pp. 503-05.

21.   J. K. Galbraith, *The New Industrial State*, Boston: Houghton Mifflin, 1968, pp. 325-47.

22.   A. H. Hansen, *Full Recovery or Stagnation?*, New York: Norton, 1938, pp. 303-318.

23.   He made these points on several occasions. See, for example, A. H. Hansen, "Change Our Economic Structure," *National Business Woman*, March 1940, p. 72.

24. This concept in negotiating styles is discussed in E. Rausch, *Win-Win: Performance Management and Appraisal*, New York: Wiley, 1985.

25. These terms are used by H. Lasswell and S. Melman.

26. Departing President Eisenhower's famous "military-industrial complex" speech (of January 1961) was written by Malcolm Moos, a political scientist.

27. C. Wright Mills, *The Power Elite*, New York: Oxford University Press, 1956.

28. S. Lieberson, "An Empirical Study of Military-Industrial Linkages," *The American Journal of Sociology*, January 1971, p. 62.

29. J. Slater and T. Nardin, "The Concept of a Military-Industrial Complex," in Rosen, *Testing the Theory of the Military Industrial Complex*, Lexington: Lexington Books, 1973, pp. 27-60.

30. *Ibid*.

31. M. Weidenbaum, *The Economics of Peacetime Defense*, New York: Praeger, 1974.

32. P. Thayer, "The Men, The Machines, The Makers," in C. W. Purcell, Jr., *The Military-Industrial Complex*, New York: Harper & Row, 1973, p. 273.

33. J. F. Gorgol, *The Military Industrial Firm*, New York: Praeger Publishers, 1972.

34. *Ibid*., pp. 25-64.

35. Lieberson, *op. cit.*

36. M. Reich, "Military Spending and the U.S. Economy," in Rosen, *op. cit.*, p. 99.

37. That policy makers are worried about dismantling the military-industrial complex suggests its existence. See G. C. Wilson, "An Age of Lower Limits," *The Washington Post National Weekly Edition*, December 4, 1989, pp. 7-8.

38. Rosen, *op. cit.*, p. 24.

39. An example is the conspiracy in the U.S. Department of State and the Central Intelligence Agency against President Allende in Chile in the 1970s. See: (1) E. B. Burns, "True Verdict on Allende," *Nation*, October 29, 1973, pp. 422-26; and (2) W. F. Buckley, Jr., "CIA in Chile," *National Review*, October 11, 1974, p. 1118.

11   TRANSPORTATION

INTRODUCTION

> In order to assist and regulate transportation activities, a governmental bureaucratic structure is required. [W. Talley, *Introduction to Transportation*, Cincinnati, South-Western, 1983, p. 12.]

Transportation is one of several regulated industries. Political economy is reflected in the regulation of transportation as well as gas, electricity, water, pipelines, water terminals, grain elevators, and other lines of commerce "affected with a public interest."[1] Transportation is one of the most glaring examples of how government creates special structures and imposes unique rules, one upon another, year after year. Two modes of transportation in particular reflect the operation of the federal government in the political economy: the century-long regulation of railroads and the regulation of airlines for roughly 50 years. In both industries, control of entry and exit has received a majority of the legislative attention given to these fields by Congress and by various administrative agencies. In the former we witness the phenomenon of continually passing legislation to overcome the failings of previous laws; in the latter, we see the classic example of sanctioning collusive action.

This chapter begins by discussing railroad entry and exit legislation passed over the course of nearly a hundred years. The discussion then turns to the case of international air transport for which cartel-like activities were challenged so that a competitive structure might hopefully be established. A consideration of transportation will add to our understanding of the processes and problems of the American political economy.

THE RAILROADS

> Government regulation of industry in the United States owes its
> origin to the problems encountered as a result of laissez-faire
> manipulation by the transportation industry. [P. Dempsey and W.
> Thoms, *Law and Economic Regulation in Transportation*, Westport:
> Quorum Books, 1986, p. 7.]

Rail transportation has been regulated in the United States for more
than a century.[2] Free-market forces are not a primary determinant of entry
into and exit out of this particular mode of transport. Statutes govern entry
and exit by establishing procedures to follow, applications to file, criteria to
meet, justifications to plead, reviews to hold, and decisions to be made by
governmental agencies and the courts. Whenever entry into the industry or
one of its geographic markets is contemplated, the determining step is a
petition to the appropriate regulatory agency for permission to enter or to
exit via certification, consolidation, discontinuance, or abandonment.

A potential rail entrant is required to apply for a *certificate of public
convenience and necessity* (PC&N).[3] Criteria used to secure the PC&N
certificate stress the need for additional transport services, adequacy of
existing service, and the impact of that new entry on competition among
existing carriers, interstate commerce, and the public interest.[4] To qualify
for and obtain such a certificate, a carrier must meet certain conditions
promulgated by a regulatory agency.[5] In addition, exit or partial exit are
monitored by special rules.

Consolidation refers to bringing together existing productive units into
an industry which is serving a market. Consolidation ordinarily occurs
through the mechanisms of merger and acquisition.[6] Whenever two or
more firms join together, not only is the number of separate, independent
competitive forces in a market reduced, but the level of concentration is also
increased in the industry.

A rail carrier may desire to cease operating a certain train along a given
route by requesting *discontinuance*. This particular cessation of service along
a route involves either total exit from the market, or partial exit of a market
sub-group. The Interstate Commerce Commission (ICC) presently considers
applications for discontinuance of service and requires that selected criteria
be met: (1) public convenience and necessity not be harmed; (2) financial
conditions of the carrier not be impaired; (3) adequacy of service not be
disrupted; (4) existing carriers not be burdened; and (5) public interest not
be hurt.[7]

Abandonment is a complete exit from a market area rather than a mere
withdrawal from one or more market sub-groups.[8] Abandonment criteria
usually are more rigid and detailed than discontinuance criteria.
Abandonment requires: (1) giving public notice; (2) providing opportunity
for purchase; (3) identifying applicant's other lines and financial conditions;

(4) calculating costs and revenues emanating from abandonment; and (5) determining whose interest will be protected by allowing or not allowing abandonment.[9]

Act to Regulate Commerce, 1887

Before 1887, rail rates were established within a framework involving subjective, on-the-spot determinations, overt collusion and special agreements from negotiations based on status. The Interstate Commerce Act of 1887 (ICA) was designed to control high and discriminatory rates, selective ratemaking, pooling and combinations. In particular, it created the Interstate Commerce Commission (ICC). Collectively, by its provisions, the Act had the purpose of begetting fair and just rail shipment rates in interstate commerce. However, the 1887 Act contained no entry/exit provisions. At the time, entry was rampant, duplication of trackage and routes existed, and predatory pricing forced some carriers to exit the industry.[10] After 1887, however, several pieces of legislation dealt with entry and/or exit.

Transportation Act, 1920

Within ten years after passage of the ICA, a series of events had emasculated that statute. Court decisions in 1896[11] and 1897[12] reduced the authority and importance of the ICC, by challenging its rate-making power and rendering ineffective the practice of rail shipment rate discrimination. In the first decade of the 20th century, three statutes were passed to strengthen rail rate-making powers: the Elkins Act (1903);[13] the Hepburn Act (1906);[14] and the Mann-Elkins Act (1910).[15] Respectively, these acts made both carriers and shippers guilty for illegally granting preferential rates, gave the ICC power to fix maximum rates and restored the provision prohibiting higher charges for short versus long hauls to deal with discriminatory rates.

The United States entered World War One in April of 1917 and the federal government took over the railroads in December of that year.[16] The U.S. Railroad Administration then operated the railroads until March 1920.[17] The immediate impetus for passing the Transportation Act of 1920, also known as the Esch-Cummins Act,[18] was to remove the railroads from this direct government operation. Congress seized the opportunity to review the entire transport regulatory policy and to modify it where necessary and possible.[19] Among the shortcomings were a lack of control over railroad capitalization and service, and labor troubles.[20] Too much entry had occurred and rail rate regulation was beginning to cause the rails to be less profitable.[21]

Emergency Railroad Transportation Act, 1933

During the 1920s and early 1930s, at least thirty-eight specific pieces of federal transport legislation were passed.[22] Most of these statutes made minor changes in the 1887 Act and the 1920 Act. Several provisions focused on water transport, safety, and special conditions of carriage. One in particular provided for temporary financial assistance to railroads during the early part of the depression.[23]

Franklin Roosevelt assumed the Presidency on March 4, 1933, and subsequently persuaded Congress to pass emergency and relief programs to aid ailing businesses, financial institutions and consumers. The Emergency Railroad Transportation Act of 1933[24] was one of these pieces of legislation. The 1933 Act attempted to ". . . relieve the existing national [transportation] emergency in relation to interstate railroad transportation, and to amend . . . the Interstate Commerce Act."[25] The Act created an office within the ICC called the Federal Coordinator of Transportation and assigned two main responsibilities: (1) to help railroads cooperate among themselves to achieve cost-economies; and (2) to determine various means of improving national transportation conditions given their poor financial shape.[26] The main posture of the 1933 Act was to prevent or forestall exit (via failure and bankruptcy) and to promote, or preserve entry (via mergers among existing carriers).

Transportation Act, 1940

By 1939, The Great Depression was decelerating,[27] and the nation was facing the possibility of entering another war.[28] Rising military expenditures expanded business activity. Due to the impending armed conflict in Europe and the Pacific,[29] Congress recognized that an adequate transportation system had become a national priority.

Both the depression and technological advances in motor and air carriage created financial difficulties for the railroads. During the 1930s, the number of operating railroads decreased from 775 to 574 and the railroad industry as a whole showed business losses of nearly a hundred-million dollars.[30] In 1938 and 1939, several ICC reports called for additional transportation laws: (1) to regulate water carriers, (2) to change the policy encouraging consolidations and combinations, (3) to recognize the suitability of specific transport modes for certain purposes, and (4) to eliminate the provision for land-grant rail rate reductions.[31]

A primary focus of the Transportation Act of 1940[32] was to coordinate all forms of transport within a total regulatory context. The plan for consolidations in the 1933 Act was eliminated and new procedures were promulgated: (1) rail carriers would be allowed to combine via their own plans; (2) the ICC could require one or more willing railroads to become part of a proposed merger plan in the same geographical area; and (3) the ICC was given power to prevent holding companies from being used as a form of corporate organization in rail consolidations and combinations.[33]

Transportation Act, 1958

After the 1940 Act was passed, the railroads prospered because of increased freight traffic generated by World War Two and the Korean War. But by the mid-1950s, railroads were again financially distressed. Congress enacted the Transportation Act of 1958[34] to provide aid to these railroads.

The 1958 Act was passed to assist the railroads with difficulties they experienced in adjusting their rates and services to the changing conditions caused by the growth of other modes of competitive transport.[35] It provided for (1) temporary loan guarantees to railroads; (2) liberalized rules for controlling intrastate rail rates; (3) possible discontinuance of rail service; and (4) a change in rate-setting procedures for rails.

4R Act, 1976

After the 1958 Act was passed, the rail situation still did not improve. The 1960s were years of increasing prosperity, due primarily to government spending on the war against poverty and the war in Southeast Asia, as well as to expansionary government monetary and fiscal policies.[36] But the venerable twin problems of competition from other modes of transport and excessive trackage could not be overcome. The Department of Transportation (DOT) Act[37] of 1966 was passed in order to develop, improve, and coordinate national transportation policy.

Between 1958 and 1969, many passenger trains discontinued their service under the new provisions of the 1958 Act.[38] Indeed, during the twelve-year period the number of operating railroad companies decreased from 412 to 351.[39] Passenger services deteriorated badly and Congress sought to upgrade their quality. In the latter part of the 1960s, several rail companies filed for protection under the bankruptcy laws.[40] In mid-1970, six railroads, making up most of the rail system for 17 northeastern states, and carrying about 20 percent of the nation's freight, were in receivership at that time.[41] Previous merger policies had not prevented these rail failures.

In the 1970s, the Rail Passenger Service Act of 1970[42] and the Regional Rail Reorganization Act of 1973 (3R Act)[43] were passed. The former created what is now called AMTRAK (for AMerican TRavel trAcK) to deal with rail passenger service problems. The latter created CONRAIL (for CONsolidated RAIL Corporation) to deal primarily with freight traffic. In both cases track was abandoned, trains were discontinued and rail services were combined.[44]   The Railroad Revitalization and Regulatory Reform Act of 1976--the 4R Act[45]--augments previous legislation: specific and detailed provisions for timing of rate changes, mergers, and abandonments, and specified dollar and percentage allocations of aid to the troubled rails.

The Secretary of Transportation has a key role in approving rail merger applications. Under 4R, a railway must submit a diagram of its system to the ICC to identify lines which are to be abandoned. No line can be abandoned until it is included on the list for four months. The ICC must postpone abandonment if any financially responsible entity, including a state government, offers sufficient monetary aid to continue the service which will contribute to a line's revenue less its avoidable costs, including a reasonable profit on the line's value.[46]

Staggers Rail Act, 1980

Serious talk began in the mid-1970s about deregulating various modes of carriage. The Airline Deregulation Act of 1978[47] was enacted and so was the Motor Carrier Act of 1980,[48] which reduced ICC controls over the trucking industry. Results of both statutes caused further difficulties for railroads.   Railroads were still considered an essential mode of transportation, but intermodal competition was strong and increasing. At a time when rail transport was needed to help combat energy shortages and inflation, the rail system continued to deteriorate and rail companies earned low rates of return on their investments in equipment. The Staggers Rail Act of 1980[49] was another attempt to establish a rational rail policy by providing financial assistance to the railroads, and eliminate unnecessary regulation. Although the Act treats rail regulatory reform mainly through the mechanism of changes in rate-making procedures, it contains several important entry and exit provisions.

The Act increases the difficulty for a competing railroad to deny track crossover permission whenever the ICC issues a certificate of PC&N for new rail line construction.[50] Another provision adds merger language to the ICC consistent with existing antitrust rules for evaluating mergers. The ICC can approve the application of a railroad to provide motor carriage prior to or subsequent to transport by rail in order to provide service to small communities.   Time requirements are accelerated for notice, evaluation, hearings and actions on rail carrier applications for consolidation, merger and acquisition. Rail abandonment process is streamlined. Procedures are established for accommodating outside financial assistance, through subsidy or sale, of prospective lines to be abandoned.[51] The time period for filing, investigating and deciding a proposed abandonment proceeding is also shortened.

Discussion

It was not until 1920 that Congress allowed the mercantilization of transport by passing special legislation. Since that time, additional statutes have been passed to correct the mistakes and abuses of previous laws and their administration. In the 1970s, the United States entered into an internal self-styled revolution, by deregulating some of what it has regulated for fifty to one hundred years.

Although air, motor and rail carriers have all be subjected to deregulating legislation, the future is unclear as to which ideological mold the railroad industry might be placed. Classical competition is probably unworkable because of economies of scale and product differentiation. Mercantilism has not worked because the industry continues to suffer after decades of governmental regulation, subsidy, franchises and protectionism. A dose of socialism might be proposed: allow for entry of a giant nationalized company with the exit of all duplicative and excessive trackage, equipment and rolling stock. Alternatively, perhaps the trackage should be nationalized and private rail carriers bid on and pay rental fees for its use. But the United States is ideologically committed to private ownership, free enterprise and the competitive market. This commitment will probably cause policy makers to continue to provide piece-meal subsidization of private rail companies from the public largesse rather than radically restructuring the tired, worn-out railroads.

INTERNATIONAL AIR TRANSPORT

[T]he regulation of competition in air transportation rested upon the twin factors of control of entry and control of rates. [R. Sampson, M. Farns, and D. Shrock, *Domestic Transportation*, Boston: Houghton Mifflin, 1985, p. 420.]

In the 1970s, after more than three decades of protectionism, the Civil Aeronautics Board (CAB) publicly began to question the need for antitrust immunity enjoyed by the International Air Transport Association (IATA). Under the leadership of Alfred E. Kahn, a Cornell University professor, the now defunct CAB was successful in sterilizing the potency of the international air cartel over the North Atlantic. This section traces the controversy between the CAB and IATA during deregulation.

In 1938, the Civil Aeronautics Act[52] established the Civil Aeronautics Authority (CAA),[53] later replaced by the Civil Aeronautics Board

(CAB).[54]   Congress granted that agency the power to exempt airlines from antitrust laws.[55] In 1946, the International Air Transportation Association (IATA)[56] was created by leading airlines of Western Europe, Canada, and the United States to coordinate disorganized air traffic over the North Atlantic.   In that same year, the CAB granted antitrust immunity to American and foreign flag airlines participating in rate-making conferences held by IATA.[57] This exemption continued for more than 30 years.   In 1978 the CAB threatened to withdraw this privilege from American air carriers and thereby discontinue the long period of stable regulated competition which had characterized international air transport. The CAB alleged that IATA was a cartel which engaged in anti-competitive collusive activities.

IATA

On August 25, 1919, the International Air Traffic Association was created to monitor international air navigation and to set up a permanent structure for its administration.[58] A short agreement was signed then to establish a central office and to pledge mutual cooperation.[59] This first IATA was an organization of airline carriers, not of individual governments; membership was voluntary but new members could be approved by a majority of existing members.[60]

As a nongovernmental organization, IATA derives legal stature from an act of Canada's Parliament which granted it a corporate charter of existence and operation.   More than 125 internationally scheduled air carriers representing nearly 100 countries belong to IATA, an organization providing technical, medical, legal, research, finance and tariff information to its members. IATA is voluntary, non-exclusive, non-political and democratic. Any airline can become a member if it has been licensed to provide schedule air service by a government eligible for membership in ICAO. Day-to-day administration of IATA is carried out by a nine-member Executive Management Board, headed by a Director General. Its budget is financed from dues paid by members, generally in proportion to the international air traffic carried by each airline.

One of the primary functions of IATA is to provide a forum for members to participate in "conferences" at which airline representative meet to discuss, negotiate and agree on rights to carry traffic on routes flown, prices charged, and standards adopted for various kinds of service. Recommendations are forwarded to respective governments of home nations of the delegates.[61] Conference results eventually become embodied in a *bilateral agreement*[62] by which fares, routes, and conditions of transport between two nations are established, published, and followed.   These agreements carry the force of law in international air travel when specific governments ratify the agreements and the filed tariffs are accepted.

The heart of IATA operations lies in a dual mechanism of Traffic Conferences and Tariff Coordination. Traffic Conferences meet on a regular basis to coordinate international fares and to establish conditions and procedures relating to fares. Tariff Coordination meetings enable IATA members to discuss matters of fares and commissions openly and collectively. World-wide Tariff Coordination conferences are held so members can review matters of overall passenger fares and air cargo rates.

U.S. Air Transport Policy

Prior to the mid-1920s, aviation was in its infancy and essentially competitive. Regulation of American civil air transport began with the passage of the Kelly Act (1925), the Air Commerce Act (1926), the McNary-Watres Act (1930), and the Air Mail Act (1934). Primary air transport policy is found in the Civil Aeronautics Act (1938)--now the Federal Aviation Act of 1958. The CAA, and its successor, the CAB, largely monitored entry and fares. Safety was assigned to several agencies but now resides in the Federal Aviation Administration (FAA). U.S. domestic air transport policy emphasized regulated competition after 1938, but its international policy since 1946 allowed for self-determination and cooperation among carriers and their nations. In the late 1970s these policies underwent a rapid change. By 1985, the CAB ceased to exist and its functions transferred to the Department of Transportation (DOT).

In November 1944, ICAO was created to promote free air traffic among nations.[63] Five "freedoms of the air"[64] were advocated, but only two were adopted because European nations wanted a tightly regulated structure. As a result, a *multi*lateral approach was avoided and a policy of *bi*lateral agreements was adopted.[65]

In April 1945, IATA was resurrected and reformulated in Havana, Cuba. Cooperation among IATA air carriers and their governments (through ICAO) was affirmed.[66] In February 1946, the CAB granted to U.S. carriers flying international routes an antitrust exemption from their participation in IATA conferences.[67] This immunity was reviewed in 1955 and continued into the 1970s.[68]

In September, 1976, President Gerald Ford began the drive for deregulation of domestic air travel when he released a report of the Economic Policy Board Task Force on International Transportation Policy.[69] A new economic philosophy of competition was initiated with multilateral discussions and bilateral agreements. IATA members were warned to allow market forces to set innovative and flexible fares, routes and schedules for *individual* carriers.

President Jimmy Carter appointed Alfred E. Kahn to be CAB Chairman in 1977. Kahn believed that air transport possesses basic competitive features: a price-elastic demand (a modest reduction in fares will increase air carriage significantly); few economies of scale (cost per ton or passenger mile is similar for fully loaded small and large aircrafts); and mobile resources (an aircraft can be moved quickly into and out of different market areas as demand changes).[70] Kahn suggested deregulating the airlines and eliminating the CAB.

Marvin Cohen, appointed by President Carter in 1979, continued as CAB Chairman under President Ronald Reagan, and pursued a policy of deregulating domestic and international air transportation. The international goal was to create a "broad based free trade zone in air transportation" based on price competition, open entry, low and innovative fares, unique services, and new markets.[71]

Although world airlines were losing money,[72] Cohen believed that the new competitive policy was not a threat to international carriers. He suggested that it is healthy in competition for carriers to "fall by the wayside" if they are not as efficient as airlines able to compete and survive.[73] Cohen attributed declines in airline profits to strikes, recessions, and higher fuel costs because of the OPEC oil cartel, not to the results of open competition.[74] Despite these words of support for the free market, international competitive policy continued to be questioned. The CAB supported a proposed Show Cause Order on IATA Conference Agreements but twice postponed the promulgation of that order at the request of the Reagan administration. The House of Representatives legislated that no funds could be spent by the CAB to enforce the 1978 Show Cause Order.[75] It was finally ordered in 1985. Smaller American airlines losing money and subsidized European airlines decrying the policy of open competition tried to dissuade the CAB from enforcement.

CAB: IATA is a Cartel

Kahn argued that IATA performs a cartel role because of its Traffic and Tariff Conferences. He labeled IATA a "smoothly oiled price-fixing cartel" and called participants in IATA multilateral negotiations "protectionists and cartelizers."[76] Kahn claimed that multilateralism among air carriers of leading Western nations, through the leadership of IATA, fixed binding floors under prices, restricted entry and capacity, and restrained competition. IATA's cartel activities were manifest in its meetings for coordinating otherwise competitive air fares which increased prices and reduced services.

Kahn believed that the CAB should repeal the antitrust immunity enjoyed by U.S. airlines participating in IATA rate conferences. He suggested replacing these conferences with *uni*lateral price determination (wherein representatives of nations negotiate and agree, *separately* but *in pairs*, as to what the overall air transport policy between them shall be).[77]

In a May 1979 statement, the CAB reiterated its belief that IATA was stifling competition in international air transportation: the multilateral conference mechanism for *discussing* rates (which are subsequently *established* and *approved*) destroys price rivalry.[78] In November 1979, CAB found that a proportional fare structure proposal of IATA amounted to manipulation for the purpose of reducing competition among its members. The CAB subsequently held that such agreements were adverse to the public interest.

In April 1980, the CAB responded to an IATA proposal to establish a two-tier structure for its organization: a Trade Association for activities other than rate-making, and a Traffic Conference for rate-making activities.[79] All IATA members were required to belong to the former, whereas membership in the latter would be optional. The purpose of such restructuring was to isolate the subject of the cartel allegations from IATA's total operations.

In May 1981, the CAB concluded that IATA was a voluntary organization of carriers (but not of governments) whose conferences *deliberately* foster uniform price agreements among direct competitors; that IATA's rate-making conferences and U.S. air carrier antitrust immunity from them reduces competition; that IATA multilateral fare setting may reduce rather than increase interlining services; and that in markets where all carriers are not IATA members, fares and services had not been disrupted.[80] The CAB did not claim that IATA was a complete cartel, but that the forum provided by IATA allowed its members to behave collusively.[81]

IATA: Not a Cartel

Director General Knut Hammarskjold of IATA contended that IATA was not a cartel engaged in anti-competitive practices. He claimed that IATA fostered world cooperation among airlines to solve the complex problems inherent in international air transportation, and that it was a *trade association* serving airlines, passengers, shippers, travel agents, and governments.[82] IATA controlled neither entry into air transport nor loading capacities on individual flights; and its pricing agreements were merely *recommendations* to governments, not binding orders to airlines. Furthermore, he argued that IATA neither required a carrier to participate in Traffic Conferences nor excluded it from them, that observers from various governments were allowed to attend IATA conferences, and that IATA opposed discrimination and unfair business practices.[83]

Hammarskjold believed that international air carriage does not possess key elements of a competition market. The commodity--the supply of air carriage--is perishable (because space cannot be stockpiled); although an aircraft is mobile and can move in and out of markets, markets themselves are immobile. Moreover, international aspects of air transportation--scheduling flights through countries with diverse laws--are not akin to competitive distribution of output in unfettered markets. As a result, international air transportation is more conducive to self-regulation through mutual cooperation and communication such as with IATA, than to open or government-sponsored competition.[84]

Resolution

In its first response to CAB's Show Cause Order, IATA described how its activities were in the public interest and called for the CAB to withdraw its tentative findings.[85] Specifically, IATA claimed that an open market for international aviation was unrealistic because foreign air transport requires a carefully integrated coordination among airlines and governments.[86] In a second response, IATA rebutted CAB's legal analysis by arguing that revised FAA rules required tariff and traffic coordination of through-rate and interline problems.[87] Moreover, IATA criticized the CAB's unilateral approach to making international air transport policy and called for an intergovernmental approach among nations to deal with the CAB's allegations.[88]

Control over price, and prevention of price cutting, are crucial to collusive cartel behavior. CAB efforts to reduce the effectiveness of IATA's alleged cartel activities was a several-pronged policy to promote competition in international air transport. The primary CAB policy weapon was the withdrawal of antitrust immunity from airlines participating in IATA Traffic and Tariff Conferences. This eliminated the central feature of cartel goals: common prices in individual market subgroups and price rivalry among cartel members. Without antitrust immunity, United States airlines participating in rate meetings are exposed to legal action for price fixing.[89]

Withdrawing antitrust immunity fosters price rivalry among international air carriers. When this goal is combined with the already existing policy of relaxed entry requirements into the industry (i.e., new carriers), and into individual markets (i.e., multiple routes), the number of air carriers increase and pressures develop for price cutting. When several airlines fly a route, it is difficult to enforce a stabilized price at a high level than when only a few fly the route.

The CAB Show Cause Order and amendments allowing United States air carriers to participate in IATA's trade association activities constituted a procompetitive policy. One of the primary features of competition is adequate knowledge of market prices, costs, productivities and capacities. These conferences allowed air carriers, especially U.S. companies, to share data with one another. This information helps all airlines make rapid adjustments to changing demand and supply conditions of fares, routes, and schedules.

The CAB Show Cause Order on Traffic Conferences was served on IATA in May 1985,[90] but some of its intended effects had already been achieved. IATA's maneuver to separate trade-association from rate-making activities was tacit recognition that price coordination took place. This result, coupled with the CAB policy of related entry requirements, both into the industry and on specific routes, introduced price, schedule, and route rivalry into international air transport. Moreover, domestic deregulation fostered a competitive climate which had spilled over into the international sector. Competitive-like forces ostensibly exist in the international air transport market. After several years of charging reduced prices, producing near capacity, and receiving minimum profits, failures and mergers in the airline industry began to cause overall prices and profits to rise in the 1990s. Already there are calls for legislation to re-regulate the industry.

CONCLUDING REMARKS

[T]here is no unified federal transportation policy statement or goal that guides the federal government's actions. [J. Coyle, E. Bardi, and J. Cavinato, *Transportation*, St. Paul: West, 1982, p. 365.]

In the political economy, there is a connection between state and market by which institutions transmitting power have developed historically over time to assign property rights, allocate resources, and distribute income for the benefit of some to the detriment of others. In transportation, the federal government has deliberately practiced political economy. For rails, the involvement has been for more than a century; for airlines, for more than a half-century. The nature and extent of involvement have been both active and direct as well as passive and indirect. The net effect of all involvement appears as an interference but turns out to be a special benefit. In the case of the railroads, the ICC and other agencies have governed and operated various rail resources and activities. In the case of international air carriers, the CAB and other agencies have monitored and approved various airline plans and proposals. For the railroad industry, direct monetary subsidies of vast sums of taxpayer funds supported private equity and debt positions. For the airline industry, indirect aid from legislation requiring restrictions or granting privileges gave an advantage to established firms over hopeful but sterile entrants. Both ways, private investors with existing monetary interests were provided protection and subsidy.

Railroading has been a declining industry since the early 1900s relative to motor and air transport. The political economy connecting state with market with respect to the rails has been to reduce the losses of private capitalists who otherwise would have foregone more property than they did under rail exist subsidy legislation. Air transport, especially international passenger traffic over the North Atlantic, has been an expanding industry, especially since World War Two. The political economy connecting state with market in this area has been to shelter a few established companies under an infant industry argument so that they might become large and powerful enough to thwart competition on their own, *sans* the protection of the state. With deregulation, such as neutralizing the effectiveness of the IATA cartel, those air carriers that were fostered and subsidized by privilege under regulation were able to achieve sufficient dominance so that under deregulation they may be able to be economic masters of their own oligopolistic destiny in terms of privilege, power, and profit. If so, then the long history of activities in the political economy will have borne the kind of bitter fruit we tended to expect.

NOTES

1.   Munn v. Illinois, 94 U.S. 113, 24 L.Fd. (1877).

2.   Act of Feb. 4, 1887, ch. 104, 24 Stat. 379 was the first real comprehensive attempt at the national level.

3.   E.g., 49 U.S.C. § 10901(a)(Supp. V 1981).

4.   P. S. Dempsey, "Entry Control Under the Interstate Commerce Act: A Comparative Analysis of the Statutory Criteria Governing Entry in Transportation," *Wake Forest Law Review*, Winter 1977, pp. 732-34.

5.   E.g., 49 U.S.C. § 10901 (Supp. V 1981).

6.   It is common usage in economics and law to refer to merger, acquisition, combination and consolidation as being synonymous. See E. Kintner, *Primer on the Law of Mergers*, New York: Macmillan, 1973, pp. 113-35; and E. Singer, *Antitrust Economics*, Englewood Cliffs: Prentice-Hall, 1968, pp. 242-54.

7.   Dempsey, *loc cit.*, pp. 732-34.

8.   R. Sampson and M. Farris, *Domestic Transportation*, Boston: Houghton Mifflin, 1979, p. 13.

9.   Dempsey, *loc cit.*, pp. 732-34.

10.   H. Scheiber, H. Vatter and H. Faulkner, *American Economic History*, New York: Harper and Row, 1976, pp. 266-67.

11.   Cincinnati, N.O. & Tex. Pac. Ry. v. ICC, 162 U.S. 184 (1896).

12.   ICC v. Alabama M. Ry., 168 U.S. 144 (1897); ICC v. Cincinnati, N.O. & Tex. Pac. Ry., 167 U.S. 479 (1897).

13.   Elkins Act, ch. 708, 32 Stat. 847 (1903) (codified as amended in scattered sections of 49 U.S.C.).

14.   Hepburn Act, ch. 3591, 34 State 584 (1906) (codified in scattered sections of 49 U.S.C.).

15. Mann-Elkins Act, ch. 309, 36 Stat. 539 (1910) (codified as amended in scattered sections of 49 U.S.C.).

16. S. Ratner, J. Soltow and R. Sylla, *The Evolution of The American Economy*, New York: Basic, 1979, pp. 118-20.

17. *Ibid.*, p. 323.

18. Transportation Act of 1920, ch. 91, 41 Stat. 456 (codified as amended in scattered sections of 49 U.S.C.).

19. D. Locklin, *Economics of Transportation*, Homewood: Irwin, 1972, p. 240.

20. *Ibid.*, pp. 240-41.

21. *Ibid.*, p. 240-42.

22. These are listed and contained in G. Udel, *Laws Relating to Interstate Commerce and Transportation*, Washington, D.C.: G.P.O., 1971, pp. iii-iv.

23. Act of Jan. 22, 1932, ch. 8, 47 Stat. 5.

24. Emergency Railroad Transportation Act, 1933, ch. 91, 48 Stat. 211 (codified as amended in scattered sections of 49 U.S.C.).

25. *Ibid.*

26. *Ibid.*

27. Although income, output and employment fell four straight years beginning in 1929, an economic recovery began in 1933. However, another contraction occurred in 1937-38. L. Valentine and C. Dauten, *Business Cycles and Forecasting*, Cincinnati: Southwestern, 1983, p. 36.

28. War with both Germany and Japan was contemplated in 1938 and 1939. See R. Barnet, *Roots of War*, Baltimore: Penguin, 1972, pp. 26-28.

29. *Ibid.*

30. U.S. Department of Commerce, *Historical Statistics of the United States, Colonial Times to 1970*, H.R. Doc. No. 78, 93d Cong., 1st Sess. 728 (1975).

31. R. E. Westmeyer, *Economics of Transportation*, New York: Prentice-Hall, 1952, p. 158.

32. Pub. L. No. 76-685, 54 Stat. 899 (codified as amended in scattered sections of 49 U.S.C.).

33. *Ibid.*, pp. 905-06.

34. Pub. L. No. 85-625, 72 Stat. 568 (codified as amended in scattered sections of 49 U.S.C.).

35. Locklin, *op. cit.*, p. 270.

36.   See W. C. Peterson, *Income, Employment and Economic Growth*, New York: Norton, 1978, pp. 459-62.

37.   Pub. L. No. 89-670, 80 Stat. 931 (1966).

38.   Sampson and Farris, *op. cit.*, p. 113 and p. 359.

39.   *Historical Statistics, op. cit.*, p. 727.

40.   Locklin, *op. cit.*, p. 276.

41.   Sampson and Farris, *op. cit.*, p. 377.

42.   Pub. L. No. 91-518, 84 Stat. 1327.

43.   Pub. L. No. 93-236, 87 Stat. 985 (1974).

44.   Sampson and Farris, *op. cit.*, p. 378.

45.   Pub. L. No. 94-210, 90 Stat. 31 (codified as amended in scattered sections of 45 and 49 U.S.C.).

46.   *Ibid.*, § 802, 90 Stat. 129 (current version at 49 U.S.C. §§ 10904-10905 (Supp. V 1981)).

47.   Pub. L. No. 95-504, 92 Stat. 1705.

48.   Pub. L. No. 96-296, 94 Stat. 793.

49.   Pub. L. No. 96-448, 94 Stat. 1895 (codified as amended in scattered sections of 45 and 49 U.S.C.).

50.   49 U.S.C. § 10901(d)(2) (Supp. V 1981).

51.   *Ibid.*, § 10905.

52.   Public Law No. 75-706, 52 Stat. 973 (1938).

53.   *Ibid.*, Section 1102.

54.   P. S. Dempsey, "The Rise and Fall of the Civil Aeronautics Board: Opening Wide the Floodgates of Entry," *Transportation Law Journal*, Vol. 11, 1979, p. 11.

55.   49 U.S. Code 1384, Section 414.

56.   IATA, *50 Years of World Airline Cooperation*, 1969, p. 6.

57.   CAB Agreement No. 493, "IATA Traffic Conference Resolution," 6 CAB 639 (1946).

58.   50 Years, *op. cit.*, p. 2.

59. *Ibid.*, p. 3.

60. *Ibid.*

61. Many western developed nations either regulate their airlines or have nationalized them. This tendency makes it easy to promulgate fares, rates, routes and schedules, especially in international aviation because such arrangements carry the force of law.

62. A "bilateral agreement" is one between two nations regarding the rights, privileges, duties and legal relations concerning foreign aviation. In international aviation, dozens of "bilaterals" exist among most western developed nations whereby each country agrees individually with every other country.

63. 50 Years, *op. cit.*, pp. 6-7.

64. The "five freedoms" involve the privilege: (1) to fly across a territory without landing; (2) to land for non-traffic purposes; (3) to put down passengers/cargo from a carrier's flag country in another; (4) to take on passengers/cargo destined for any State and (5) put passengers/cargo down in any other State. See B. A. Sims, "International Air Transportation: The Effect of the Airline Deregulation Act of 1978 and the Bermuda II Agreement," *Transportation Law Journal*, Vol. 10, 1978, p. 240.

65. 50 Years, *op. cit.*, pp. 6-7.

66. IATA, *Trends in International Aviation and Governmental Policies*, 1979, p. 10.

67. *Ibid.*, p. 14.

68. CAB Order E-9305, June 15, 1955.

69. President Gerald Ford, *Statement of International Air Transportation Policy of the United States*, 1976. p. 9.

70. A. E. Kahn, *The Economics of Regulation*, (New York: Wiley, 1971), pp. 209-220.

71. M. Cohen, *Competition in Air Transportation on the North Atlantic*, Third International Aviation Conference, Paris, 1981, p. 14.

72. *Ibid.*, pp. 2-3.

73. *Ibid.*, p. 9.

74. *Ibid.*, pp. 4-6.

75. Private correspondence, Office of Aviation Operations, U.S. Department of Transportation, Washington, DC.

76. A. Kahn, "Protecting Airlines from Freedom," *Washington Post*, November 5, 1981, p. A29.

77. *Hearings Before House Committee on Public Works and Transportation on International Aviation Policy*, 97th Congress, 1st Session, 1981, p. 12 (from "Statement of Alfred E. Kahn").

78. CAB Order 79-5-113.

79. CAB Order and Statement of Tentative Conclusions 80-4-113.

80. CAB Final Order Terminating Proceeding 81-5-27.

81. CAB Order 8-4-113, p. 9.

82. Statement of Knut Hammarskjold, *Hearings Before the House Committee on Public Works and Transportation on International Aviation Policy*, 97th Congress, 1st Session, 1981, p. 1-4.

83. *Ibid.*, p. 1.

84. IATA, "This 'Cartel' Nonsense," 1980, pp. 1-2.

85. IATA, Response to Board's "Order to Show Cause," Docket 32851, Agreement CAB 1175, 1978, pp. 1-5.

86. *Ibid.*, p. 82.

87. IATA, Comments on the Board's "Statement of Tentative Conclusions," in Order 80-4-113, 1980, pp. 1-16.

88. *Ibid.*, pp. 116-117.

89. Public Law No. 190, 26 Stat. L. 209, 1980.

90. G. Feldman, "IATA Could Finalize Restructuring at Geneva AGM," *Transportation World*, 1978, pp. 25-28.

12   HIGHER EDUCATION

INTRODUCTION

There is no question that college and universities, public and private, face one of the most challenging periods in their history. [J. Gilley, K. Fulmer and S. Rethlingshoefer, *Searching For Academic Excellence*, New York, Macmillan, 1986, p. 3.]

Why do critics attack education today? Why have politicians threatened to regulate hours and working conditions at public institutions of higher learning?[1] Why are legislators introducing bills to evaluate teachers, reduce budgets, or control specific expenditure categories of schools and universities?[2] Why the increasing rhetoric about eliminating tenure, redefining academic freedom, and dismantling faculty government?[3]

A singular response redounds ostensibly common to all these questions: namely, that certain political and economic forces embedded within modern American capitalism seek to restructure the Academy. As technology improved during the middle of the twentieth century, pressures have mounted to change the nature of the university as a social institution.[4] The business sector profits from scientific advancements for economic growth; and the university system--the Academy--has become a primary source of research, development, and technical knowledge as well as its dissemination. It is a contention of this chapter that the Academy is being victimized by this relation, and the result portends a loss of scholarly independence the Academy has enjoyed for several centuries. During the 1970s, when the political economy of higher education came into sharp focus, universities felt the impact of societal unrest and dissent.[5]

Recent Disorder

The United States has been beset recently by frustration and turmoil.[6] For the second time albeit a century and a half apart, a war was lost.[7] Inflation and unemployment ravaged the economy simultaneously.[8] Rebellious youth violently rejected prevailing cultural values.[9] Revisionists told us that the emergence of the United States as a world power was not true, that our entry into World War Two was not as innocent as most people thought.[10] Church attendance began to decline; but whereas members of some denominations rejected higher religious authority, evangelism started to flourish once again.[11]

Many people consider members of American institutions to be suspect because growing evidence indicates dishonesty and corruption. Indeed, the word "politics" increasingly carries a negative connotation.[12] Even the esteem held for physicians has fallen in the rating polls.[13] Business executives have already lost some of the prestige they once held.[14] This loss stems from a set of interrelated factors: the arms race and sale of weapons to sparring third-world countries; huge cost overruns being paid to defense contractors; bribery scandals involving big-business payoffs to foreign officials; governmental bailouts to several large corporations; illegal campaign contributions to political candidates during and after the Watergate crisis; successful lobbying for tax loopholes; the withering of the corporate income tax; the savings and loan crisis.[15]

The Academy has both fathered and borne the burden of a large part of this recent unrest and distrust. Most of the social and political points described above emanated from university scholarship and publication. For shattering the comfortable myths, professors are often denounced as being troublesome.[16] In addition, many young people today consider the college diploma to be an entitlement to income, consumption, and the "good life." Human capital research and the positive correlation between income and education contribute to that expectation.[17] But there has been limited access to the Academy and its fruits, especially for minorities. During the 1960s and 1970s, universities were the primary scenes of counter-culture demonstrations.[18] The Southeast Asian War and United States involvement became an important focus of campus disorder. University research in support of military weaponry and operations fomented discontent.

Business Influence?

The Academy has been criticized not only by the counter-culture but also by the establishment. When students rebelled, many faculties appeared unwilling or unable to contain them; moreover, pronouncements of iconoclastic professors attested that the Academy itself did not fully support the goals and values of the industrial system. In light of this unacceptable alignment, business responded by exerting influence on the goals of higher education. Several large corporations endowed professorships for "Chairs of Free Enterprise" while others maneuvered to control the Center for Economic Education at various universities. Influential business institutions supplied plethora of materials describing the role of business and its *proper* place in society to these professors and centers, their destiny being inculcated into pupils and students across the nation. In the midst of all these frantic efforts, we continued to debate who should rightfully be in charge of the Academy. Historically, the twin institutions of academic freedom and tenure have supported faculty governance at the Academy; hence it is not surprising that these arrangements are at the heart of the recent attack on that venerable institution.

FACULTY GOVERNANCE

> The faculty has primary responsibility in . . . curriculum, subject matter, methods of instruction, research faculty status, and . . . aspects of student life, [*AAUP Policy Documents and Reports*, 1984, p. 109.]

Faculty participation in university government remains a conservative, not a radical, idea. The evolution of the university as an academic organization attests that the principle of faculty governance was accepted centuries ago. Moreover, the faculty has retained its role in university policy-making down through the ages. Even though constitutions and statutes of several states cite faculty governance, still educators currently struggle to preserve this democratic institution against the encroachment of autocratic control.

History

Faculty governance began with the rise of the university in Europe. During the Middle Ages, the university formed a society of masters and scholars, much akin to an apprentice system in which teacher and student jointly investigated knowledge. Not only was the Medieval university "self-governing as well as self-respecting,"[19] but the institution was also characterized by professorial control. Our contemporary university, rooted in the Medieval universities of Paris and Bologna, is a direct descendant of the German university.[20]

In the early American university, the faculty decided basic educational matters. At Harvard (founded in 1636), "it had been the clear intention of the founders . . . to carry on the English tradition of resident faculty control".[21] Clark Kerr reports that for the United States, "the first great grant of power to the faculty of a major university was at Yale."[22] Concerning the American university of the twentieth century, Jacques Barzun points out that "the faculty supplies that ultimate directives from above [because] any central administrator who knows his job takes it for granted that his function is to serve the purposes of the faculty."[23] In these ways, the American heritage of the tripartite functions of democratic government--legislative, executive, and judicial--are operative at many universities. The faculty legislates policy, the administration executes it, and a governing board passes judgment on both. The central feature of this relationship remains necessarily the role of the faculty.

Faculty Responsibility

That the faculty makes policy and the administration carries it out according to the intent of the faculty represents the essential principle of university government.[24] The role of the faculty in discharging the stated functions of a university--teaching, research, service--has received scant attention outside the Academy. A faculty accepts basic responsibility for these three activities. The faculty decides on rules and regulations necessary to university government and discipline, including the library and laboratories. After the faculty determines policy matters, it then delegates authority to the administration to execute these policies. The faculty has a responsibility to accept and retain these duties, but it must also have the freedom to exercise authority to discharge them. The university's most precious resource lies in the quality and quantity of faculty effort. All agencies within the university should be marshalled toward wisest possible use.

The *raison d'etre* of any university is to create, disseminate, and store knowledge, and to provide an environment to enhance the professional development of faculty members. The existence of a university in a democracy means that society has allocated part of its productive resources to house the collective wisdom of the ages, to provide for open inquiry into truth, and to foster creativity and independent expression. Indeed, the scholarly research of a university faculty becomes *the* catalyst which contributes to the intellectual process and progress of humanity.

In a university, faculty members are expected to be competent, motivated, and committed to standards of personal integrity and professional excellence. These characteristics include tolerance, intellectual curiosity, a sense of responsibility, and dedication to furthering knowledge to enhance human welfare. To be subjected to detailed supervision and discipline by administrative officials to serve the latter's goals becomes counterproductive to independent scholarship. Indeed, a faculty member is a responsible officer of a university, not a subordinate employee of it. Guidelines concerning the duties of the faculty must be established democratically by members, using standards of professional expertise and judgment which they deem appropriate. The nature and objectives of the university are not identical with those of authoritarian structures; thus, procedures for developing university policy are not appropriately drawn from the experiences of the military, business corporations, or governmental bureaucracies.

Administrative Duties

A misunderstanding persists as to the distinction between policy-making and its execution, especially the proper roles of the faculty and of the administration. Policies refer to those basic rules, having a distinctive character from procedure and practice, which become institutionalized over time as accepted matters of principle.[25] Policies help decide individual issues, avoid repeated analyses, and provide cohesiveness for the objectives of an organization. A matter appropriately becomes an item of university policy if it affects the goals of the institution, as well as the content, composition or direction of instructional, research, and service programs. Issues which require policy formulation include establishing educational programs and their priorities, setting resource allocation guidelines for program achievement, fostering the professional development of faculty members, and promoting the educational talents of students enrolled in the university. The faculty retains jurisdiction to decide these matters with the counsel of the trustees or governing board. University, college, and departmental administrators have a duty to execute these policy decisions according to the will of the faculty. Whereas the faculty must engage in continuing dialogue with administrators, a university administration should serve the faculty and students, not vice versa.

Administrative execution of faculty-made policy requires more planning and coordinating than policy making by administrative fiat. The presence of administrators who reject the former and opt for the latter undermines the essence of the academy. Some administrators engage in the humbug of promoting a self-serving category called "administrative policy." This, too, threatens the survival of the Academy. Rather than tolerating administrators who give mere lip-service to the legitimacy of faculty governance, the Academy can only do its job properly when they honestly support the principle that the faculty makes policy and the administration executes it.

TENURE AND ACADEMIC FREEDOM

Academic freedom is closely related to the freedom of expression guaranteed by the First Amendment to our Federal Constitution. [R. Nixon, "Academic Freedom," *Vital Speeches*, July 1, 1966, p. 550.]

The academy has continually struggled to preserve two qualities of traditional German universities--*Lehrfreiheit* and *Lernfreiheit*.[26] The former quality gave professors the right to create and disseminate knowledge freely; the latter gave students the right to pursue and question knowledge openly. Just as student councils grew out of *Lernfreiheit*, so tenure, academic freedom, and faculty government reflects *Lehrfreiheit*.

Professing Scholarship

Academic freedom allows a professor to teach what scholarship suggests is the truth in one's particular field of expertise. This right encompasses freedom of research, published results, and questions of what others believe to be settled. The concept of academic freedom, which does not appear in the United States Constitution, is neither defined, sanctioned, nor upheld by statutory law. Accordingly, to seek and receive the aid of the courts whenever academic freedom is violated becomes difficult. At best, academic freedom remains a part of the common law, although undoubtedly a constitutional right under the First Amendment.

Members of the Academy may be threatened with dismissal or punitive action for expressing unpopular opinions as they pursue knowledge and truth in a free society. Permanent tenure--a practice of granting continuous appointment to a professor--exists to support academic freedom. A professor ordinarily receives permanent tenure only after a lengthy probationary period during which time the candidate must demonstrate dedication, integrity, effectiveness, and scholarship. Traditionally, tenured faculty members nominate their peers for tenure, and then vote on the candidate for admission to that status, yet another prerogative of faculty governance consistent with the notion of *Lehrfreiheit*.

Some critics believe that rights and privileges associated with tenure and academic freedom allow a professor to be irresponsible, unproductive, and meddlesome, with no sanction or punishment. But neither tenure nor academic freedom ring absolute. Most tenure and academic freedom statements contain qualifying sections delineating proper occasions to speak or write as a citizen, rather than for the institution, and how to confine tenure-protected remarks to areas of one's expertise. Moreover, at many institutions, tenure becomes subject to revocation whenever an individual's level of performance has declined significantly over the years and falls below expectations specified for professional duties.

In a democratic society, responsibilities ordinarily accompany rights and privileges. Accordingly, scholarly activities at the Academy require that professors be unbiased as they engage in scientific and philosophical inquiry. Above all, we presume that the pursuit of intellectual matters will not be compromised by special interest connections. Indeed, *Lehrfreiheit* embodies a quality of detachment, the expectation that tenure and academic freedom will be granted *only* to those who are disassociated from private special interest groups.

Research Activities

Research activities represent one of the most important functions of the Academy; in fact many modern-day universities are just as heavily research as teaching institutions. Land-grant universities especially have been committed to teaching, research, and community service involvement for more than a century. Research, by its nature investigative, involves the establishment of new cause-and-effect relationships based on objective analyses of facts. Scholars at the Academy, to be able to practice free inquiry, must not be shackled or controlled as they assume their responsibility to conduct research, especially at the theoretical and basic levels. Research involves the creation and production of knowledge (whereas teaching and service involve its dissemination). Producing knowledge is not akin to producing most other goods and services because scholars do not employ the market-and-price system in the same way as the private sector. The profit motive does not directly govern research at the Academy, as can be seen, for example, by the fact that most professors contribute journal articles to academic rather than commercial publications. In the ratings of the outstanding academic institutions, the leaders are usually universities that produce important research results. Nobel Prizes, for example, are usually won by university professors for their pathbreaking research, rather than corporate laboratory researchers.

The economic growth of America has been a direct result of technological and scientific advances, most of which academic researchers generated. An important question arises: Where ought knowledge-creation be conducted? Should research, invention, technology, and new ideas emanate from colleges and universities (where there exists at least some pretense of freedom of thought) or from business and/or government (where special interest provides incentive for power and influence of the few over the many)? Can we tolerate research overseers who tell researchers what and how to investigate? Would not that arrangement stifle creativity and independent inquiry in a democratic society?

FROM ACADEMY TO BIG EDUCATION

Since it does not sell a product or otherwise generate income, academic science must rely on external support . . . [R. Solo, *The Positive State*, Cincinnati: Southwestern, 1982, p. 153.]

In *The New Industrial State*, Professor John Kenneth Galbraith argued that American capitalism has become a political economy in which leading industrial corporations, the military, large unions, and the federal government comprise a self-serving coalition organized to operate the economy.[27] Indeed, Galbraith's "new industrial state" *is* that coalition. On this basis, in modern American capitalism large organizations and government--the Industrial System--rule the economic, political, and social affairs of the economic system in order to facilitate planning, control, and their own survival.

A Coalition

In the new industrial state, Big Business has formed an alliance with Big Government, and has shared control with Big Military and Big Union; however, one important component is not yet widely recognized as a full-fledged member--the college-university sector, Big Education. The latter already contributes significantly to the industrial system and to the service of Big Government, in the form of federally-sponsored research contracts and grants, federal programs to aid higher education, and operational procedures followed in order to continue receiving federal funds. In fact, public higher education increasingly serves state agencies and legislatures for the same reasons.[28]

Big Education serves Big Business by providing factors of production--training, skills, and knowledge--vital to the operation of the industrial system. Technology has advanced so dramatically during recent decades that Big Business requires highly educated and specialized manpower, not only to assist planning and decision making, but to conduct its operations. Big Education, for many years, has been supplying the industrial system with technical know-how at nominal cost to Big Business, though Big Education does not ordinarily produce knowledge, as a factor of production, in the market place. At public institutions, middle-class taxpayers essentially support university undergraduate and graduate education through property and sales-tax levies, both regressive forms of taxation. However, because most universities have been supported by either local or state governments, and recently in no small part by federal grants, the argument may be extended to contend that education is actually produced and distributed by the market. Education has been essentially socialized primarily because state and local governments own, operate or finance most educational resources: buildings, laboratories, libraries, computer centers, and faculties.

Influential public-policy makers seek diverse goals with respect to controlling the Academy, but the ultimate effects of each are similar. On the one hand, some persons want the Academy to provide the industrial system with inputs of specialized knowledge and technically-trained persons. For them, the output of the university must be "functional," that is, contribute directly to the profit motive and related business objectives. If not, business can accuse the Academy of misuse of scarce resources and then maneuver the university into the service of the Industrial System.

On the other hand, certain groups want to reduce the size of the Academy because they define it as a useless entity per se. This mentality reflects a national cultural gap shared by the masses who either dislike or distrust the Academy for several reasons.[29] First, they neither understand nor appreciate the importance of intellectual endeavors in a technological, business-oriented society; a second group never sought or seized the opportunity to taste the fruits of the Academy. Both harbor negative attitudes toward the Academy. The former group wants to augment the basic and applied scientific areas to the detriment of the arts, humanities, and social sciences whereas the latter wants to destroy the Academy based on spite and shortsightedness. As these two groups increase in size and influence, they hasten the decline of the Academy.

Big Education, now only partly in the service of the industrial system, has resisted adaptation to the new industrial state because the former refuses to be dominated by the latter. Two arrangements must be displaced before Big Education can become inalterably drawn into the industrial system and completely controlled by it: (1) the twin institutions of tenure and academic freedom, and (2) faculty participation in university government. University professors of liberal temperament and persuasion are ordinarily individualistic, independent, and iconoclastic. As social critics, they envision the Academy to be an instrument of social change. In their search for truth, a description of the world as it is, they may not have in mind those objectives which are consistent with the goals of the industrial system. Recent attacks on social criticism expressed by faculty members and recent attacks on tenure and academic freedom are not unrelated. The accumulated effects of both tend to undermine faculty control and to align the Academy with the goals of the industrial system.

Capturing Big Education

A subtle mechanism, which drives Big Education into the service of the industrial system, operates on four fronts. First, the federal government, through contract and grant programs, provides a substantial amount of funding to colleges and universities. Some of these monies support research to enhance the industrial system. As a result, Big Education is exploited to generate a large portion of the technology used by the industrial system.

Second, state legislatures starve the Academy by cutting programs, reducing funds, and allocating monies for itemized budgets. As a consequence, in order to carry on their programs, university administrators and researchers look to outside sources of funding for contracts, grants, and gifts.

Some scholars even exploit themselves by seeking financial support from business firms, trade associations, unions, foundations, and various agencies of government in order to continue their projects. Funding-generated research more and more supplants that generated by curiosity. To the extent that legislatures or businesses attach dictated conditions to the acceptance of funds from the vested interest groups, the Academy becomes aligned with various facets of the industrial system. The specter of attachment to special interests displaces the detached character of scholarship at the Academy.

Third, business corporations endow professorships, build facilities, and provide research funds for special purposes at many universities. Administrators at the Academy begin to look upon these funds as a normal part of support and ultimately count on their continued receipt; as a result, the Academy adapts itself to the industrial system or anything else. Some university administrators even plead for a partnership between the Academy and the business sector. At institutions where administrators, rather than the faculty, make policy, these efforts have been extremely detrimental to the Academy.

Fourth, underfunding the Academy has caused the purchasing power of faculty salaries to decrease for more than a decade. Accordingly, many highly qualified professors are paid below their opportunity costs in business and industry. The recent exodus of top scholars in physics, mathematics, chemistry, and computer science, for example, to accept higher-paying jobs in America's leading corporations, seems a *fait accompli* of the absorption of Big Education into the new industrial state.

There are other mechanisms at work which threaten the Academy. For one, the tenure/academic freedom system makes difficult but not impossible the process to discharge faculty who already have been granted tenure. Professors are potentially free, through academic freedom, to speak out on issues which may be critical of the industrial system. Faculty participation in policy making, as well as faculty control over tenure and academic freedom, have become inconsistent with the goals of the industrial system (which is to promote its own power, prestige, security, and survival). Each year, various state legislatures attempt to abolish or limit tenure, and some even pass such legislation. Whereas attempts to draw Big Education into the new industrial state by controlling tenure, academic freedom, and faculty governance may not constitute a deliberate conspiracy against democratic values, they do represent a drifting cultural tendency toward the demise of the Academy. The erosion of academic freedom at the Academy can also be noted in the activities of watchdog groups, secrecy in federally funded research, and the disrespect for free speech by certain students, administrators, and even some faculty.

Supporters of the new industrial state portray a self-righteous posture of the divine right of efficiency. Notwithstanding that efficiency means maximizing net social benefits, this tortured notion persists. Proponents tend to judge importance by functionalism. In order to be worthwhile, an idea must have direct pecuniary value to the members of the industrial system; its corollary is to eschew criticism. Thus, criticism of the industrial system becomes invalid unless the critic offers a positive alternative. Above all, it is believed, intellectual effort must offer constructive ideas rather than destructive thoughts. But those who plead for positive statements rather than negative ones have succumbed to that fallacy of logical argument which discredits criticism on grounds that the critic was not helpful. Nevertheless, to prevent the Academy from being an instrument of social change and its members as social critics, such contentions are consistent with a drive to capture Big Education.

The Academy is also subject to decline from within its own walls. Faculty, administrators, and students share in these efforts. Some faculty abrogate their governance responsibilities by deferring policy making to administrators. In addition, the Academy is increasingly staffed by administrators who spent little time in the classroom and did not advance through the ranks. Finally, the Academy has felt incursions from the Left as well as the Right. For example, some ideological zealots have been successful with supplanting education with political indoctrination by altering campus rules and curricula.[30] All these developments demonstrate a lack of appreciation for faculty governance and will accelerate the demise of the Academy.

CONCLUDING REMARKS

> There is nothing so important for American higher education now as the reemergence of thoughtful educators, of academic executives who are farsighted statesmen . . . [G. Keller, *Academic Strategy*, Baltimore: John Hopkins Press, 1983, p. 174.]

The unique march of technological events in modern American capitalism lies behind recent attacks on the Academy and its possible decline. If the Academy becomes a formal part of what President Eisenhower called *"the military-industrial complex,"*[31] it will undoubtedly happen after the effectiveness of tenure, academic freedom, and faculty governance has been reduced for those institutional arrangements. After all, in order for the elements of a system to be effective, few internal inconsistencies can exist among constituent parts.

The word "university" is related to these Latin roots: *unis* (one) and *veritas* (truth). The traditional concept of the university signifies a unified search for knowledge wherein professors are encouraged to inquire and investigate openly and freely. In this endeavor, a university becomes a community of scholars in the sense of shared values with little or no outside, centralized control over teaching and research. If Big Education falls into the service of the Industrial System, then these interrelations become severed.

As the Academy declines, members will find it increasingly difficult to remain detached. Indeed, *attachment* already poses a threatening condition which could envelope the Academy, especially through the research/consulting contracts and grants system. Academic researchers must be on guard to prevent public and private support of specific research programs from aligning them with funding sources to perform specific, result-determined research. If professors at the Academy work with and for the benefit of private special interests, the ultimate effect may pervert the venerable tradition of *Lehrfreiheit*.

Legislatures, to the extent that legislators align with the Industrial System, do not have to attack directly the Academy to drive it into decline, or even to eliminate tenure, academic freedom, and faculty governance. Much as modern warfare relegates killing to impersonal status compared to former times when hand-to-hand combat forced the victor to witness the anguish of a slain or injured enemy, legislators need only covertly threaten the economic security of the members of the Academy--the faculty, the scholars, the academicians. By reducing programs, faculties, and budgets, those professors with options will leave the Academy. Heavy work loads, reduced real incomes, and increasing frustration will drive out those at the upper echelons of competency, who will then ultimately serve the Industrial System. But such exiting has high social purpose for the industrial system because it needs the technology wrought by the Academy to perpetuate the goals of the former. Whether these goals are achieved directly or indirectly, the result remains essentially the same.

What can be done to restore the traditional institutions and functions of the Academy? Should they be preserved? Or will the Academy inevitably continue to fall into the service of the industrial system? Would such a fall not be in the best interest of society, especially if the electorate wants the Academy to serve the system? Do the Academy and its faculty know best for society? Are the Academy and its faculty so unique and important that they deserve special status? Recall that prior to the Protestant Reformation, priests set themselves apart from the masses! Are the faculty--university professors--so different that they require special privileges or know better than the electorate? If the Industrial System serves the people by providing employment and output, would they not be best served if the Academy did fall under the control of the industrial system? However these questions are ultimately resolved, our society as a whole must identify and debate their implications and effects openly before the traditional institution of the Academy becomes unsalvageable.

NOTES

1. L. Stephenson, "Our Kept Universities," *The Progressive*, March 1973, pp.46-49.

2. O. Carey, "Evaluating the Total Contribution of Faculty," *Collegiate News & Views*, Spring 1974, pp. 13-16.

3. K. Brewster, "Should Colleges Retain Tenure?" *Wall Street Journal*, October 2, 1972; and "Tenure in Trouble," *Newsweek*, June 10, 1974, pp. 75-76.

4. P. H. Abelson, "Evolving State-University Relations," *Science*, January 24, 1986, p. 317; and M. Tishler, "The Siege of the House of Reason," *Science*, October 1969, pp. 192-94.

5. W. Brock, "Congress Looks at the Campus . . .," *AAUP Bulletin*, Autumn 1969, pp. 327-36; and M. Tessler and R. Hedlund, "A Hard Look at Campus Dissent," *The New Republic*, September 12, 1970, pp. 17-18.

6. Most of the problems besetting American society in the 1970s and early 1980s are covered in S. Bowles, D. M. Gordon, and T. E. Weisskopf, *Beyond the Wasteland*, Garden City: Doubleday, 1983.

7. In 1812 *and* 1974. See J. A. Lower, *Canada*, Toronto: McGraw-Hill Ryerson, 1966, pp. 73-79.

8. Between 1974 and 1980, the unemployment rate averaged more than 7 percent annually whereas the inflation rate average more than 9 percent annually. *Economic Report of the President*, 1989, pp. 352 and 377.

9. J. Mann, "Traditional Values: On the Rebound," *U.S. News and World Report*, February 28, 1983, p. 46; and N. Lemann, "Values, Personal Choice, and the Failure of Liberalism," *Washington Monthly*, December 1983, pp. 33-35.

10. See J. M. Swomley, Jr., *American Empire*, New York: Macmillan, 1970, pp. 84-98.

11. L. Albrecht, et al., "Thunder on the Right. . .," *People*, October 13, 1980, pp. 32-7; and N. Shuler, Jr., "New Right Attacks Humanism," *Humanist*, September-October 1980, pp. 38-39.

12. "Corruption's 'Good Old Days' Are Back," *U.S. News and World Report*, August 24, 1987, p. 10.

13. M. Cohen, "My Mother's So Ashamed. Her Son's a Doctor," *Gentlemen's Quarterly*, December 1988, pp. 91+.

14. For example, see S. Blotnick, "I Don't Get No Respect," *Forbes*, September 22, 1986, pp. 234-35.

15. In 1955, the corporate income tax contributed 22 percent to all government receipts, but by 1980 it formed only 10 percent. *Economic Report of the President*, 1989, p. 402.

16. M. Ways, "The Faculty is the Heart of the Trouble," *Fortune*, January 1969, pp. 94-97.

17. See Bureau of the Census, *Earnings by Occupation and Education*, Washington, DC: U.S. Department of Commerce, Vol. 2, PC80-2-8B, May 1984.

18. "The Causes of the Student Unrest During the 1960's," *Phi Kappa Phi Journal*, Fall, 1971, pp. 39-42; and S. Hayakawa, "The Real Root of Student Disorder?" *Readers Digest*, November, 1970, pp. 167-68.

19. C. H. Haskins, *Rise of Universities*, Ithaca: Great Seal, 1963.

20. J. Ben-David, "Universities," *International Encyclopedia of the Social Sciences*, Vol. 16, New York: Macmillan, 1968, pp. 191-198.

21. F. Rudolph, *The American College and University*, New York: Random House, 1962, p. 166.

22. C. Kerr, *The Uses of the University*, Cambridge: Harvard, 1963.

23. J. Barzun, *The American University*, New York: Harper & Row, 1968.

24. For example, this relation is statutory for Colorado (C.R.S. 23-31-114 and C.R.S. 23-31-115).

25. M. H. Mescou, M. Albert, and F. Khedouri, *Management*, New York: Harper & Row, 1988, pp. 300-305.

26. Freedom to teach and to learn. See D. Fellman, "Academic Freedom," *Dictionary of the History of Ideas*, New York: Charles Scribner's, 1973, pp. 9-16.

27. J. K. Galbraith, *The New Industrial State*, Boston: Houghton Mifflin, 1968.

28. Some insight with these views can be gained from C. Jencks and D. Riesman, *The Academic Revolution*, New York: Doubleday, 1968, pp. 480-509.

29. S. Kaplan, "Big Man on Campus," *Common Sense Magazine*, November-December 1986, pp. 27-31.

30. G. Will, "Left Holds Sway on Campus," *Rocky Mountain News*, September 16, 1990, p. 67.

31. See Chapter Ten, above. D. Eisenhower, "Eisenhower's Farewell--A Prayer and a Warning," *U.S. News and World Report*, January 30, 1961, p. 69.

13   MEDICAL CARE

INTRODUCTION

> There are sophisticated reasons why the pluralism for which we aim
> is not only ineffective but . . . undemocratic and . . . inadequate for
> dealing with situations of medical need. [G. Silver, *A Spy in the
> House of Medicine*, Germantown: Aspen, 1976, p. 58.]

A continuing health-care crisis in the United States is reported almost
daily in print and broadcast media.[1] Limited access to medical care for the
poor, skyrocketing hospital costs and health insurance rates, an alleged
shortage of nurses, malpractice lawsuits against physicians, early death or
incapacitation from a variety of illnesses, especially among certain ethnic
groups, and overuse of prescription drugs are among the many health and
medical care issues heralded in this country. Citizens' groups, heads of
governmental agencies, politicians, insurance executives, medical
professionals, and other involved persons have spoken out about these and
other problems in one way or another. For more than a generation, both
speculation and the results of scholarly research have identified problems,
symptoms, causes, and possible solutions. Most recommendations call for
additional programs, resources, expenditures, and controls, usually under the
direction of the federal government. Ironically, but not surprising, many
proposals treat symptoms rather than problems and their causes. Moreover,
and still not surprising, many recommended solutions call for extensive
governmental involvement in both production and delivery of medical care
to deal with what is considered a second-rate health status of the United
States. But the record shows that government is already substantially
involved in health and medicine. Indeed, some observers suggest that
government itself may be the chief cause of many symptoms of the alleged
medical-care crisis.[2]

Political economy refers to a nexus between private and public interests, especially in terms of the creation and transmission of power, of its impact on property, resources, and incomes, and of why class disparities which tend to arise need correction. The production and delivery of medical care is ripe for this kind of inquiry. Contrasted with other repositories of political economy, medical care contains unique and peculiar characteristics. These special institutional arrangements can be noted by the way that organized medicine has maneuvered government into assigning it privilege, authority, and power.

The political economy of health and medical care in the United States can be understood by identifying connections among components of the medical-care sector and government. In general, the production, delivery, and consumption of such items as drugs, services of health professionals, and hospitalization are the primary resources to be considered. Because the medical doctor is at the center of decision making, it is the historical role of "organized medicine" in the form of physicians' groups, including their influence on both legislation and public opinion, that is the primary area highlighted below.

The inquiry into medical care begins by identifying resources allocated to this sector and indicators of health status in the United States vis-a-vis other developed nations. Next, a brief history of medical-care delivery is presented by considering the role of organized medicine, including the authority that physicians have over medical-care decisions. The discussion then turns to the efforts of organized medicine to influence public opinion on certain forms of governmental involvement in medical-care delivery.

PRELIMINARY CONSIDERATIONS

[T]he United States really has a "sickness care" system, not a "health" system. [S. J. Williams and P. R. Torrens, *Introduction To Health Services*, New York: Wiley, 1984, p. 481.]

The political economy of medical care can be evaluated against a backdrop of health status and resources allocated to its production and delivery. How does the United States compare to other developed nations in the world with respect to health?

Overview

Before proceeding, it is useful to distinguish between concepts of health and of medical care. Health and health care are broad concepts whereas medical care is but one contributor to health. Health care deals with all aspects of illness and wellness. Improving diets, exercising regularly, controlling stress, reducing pollution, and receiving medical attention augment human health status. Although it is only one part of the total health scene, medical care has been considered as the primary contributor to good health. In the United States, there has been a tendency to equate health care and medical care, and the latter with physicians' services. From that connection, there has been a tendency to blame the health crisis on medical doctors, especially on insufficient numbers, inferior training, and poor performance. No doubt, Americans suffer an unduly high amount of disease and illness--cancer, heart and lung disease, hypertension, broken limbs, and damaged body parts. However, many of us eat, drink and smoke too much, drive too fast, act recklessly and carelessly on the job and at play and in the home, engage in sexual activities without adequate precautions, use too many resources without proper disposal, and exercise too little. When health problems occur, many persons expect physicians to be able to correct them quickly. If they cannot or do not, it is often concluded that because of them, the quality of medical care is poor or has deteriorated. But this is a superficial criticism of the role of physicians, a point which will be considered below. Nevertheless, the focus of this chapter is on medical care rather than health care in the broad sense.

Medical-Care Resources

Among the world's industrialized nations, the United States has the largest Gross Domestic Product (GDP), and ranks near the top for GDP per capita.[3] During 1990, there were more than 600,000 physicians and 1,200,000 hospital beds in the United States, and the country spent in excess of $500 billion on health and medical care.[4] However, on a relative basis compared to other advanced nations, the allocation of American medical resources raises some vexing questions.

Table 13.1 indicates that in 1989, the United States devoted more of its GDP on health than any other country (11 percent), as well as more on a per capita basis ($2,051). Although the United States experiences respectable ratios for population per physician and per hospital bed, they are not as favorable as in some other developed countries. With 549 persons per physician, the United States ranks worse than Australia, Canada, the Netherlands, and Sweden. Moreover, the United States ranks last among the eight countries by the measure of 171 persons per hospital bed. These are two crucial resources, and despite the fact that such a large share of the world's highest GDP is allocated to health and medical care, its application in America appears to be less effective than in several other nations.

Table 13.1   Indicators of Medical Care Resources, Selected
                Developed Nations, 1980-1989

Nation	Health Expenditures		Population Per Physician	Population Per Hosp.Bed
	Percent of GDP	Per Capita		
United States	11.2	$2,051	549	171
Australia	7.1	887	524	157
Canada	8.6	1,376	548	129
Germany	8.2	1,502	431	89
Japan	6.8	1,347	735	84
Netherlands	8.5	1,233	510	82
Sweden	9.0	1,690	500	67
United Kingdom	6.1	723	711	119

Source: *Statistical Abstract of the United States*, Selected Issues.

Health Status

Among 100 nations of the world, the United States ranks surprisingly
low for some basic indicators of health status: 35th for crude death rate,
16th for life expectancy at birth, and 15th for infant mortality.[5] Among
these 100 nations, many are Lesser Developed Countries, but even among
developed countries, the United States does not fare so well.

From Table 13.2 it can be noted that with 8.8 deaths per thousand
persons in 1989, the United States ranks 5th among leading developed
nations. Yet, for life expectancy at birth and for infant mortality, it ranks
virtually last among these eight countries. Whereas reasons why this poor
standing exists have not been thoroughly established, it is cause for concern
that the United States allocates so much of its GDP to health and medical
care but has not achieved a higher health status than it enjoys.

The same picture appears for death rates from disease. Table 13.3
shows several leading causes of death, measured as rates per 100,000 of the
population, in eight developed nations. By measures of deaths from heart,
lung, breast, and liver diseases, the United States ranks worse than several
other countries. On the one hand, data may support a contention that race,
income, diet, and life style are largely responsible for the poor American
health status. However, on the other hand, it may indicate that health and
medical-care resources in the United States are allocated more for
therapeutic than preventative purposes.

Contrasted to conditions among nations, consider some aspects of
American health posture internally. Table 13.4 contains data on selected
average measures of health status by race. Reported statistics indicate that

Table 13.2   Basic Indicators of Health Status, Selected Developed
                    Nations, 1989

Nation	Death Rate Per 1,000	Life Expectancy At Birth	Infant Mortality Per 1,000
United States	8.8	75.4	11
Australia	7.7	76.2	8
Canada	7.4	77.2	7
Germany	11.8	75.9	7
Japan	6.8	79.0	5
Netherlands	8.6	77.2	7
Sweden	11.6	77.4	6
United Kingdom	11.8	75.3	9

Source: *Statistical Abstract of the United States 1990.*

Table 13.3   Death Rates from Serious Diseases, Selected
                    Developed Nations, 1986-1987

Nation	Death Rates Per 100,000 Population			
	Heart Disease	Lung Cancer	Breast Cancer	Liver Disease
United States	200.8	53.9	31.8	12.0
Australia	216.2	39.4	29.5	8.4
Canada	197.7	51.6	35.0	9.9
Germany	158.8	35.2	33.1	19.6
Japan	39.9	25.8	8.0	13.7
Netherlands	158.8	56.7	37.7	5.6
Sweden	236.5	22.6	25.2	6.9
United Kingdom	229.7	55.1	41.9	5.0

Source: *Statistical Abstract of the United States 1990.*

for the categories shown, members of the Black population in the United
States lag behind members of the White population. Blacks visit a physician
less frequently than Whites, and their life expectancy is shorter, death rates
and infant mortality higher, and deaths due to leading causes greater than
for Whites. A conclusion drawn from Table 13.3 and Table 13.4 is that not
only do medical-care results in America lag behind other developed nations,

Table 13.4   Health Status by Race, Selected Characteristics,
                  United States, 1987

Characteristic	White	Black
Physician Visits, Per Person, Per Year	5.5	4.9
Life Expectancy At Birth	75.6	71.3
Death Rate, Per 1,000 Persons	5.1	7.8
Infant Mortality Rate, Per 1,000	5.5	11.7
Deaths, Heart Disease, Per 100,000	165.0	226.9
Deaths, Cancer, Per 100,000	30.1	172.2
Deaths, Liver Disease, Per 100,000	8.4	14.9

Source: *Statistical Abstract of the United States 1990.*

but there are barriers to access to medical care among the citizens of the
United States. Whereas differences in life circumstances may account for
the lop-sided data, it must be remembered that in the United States medical
care is essentially a consumer good and consumption occurs out of income,
and White income, on average, is one-third larger than Black income. This
suggests another conclusion--namely, that the structure of the American
medical-care delivery system, based as it is on a market-price system, may be
partly responsible for the health disparities between White and Black
people.

EVOLUTION OF POWER

The AMA is more a force as a lobbyist than as a disciplinarian; it strikes
fear into the hearts of politicians. . . [C. Inlander, L. Levin, and E.
Weiner, *Medicine in Trial*, New York: Prentice-Hall, 1988, p. 181.]

The political economy of medical care in America involves physician
control backed by governmental agencies. The history of how American
medicine sought and obtained this control can be divided into three broad
periods: before 1910; 1910 to World War Two; and the post-World War Two
era.

Early American Medicine

In colonial America, medical care was based more on prevention than
cure. Folk and patent medicines as well as home care were the main

contributors to health at that time. In large eastern cities, physicians trained in British and European universities challenged these methods and promoted "an academic, intellectual style of medical care."[6]   A class-system existed--English-trained "elite" physicians and a "lower order" of surgeons and apothecaries.[7]   Health and medicine were not addressed in the Constitution, so the fee-for-service system developed rather than a government-sponsored mechanism.[8]   This method for remunerating American physicians persisted as the primary means down through the years.

The first medical school was established in the United States in 1765 at the University of Pennsylvania.[9] During the early part of the 19th century, due to a lack of physicians, the proprietary profit-seeking medical school was created. The number of medical schools proliferated so that by 1850, there were 42 in the United States (but only three in France).[10] A number of small medical schools even located in the midwest.

During the latter part of the 19th century, additional medical schools and hospitals were set up, students in the former being trained in the latter. This connection gave rise to physician control of hospitals. Prior to the Civil War, lay practitioners provided medical advice. Many states began to enact licensing legislation to prevent untrained persons from practicing medicine, and physicians organized into state and national medical societies as an attempt to drive out the haphazard practice of medicine. The American Medical Association (AMA) was founded in 1847, and until around 1900, it was mainly concerned with education of its membership.[11] From 1850 to 1900, through AMA lobbying, "the medical profession sought and received licensure in each state [which] delegated this . . . authority to medical licensing boards."[12]   In 1901, the AMA was reorganized and several "councils" were formed.[13]   During the latter part of the 1800s nearly 400 medical schools existed in the nation, many of which were nothing but "diploma mills" largely organized on an apprenticeship basis.[14] By 1900, there were approximately 147 medical schools. The quality of medical education and practice was uneven and many inferior physicians were delivering shoddy medical care. Conditions were ripe for change.

The Flexner Report

In 1904, the AMA founded a Council on Medical Education and charged it to improve the quality of education in America's medical schools. A survey was conducted in 1906 and the Council found that barely half of the 160 medical schools in the country offered an "acceptable" medical education.[15] The Council convinced the Carnegie Commission to conduct a survey, which the latter assigned to Abraham Flexner.

Flexner was not a physician but "unwittingly served the highly parochial interests of organized medicine."[16]   While performing his study, he conducted a whirlwind inspection of medical schools, some in only an afternoon.[17] His ideal for training a physician was based on the program at Johns Hopkins University rather than the tasks that a medical doctor should be able to do.

The Flexner Report, a harsh exposé of how medical education lagged behind medical science, was released in 1910.[18] Flexner, as a result of his inspections, reportedly found: untrue catalog claims; non-existent or ill-equipped laboratories; unsanitary conditions; libraries that lacked books; and professors located in their own practices rather than the classroom.[19] He reached three conclusions: (1) there were too many physicians in the United States; (2) a large number of the medical schools should be closed; and (3) the standards for a medical education ought to be improved in schools allowed to continue operating.[20] These goals were in the public interest--"fewer doctors who were better trained."[21] Not surprising, his report "hastened the schools to their graves. . ."[22]

As a result of the Flexner Report, many existing medical schools went out of business. Most state legislatures used it as the basis for passing legislation to confer on the AMA additional authority over medical education and the practice of medicine. The key to control was given to the AMA Council on Medical Education.

Tightened Physician Control

Organized medicine established a foothold for its present control over the production and distribution of medical care between the time that the Flexner Report was released and the end of World War Two. That foothold became a stranglehold. In 1906, 162 medical schools existed in America but the number gradually decreased to 85 in 1920, 76 in 1930, and 69 in 1944.[23] The AMA created substantial barriers to entry into the medical profession by influencing, with the force of law, the following areas: establishing standards for medical education; creating new medical schools; controlling medical-school enrollments; requiring graduation from an approved medical school prior to applying for a licensing examination; limiting the number of licensure examinations to be given; insuring that examinations are designed and scored "properly" prior to obtaining a state license; monitoring state medical licensing boards; deciding the required training before a medical-school graduate can practice medicine; dictating the length of time spent for internships and residency after graduating from medical school.[24]

Today, the primary decision maker in medical-care delivery is the physician. Only licensed medical doctors can prescribe drugs, order laboratory tests, admit (release) a patient to (from) the hospital, determine treatment, and perform most medical procedures (some of which nurses and other health professionals are capable of doing and allowed to do only under supervision).

Authority, power, and control encompasses more than just the direct practice of medicine. Physicians are organized into local medical societies. Prices charged under the fee-for-service mechanism are cross-coordinated on a cost-accounting basis. "Value points" for each specific medical procedure a physician might perform on a patient are recommended by the AMA based on its research.[25]   As a result, physicians have a common basis for charging patients. Local medical societies "suggest" for physicians in the community what each point "should be" worth. For example, if removing a wart from a patient's hand has 8 points, and the suggested value of a point is $5, then the fee would be $40. It is obviously to the economic advantage of physicians in the community to follow this pricing procedure and thereby avoid price competition.

Control by the AMA over medical-care production and distribution since the Flexner report has created significant barriers to entry into the physician's industry. The combined result of three state-sanctioned AMA requirements--certifying medical schools, requiring graduation from one prior to examination and licensure, and lengthening the internship and residency times--is to reduce the number of physicians. Combined with control over both the direct practice of medicine and the conditions under which patient care is delivered (such as the traditional fee-for-service method of payment), the net result is to raise prices for medical care, reduce the quantity of such care that is demanded and supplied, and to increase physician's net incomes.

FURTHER INFLUENCE BY ORGANIZED MEDICINE

[A]n effective and often-used technique in mobilizing public opinion, the appeal to crisis impedes the appraisal of competing policy measures. . . [M. Bowler, R. Kurdie, T. Marmor, "The Political Economy of National Health Insurance," *Journal of Health Politics, Policy and Law*, Spring 1977, p. 103.]

The political economy of medical care involves the historical background of how organized medicine has successfully obtained control over its production and distribution in the United States. The AMA and other organizations have used their prestige, power, and position in various ways to perpetuate control over the delivery of medical care and the price of physicians' services, which denies some people access to medical care and which raises the incomes of individual medical doctors. Probably the most effective use of power has been to influence legislation affecting medical training, licensure, and hospital privileges. In two other forums physicians' interests have been successful at influencing decision makers in their favor. One situation is inside the hospital; another is among the polity. The first will be briefly reported, whereas the latter requires some elaboration.

Responses to a sample survey of more than 500 voluntary, non-profit hospitals, the most influential voice heard in the medical-equipment purchasing decision was from staff physicians. Hospital officials--head nurses, chief administrators, and purchasing agents--reportedly played a minor role in deciding and recommending which type and brand of medical equipment items a hospital should purchase. Whereas the most desired locus of purchasing selection responsibility was admittedly in the hands of the hospital administrator, it is not surprising that more than three-fourths of the hospital staff physicians responding to the survey claimed that they ought to be in charge.[26]

Distortions

Probably the most intellectually dishonest strategy pursued by medical and physicians' interests has been to have successfully convinced a majority of the citizenry of the undesirable consequences of government becoming directly involved[27] with producing, financing, and distributing medical care.

Since the end of World War Two, statements made by physician, hospital, and private health insurance groups have criticized proposals for national health insurance. In particular, government participation in providing medical insurance has been called socialized medicine, supposedly leading to: 1) a decline in the quality of medical care delivered; 2) overuse of medical care resources; 3) delays in obtaining physician's appointments; 4) long waiting lines in physician's offices; 5) inability to select the physician of one's choice; 6) insufficient time to tell a physician about one's illness; 7) a deterioration of the physician-patient relationship; and 8) difficulties in securing immediate emergency attention.[28]   These eight undesirable consequences were treated as hypotheses to be tested through empirical research by comparing medical care in British Columbia with that in the United States.[29] Results suggest that organized medicine has fooled the American public into believing something that is not so.

British Columbia does not have *socialized medicine*. Physician's offices, clinics, and hospitals are neither owned nor operated by the provincial government. Moreover, most physicians and nurses are not government employees. British Columbia does have *socialized medical insurance*, however. Since 1949, this Canadian province has operated a government-owned and -operated hospital reimbursement plan; and since 1968, it has administered a government owned and operated medical insurance plan for the provision of physicians' services.

To investigate the hypothesis that government medical insurance leads to the eight undesirable consequences (EUCs) cited above, a questionnaire was designed and administered on two separate samples, one in Vancouver, British Columbia, and the other in northern Colorado. The common questionnaire, adjusted only slightly for geographic and institutional differences unique to each area, contained questions relating to demographics and the issues under investigation. In Canada, responses were evaluated for former Americans who were living in British Columbia.

Research Results

Respondents to the Colorado survey have medical-care expenses typical of many persons across America. Persons responding to both surveys exhibited very similar demographic characteristics.

GP Physician Visits. The assertion that government health insurance encourages people to overuse medical care resources was tested by asking the number of visits made to a regular family practice (GP) physician in the past year. The weighted arithmetic mean was 7.8 visits per family in British Columbia versus 6.9 visits in Colorado. British Columbia residents appear to use physician care resources only slightly more people than in the United States.

Nonemergency GP Physician Appointment. The allegation that socialized medical care arrangements requires a lengthy waiting time before obtaining a physician's appointment, especially under nonemergency conditions, was tested by asking how long one had to wait before gaining admission to the GP physician's office. More than 39 percent of the British Columbia respondents obtained a nonemergency general practitioner's appointment within one day of request, compared with only 28 percent in the Colorado survey. The weighted mean for *each* distribution was 2.6 days, much less than the four-day waiting time reported by the American Medical Association.[30]

Nonemergency Office Waiting Time. Another contention is that government-sponsored medical arrangements cause patients to wait in a physician's office for an unreasonable length of time. Research results showed that a larger percentage of British Columbia than Colorado respondents reported waiting *less than* 30 minutes. The average wait in a GP physician's office was 24.8 minutes in British Columbia. For Colorado the time was 31.2 minutes, close to the National Center for Health Statistics' estimated waiting time of 30.4 minutes,[31] and the American Medical Association's reported waiting time of 27 minutes.[32]

Nonemergency Visits. Government medical insurance has been criticized as leading to a lack of choice, adequacy of time, and satisfaction with diagnoses when visiting a physician. These claims were tested by asking whether during the last visit one was able to see the desired physician, be with him/her long enough to relate symptoms, and feel satisfied with the examination. Experiences reported in British Columbia were slightly better than experiences in Colorado.

Emergency GP Visits. For socialized medical arrangements under emergency conditions, a patient allegedly is unable to obtain immediate attention. This allegation was tested by asking if in an emergency situation, one was able to see the desired physician; received an appointment the same day; and was satisfied with the examination. All respondents in British Columbia reported that they were able to obtain an emergency appointment within two days, but Americans had to wait somewhat longer than that, on average.

Obtaining Specialist Appointment. Length of time necessary to obtain a specialist's appointment was tested by asking how long one had to wait the last time a specialist's appointment was sought. More than one-half of the Colorado respondents obtained a specialist's appointment within one week, but the figure was less than 40 percent for patients in British Columbia. The American Medical Association reported an average wait of 10.2 days for a specialist's appointment.[33] Based on both sample surveys and AMA studies, time required to obtain a specialist's appointment under government medical insurance in British Columbia is probably not different from the American medical care delivery system.

Waiting in Specialist's Office. Waiting times were evaluated for specialist physicians by asking how long one had to wait in the specialist's office before being examined by the specialist. Results suggest that specialist waiting times might be less in British Columbia than in the USA. The weighted mean was 20.8 minutes waiting time in that Canadian province and 23.3 minutes for northern Colorado. The American Medical Association reported a figure of 22.3 minutes in the United States.[34]

Visits to Specialist Physician. Three specific activities associated with visiting a specialist physician's office were investigated by asking whether during the last visit to a specialist physician, one was able to see the desired specialist; be with the specialist sufficiently long to explain problems; and experience a satisfactory examination. A majority of respondents to both surveys were able to see the specialist of their choice, but slightly more in British Columbia. Likewise, a near-total majority of both sets of respondents indicated having sufficient time to communicate symptoms to a specialist physician. Based on the Colorado survey and other sources, it can be concluded that no difference probably exists between physician care delivery under government medical insurance in British Columbia and the system in the United States.

Implications of Research Findings

Public policymakers should consider seriously the validity of traditional beliefs about an emotionally loaded subject. Current alternatives being debated in Congress involve substantial governmental involvement in the financing mechanism for the production and distribution of medical care. But government in the United States has already been substantially involved in the health and medical care sector for some time. Most hospitals are nonprofit organizations, many owned and operated by local governments. Occupational licensure, resource allocation by state-sanctioned boards, price fixing, and deliberate influence by the medical profession over entry and supply characterize both the production and distribution of physician and nursing services. Federal, state, and local governments subsidize, foster, and protect segments of organized medicine, mostly at its own request.

Two important questions concerning current medical care production and delivery are, first, whether *additional* governmental involvement into the delivery system will treat the health care problem or merely its symptoms, and second, whether power and control by organized physicians' groups will be enhanced or diminished. The political economy of medical care has been distorted by propaganda tactics, noted by the fact that the EUCs appear to be neither problems nor symptoms. This tendency ought to be recognized so that time, effort, and resources are not diverted from other crucial matters.

CONCLUDING REMARKS

Prospects for the health of Americans will be determined by public policy, by those decisions which shape contemporary environments in communities, workplaces, homes, and schools. [N. Milo, *Promoting Health Through Public Policy*, Philadelphia: Davis, 1981, p. 3.]

In American capitalism, many decisions concerning resource allocation, production, and exchange involve interaction between the market economy and the political economy. In the former, unmitigated forces of supply and demand allocate factors of production to create goods that people who have money to spend believe subjectively they want most. In the latter, resource diversion and creation of output in a market are influenced, in part, by privilege, on behalf of producers or consumers, assigned by the State. Political economy can manifest itself in various ways. Government may regulate an industry directly, actually own and operate the industry's facilities, become a sole purchaser of resources and industry output, or endow selected industry participants with certain rights for self-determination. Whatever role government plays in the political economy there is a tendency for a dichotomy to develop--some persons benefit more than others.

The political economy of medical care depicts an organizational and behavioral pattern somewhat different from other sectors of the economy. Medical care portrays a unique combination of the market augmented by grants of power and privilege from the State. Industry participants who possess power operate under the guise of the market so that political economy becomes expressed two ways, each reinforcing the other.

First, organized medicine--physicians and their trade association, the AMA--initially set up conditions for power and secured State privilege to mutually cross-coordinate medical-care delivery among themselves with legal backing by government.   Privilege begat authority and assigned that organization extensive control over conditions for the production and distribution of medical care. Privilege, authority, power, and the fruits of successful rent-seeking gave rise to social status.

Second, authority, and respect conferred by cultural position allowed organized medicine to operate under a guise of concern for health and safety to influence public opinion against governmental medical-care programs known to be successful in other developed nations. These efforts, although often challenged, have been effective to forestall meaningful restructuring of organized medicine's control over the production and distribution of medical care in the United States.

Different mechanisms for medical-care delivery are used in other developed nations whose health status is often superior to that in America. Portions of these mechanisms, if adapted to American institutions, might help the nation improve the well-being of its citizens. However, rigidities in the political economy which benefit organized medicine will be difficult to relax for some time.

NOTES

1.   For examples, see: (1) "The Rising Cost of Health Care," *School Update*, April 20, 1987, pp. 2-12; (2) V. Cahan, "The Real Health Care Catastrophe," *Business Week*, February 9, 1987, p. 29; and (3) S. Shortell and E. Hughes, "What Price Cost Controls?" *Scientific American*, August 1988, p. 16.

2.   One illustration of this point is: "Congress' Health Care Woes," *U.S. News and World Report*, July 31, 1989, p. 45.

3.   *Statistical Abstract of the United States 1990*, Washington, D.C.: U.S. Government Printing Office, 1990, p. 840.

4.   *Ibid.*, pp. 101 and 106.

5.   *Ibid.*, pp. 92, 822, and 835-36.

6.   E. F. Oatman, *Medical Care in The United States*, New York: Wilson, 1978, p. 14.

7.   P. Starr, *The Social Transformation of American Medicine*, New York: Basic, 1982, p. 37.

8.   R. B. Greifinger and V. W. Sidel, "American Medicine," *Environment*, May 1976, p. 8.

9.   G. A. Silver, *A Spy in the House of Medicine*, Germantown: Aspen, 1976, p. 4.

10. Starr, *op. cit.*, p. 42.

11. Oatman, *op. cit.*, p. 19.

12. P. J. Feldstein, *Health Care Economics*, New York: Wiley, 1983, p. 381.

13. Oatman, *op. cit.*, p.

14. Silver, *op. cit.*, p. 5.

15. Starr, *op. cit.*, p. 118.

16. R. A. Kessell, "The A.M.A. and the Supply of Physicians," *Law and Contemporary Problems*, Spring 1970, p. 268.

17. *Ibid.*

18. A. Flexner, *Medical Education in the United States and Canada*, New York: Carnegie Foundation, 1910.

19. Starr, *op. cit.*, p. 119.

20. R. A. Kessell, "Price Discrimination in Medicine," *Journal of Law and Economics*, October 1958, pp. 24-27.

21. *Ibid.*

22. Starr, *op. cit.*, p. 120.

23. Feldstein, *op. cit.*, p. 382.

24. Kessell, "Price Discrimination . . . ," *op. cit.*, pp. 28-31.

25. This practice has existed for some time. See: A. E. Nourse and G. Marks, *The Management of a Medical Practice*, New York: Lippencott, 1963, pp. 299-319.

26. See R. D. Peterson, "Buyer Conduct for Medical Equipment," *Journal of the National Medical Association*, May 1972, pp. 255-76.

27. See B. C. Martin, (ed.) *Socioeconomic Issues in Health*, Chicago: American Medical Association, 1979, pp. 13-24. For examples of the latter, see: S. R. Helmers, "Why Not a Nationwide Doctor Strike?" *Medical Economics*, Sept. 1, 1975, pp. 82-91; and, "We Can't Fight Uncle Sam All By Ourselves," *Medical Economics*, Jan. 26, 1976, pp. 213-217.

28. See AMA testimony, Hearings on Health Services for the Aged Under the Social Security System, Committee on Ways and Means, U.S. House of Representatives, Aug. 2, 1961, pp. 1317-1326 and 1344-1350. Other excellent sources that documents the medical profession's contentions about the EUCs are P. R. Hawley, "Economics of Medical Care," *Vital Speeches*, pp. 420-425; "The Truth from Canada," Denver: Colorado Medical Society, 1976; and R. C.

Newman, "For Women Only," *Contemporary Magazine, The Sunday Denver Post*, Oct. 15, 1978, p. 4.

29.   This section is based mainly on R. D. Peterson, "Patient's Experiences with Government Medical Insurance In British Columbia," *Inquiry*, Spring 1980, pp. 72-84.

30.   J. R. Cantwell, (ed.). *Profile of Medical Practice*, Chicago: AMA, 1976, p. 149.

31.   "Sunday Magazine," *St. Louis Globe-Democrat*, Apr. 4, 1976, p. 36.

32.   *Profile of Medical Practice, op. cit.*, p. 149.

33.   *Ibid.*

34.   *Ibid.*

14 IMPRESSIONS

INTRODUCTION

[T]he dualistic nature of the capitalist economy requires a revolutionary synthesis in which the limits to the relevance of the classical frame of reference are clearly defined. [B. Gerrard, *Theory of the Capitalist Economy*, Oxford: Basil Blackwell, 1989, p. 90.]

The preceding inquiry into modern American capitalism raises several basic questions. How has the present status of the American economy been influenced by its past? Where is the system heading? Are market forces really at work in the United States? What constitutes "the political economy"? How does it interact with the market? After summarizing highlights of previous chapters, some possible implications for the future of American capitalism are discussed.

Perspective

A definition for political economy was cited several times in various passages above. Key terms embodied in that definition consistently stressed historical development, possession and transmission of power, assignment of property rights, allocation of resources, distribution of income, connections between State and market, and creation of disparities. These concepts have guided the analysis because discussions of American capitalism and its antecedents thus have treated, alternatively, history, power, property, the State, the market, and disparities.

Basic Connection

In *The Theory of Monopolistic Competition*,[1] Edward H. Chamberlin pointed out that product differentiation, to the extent that it can be accomplished and to the degree that it motivates buyers, confers an element of monopoly power on the seller. This tendency creates some exclusivity for selling the differentiated item. As a result, the seller tends to receive a price and profit somewhat higher than under competition. However, above-normal profits continue only until entry, price competition, or reciprocal product differentiation by rivals eliminate them.

In the political economy, private interests pursue a similar strategy. If the State grants special status to members of some particular group, often at their behest, an element of monopoly power is conferred on them. Moreover, that privilege increases the income-generating ability of a recipient's property on a continual basis when the backing of the State protects higher prices and profits rather than allowing them to be reduced by pressures of the market. To illustrate, Chapter 13 indicated that physicians have acquired special status to control both entry into the industry and work rules. As a result, physicians' fees and the rates of return on investment in medical education are higher than they would be without such privileges. Likewise, Chapter 12 reported that American air carriers flying international routes enjoyed antitrust immunity from agency rule until deregulation removed it. While in effect, participating airlines enjoyed both higher prices and profits than without the immunity.

KEY CONCEPTS AND SOME CONCLUSIONS

Economic development is not primarily an economic but a political and a social process. [R. Heilbroner, *The Great Ascent*, New York: Harper & Row, 1963, p. 16.]

A number of tentative conclusions can be drawn from the narrative in previous chapters. The point of view is the manner by which political economy affects American capitalism.

Basic Elements

An elemental historical treatment has guided the presentation of topics. Indeed, evolutionary features affecting the American economy were presented relative to seeking, obtaining, and benefitting from status. These features can be noted not only in discussions of political economy and economic systems, but in specific areas where political economy is practiced. Moreover, disparities affect persons both inside and outside an industry. For example, physicians much greater influence on the structure of the medical-care delivery system than nurses and pharmacists; and Whites enjoy special status compared to Blacks because medical care is unevenly distributed by race.

Political Economy

Whenever the "political economy of" a particular topic is cited, two interrelated questions naturally arise: What is government's policy on the matter; and how has the policy filtered down to shape private actions on the matter? Answers serve to identify the type of advantage transferred to whom, the procedure by which beneficiaries were successful in persuading the State to grant an advantage, and the manner by which that advantage is protected, promoted, and policed by the State. It also calls into question the precise mechanism which endowed the property controlled by the favored group with more income-earning ability than others.

Power and Legitimacy

One important dimension of political economy is power, a quality which does not necessarily imply absolute control. Power means the ability to achieve one's goals (such as obtaining a franchise to assign favorable property rights to the seeker-holder). For example, the corporation has obtained favorable ability-enhancing privileges from the State vis-a-vis other types of business organization.

For more than a half-century, social critics have questioned whether the corporation is an internally consistent, rightfully constituted market institution. Observers suggest that the corporation will not be a legitimate entity until it becomes a responsive vehicle for positive social change. The primary importance of legitimacy is the intellectual basis it provides for challenging the propriety of institutional arrangements found in capitalism.

Economic Organization, Property, and Government

Feudalism was essentially a system for governing. American capitalism has feudalistic roots, mainly in a number of legal relationships which characterize its business system. Usury laws, price-cutting, and minimum wages can be traced to the feudal era. So can many of the rules for holding, using, and distributing real property.

Several features of *mercantilism* from Europe's history resemble those in modern American capitalism. As with 18th century England, governments in the United States today become directly involved in setting prices, allocating resources, licensing occupations, enacting foreign policies to foster economic interests in other countries, and otherwise subsidizing and protecting businesses so they can consolidate power and accumulate property.

As a system of economic organization, *fascism* is a continuation of mercantilist policies under conditions of rapidly advancing technology. In this setting, the State often takes the initiative in bringing business, labor, consumers, and administrative agencies together for joint decision making. The result is coordination of resource allocation, production, and distribution into selected market areas. These practices are not unknown in the political economy of American capitalism.[2]

The State is directly involved with what some would term *socialist* production and distribution. Government ownership and operation on the production side, although prominent in public education and roadways, for example, does not, however, characterize American capitalism. On the distribution side, social welfare programs are administered under socialism to satisfy basic human needs, but only on a modest basis in the United States relative to Western democratic socialist countries.

Economic Sectors

Chapters 10 through 13 examined the activities of only four areas within the American economy. However, the *Standard Industrial Classification Manual* contains data on more than 450 four-digit industry groups and on approximately 100 two-digit sectors in the American economy.[3] There is room for additional inquiry to determine the extent to which political economy is at work in other parts of the system. Even without information on other industries or sectors, most informed citizens are aware that government influences and affects those areas. In Food and Kindred Products, Petroleum Refining, Metals Mining, Construction, Finance, Insurance and Real Estate, to name but a few areas, governments at all three levels augment the market through a variety of policies and programs. For these and other industries, there is little reason to expect that connections between State and market will be reduced during oncoming decades. On the contrary, an expanding role can be expected for political economy but its practice for each sector will undoubtedly find expression in its own unique way.

Within the four sectors examined, slightly different perspectives on political economy can be detected. For the military-industrial complex there is a broad-based, informal coalition involving members at all levels of business, government, labor, and society. In transportation, government has striven to protect or expand an infant industry (now well into its mature years). The Academy produces something essential to the industrial system, so the political economy appears to be in the process of bringing higher education into its service and under its control. But for medical care, there has already been a skillful, deliberate takeover by selected participants in the industry with the backing of the State. In these ways, each individual area demonstrates that the practice of political economy is necessarily tailor-made for the peculiar institutions and problems within each industry or sector.

THE ALCHEMY OF THE AMERICAN ECONOMY

[T]he level and direction of economic activity in an advanced industrial society depends crucially upon political decisions. [T. Bottomore, *Theories of Modern Capitalism*, London,: George Unwin, 1985, p. 77.]

Political Economy and American Capitalism presents the position that the economic system of the United States is a unique blending of what some writers refer to as "the mixed economy." However, the interface between the market and the political economy is not an ordinary mixing, but a chemical blending.[4] Whereas the elements of capitalism are still present, the role of government is not *laissez faire* but exhibits an activist posture within a democratic framework in which the State responds to the petitions of private interests under their First Amendment rights. Nor is the mixing one of private and public ownership, or even of public direction of private enterprise. Even for public utilities, which comprise a minor share of value added in the American industrial structure, regulatory agencies are often the pawns of the utility companies. Yet, this relation is but another dimension of the market and political economy in American capitalism.

Market Forces

That American capitalism is a political economy does not mean that the market is dormant or dead. The market is very much alive, and to suggest otherwise would be naive. However, it functions differently in various sectors of the economy. In some corners of the system, as Galbraith[5] has noted, the market may operate by the textbook model. Some examples are yeoman farmers and ranchers, small retail shops, and local service firms. In other corners, the classical market may be propped up with government aid, and in still others, the market is either the handmaiden of the political economy or is overwhelmed by it.

Prices determined by conventional market forces of supply and demand in a competitive context occur in certain key parts of the American economy. At the base of the economic system are the primary commodity and financial markets. Here, many of the elements of a competitive market are present, and price determination is accomplished under circumstances in which government attempts to maintain and insure that competitive conditions are allowed to function. Items sold in these primary markets are usually standardized and graded. Hundreds--even thousands--of relatively small-scale buyers and sellers (or their agents) interact and respond to an auction-like bidding process, under conditions of widespread information, to transact in both the cash and futures markets. As a result, prices are formed for each basic commodity: grains, animal products, petroleum, fruits, vegetables, precious metals, minerals, lumber, corporate securities, and foreign currencies. These market-determined prices are paid by processors and manufacturers who add value to them while carrying on economic activity. Although free market forces establish basic prices in this context, the political economy is still present to some extent. For example, the farm sector benefitted from outlays of nearly $27 billion in 1987[6] by the federal government, and numerous pieces of farm legislation establish quotas, restrictions, controls, and other rules for planting, growing, importing, and marketing crops and livestock.

Moving up the economic structure, away from the raw materials and extractive levels, toward to the processing, manufacturing, and distributing levels, the practice of political economy accelerates. There is a tendency for processors, manufacturers, and distributors, many of them serious accumulators of capital under a corporate umbrella, to be better organized and more successful at lobbying and securing favors from the political economy than are enterprises at the raw materials and extractive levels.

Roots of Political Economy

Political economy emanates initially from the legislative body of the State, and is carried out by the latter's agencies or departments administered by an official of the State. In one dimension, these offices exist at each level of government: federal, state, and local. In another dimension, at each level, the three traditional functions of democratic government--legislative, executive, and judicial--assist the practice of political economy.

The primary wherewithal for political economy is the administrative agency structure of government. Under the invitation of the First Amendment, citizens seeking special favors, privileges, or status petition elected officials--senators, representatives, assembly persons, council members, zoning commissioners--to enact statutes (or ordinances) and make rulings which will endow their properties with special income-generating power. Generally, but not always, an agency of some level of government is set up and charged with the responsibility of administering the favorable legislation. As examples, state medical licensing boards, defense procurement agencies, boards of regents, and the Interstate Commerce Commission are administrative entities which foster, protect, monitor, aid, and otherwise guide the group which originally sought and obtained the favor. Administrative agencies--boards, offices, commissions--were designed to serve the public interest, and generally do so with professional zeal. Nevertheless, these entities also cater to special private interests.

At each level of government there are numerous administrative agencies created by a legislative body, and originally established in deference to the delegation clause of the federal Constitution.[7] They were set up because technology advanced to a point that highly complex, complicated, and technical areas of business, economic, or social activity had emerged and needed control or guidance for the public interest. Congress had neither the time nor expertise to meet, debate, and decide continuously on all the problems which might arise when the newly devised technology was being exploited in its own arena of production and distribution. In response, legislatures created a body of technical experts--an administrative agency--to coordinate and guide activity in that arena.[8] One of the first administrative agencies was the Interstate Commerce Commission, established in 1887. Two others are the Federal Aviation Administration and the Federal Communications Commission. There are many more.

In carrying out the responsibilities assigned to them by legislative bodies, as approved by the executive and upheld by the courts at some point, administrative agencies engage in rule making and adjudication.[9] Many have subpoena and enforcement powers. In doing so, they become their own legislative, executive, and judicial branches (subject to appeal and review by the regular court system, and to oversight during the next legislative session). In the adjudication process for some (but not all) administrative matters, the burden has been shifted from requiring the agency to prove an allegation to requiring the accused citizen to prove that it is not so (as for the Internal Revenue Service with respect to suspected non-complying taxpayers). An obvious potential for creating and exercising power exists. In some agencies, ineptness has caused enormous losses of public and private funds. Consider the accusations against President Reagan's Secretary of Housing and Urban Development the lost billions of depositor (and eventually, taxpayer) dollars due to the lax auditing and supervision procedures by the Federal Savings and Loan Insurance Corporation.

Implications of Political Economy

American capitalism has experienced a type of organic growth during which countless social, economic, and political changes have occurred. It is an understatement to assert that the system will undergo additional changes in the decades ahead. This organic growth is obviously a result of human action and reaction. The fundamental framework for these sequential events has been advances in technology and institutional adjustments which react to them. Technology is a human activity, and so is the process of institutional adjustment. What matters, of course, are the values and goals characterizing those persons influencing both technological development and institutional adjustment.

The American economy has been plagued with either slow growth, inflation, unemployment, or low productivity since the mid-1950s. A number of government-policy remedies have been proposed, enacted, and applied over the years. New administrative agencies have been created, and existing ones have been given expanded powers. As the technologically advanced system of industrial capitalism in America continues to mature and develop, its potential for further growth of output will be based on vast output capacity and capability it has already accumulated. If problems with efficiency and productivity persist, the economic system will probably continue to fail to reach its potential. As this happens, additional governmental programs, policies, taxes, incentives, controls, and privileges will be instituted and installed. Along with them will be created additional administrative agencies. The result will be additional connections between the State and the market--a mushrooming political economy.

CONCLUDING REMARKS

By expanding, capitalism alters its environment. Expansion may also transform the way that capitalism works. [S. Bowles and R. Edwards, *Understanding Capitalism*, New York: Harper & Row, 1985, p. 18.]

As the new century dawns, technology can be expected to advance at a steady pace, perhaps at a trot or even a gallop. The basic sciences--physics, chemistry, biology, mathematics--will undoubtedly be the sources of new discoveries. Increases in the level of knowledge will also occur in the arts, humanities, and social sciences. In the past, large-scale plant and equipment have been installed to exploit new scientific achievements. Highly capital-intensive technology is usually adopted first because it is most expansionary on the economy. Significant scientific breakthroughs in social science, for example, do not receive the emphasis as do breakthroughs in the physical sciences because the former are less capital-intensive than the latter. Given the tendency of an obsession in capitalism for accumulating capital and wealth, as Heilbroner[10] indicates, those items that are capital intensive have been and will probably continue to be emphasized. Whenever capital accumulation occurs, it tends to require a large-scale factory with heavy, complicated machinery, undoubtedly under the control of the corporation, as Galbraith[11] describes. It remains to be seen whether sufficient fruits of technology will filter down to the masses from a socially oriented corporation, as Bell[12] hopes. But that corporation, as Drucker[13] suggests, will probably have extensive decision making powers which are granted, approved, and backed by the State and the political economy.

As new technology is developed and new processes, products, and industries arise in response, there will be a tendency to increase the number of administrative agencies. Lawmakers at various levels of government, to accommodate the new technology, will tend to establish an administrative agency to coordinate, control, foster, subsidize, protect, manage, and guide the exploitation of that technology, hopefully for the benefit of the general public, but surely at least for private interests. In performing these functions, the administrative agency will necessarily operate in a combined role as all three branches of government--legislative, executive, and judicial. The agency will make rules, administer those rules, and adjudicate whether the rules so administered were carried out properly according to the intent of the congressional body which created the administrative agency and empowered it with its comprehensive tripartite functions. Moreover, additional lobbyists will be needed to petition lawmakers and administrative agencies for special status. In the course of all this, political economy will be practiced because the State, or an agency of it, will interface with the market to grant some property owners with special privileges, but deny favors to others.

Institutional adjustments to advancing technology by way of creating new administrative agencies and expanding the powers of existing ones, may potentially become uncontrollably authoritarian and overly partial. One cannot help but observe, however, that American democracy has been strong and resilient, and flexible but stable. The spirit and power of the Constitution, including its Amendments, as well as the expectations and demands of the citizenry, will hopefully prevent American capitalism from evolving into tyranny or at least from becoming increasingly bureaucratic. Indeed, to these ends:

> From the standpoint of economics, the problem is not government but the need to further develop democracy so that government is increasingly democratic. [M. Lutz and K. Lux, *Humanistic Economics*, New York: Bootstrap, 1988, p. 220.]

NOTES

1.   E. H. Chamberlin, *The Theory of Monopolistic Competition*, Cambridge: Harvard University Press, 1962, pp. 56-116.

2.   During the spring and summer of 1990, the Honorable Roy Romer, Governor of the State of Colorado, organized, arranged, and chaired several meetings at which baseball commissioners, national league executives, and professional baseball investors discussed the possibilities of a major league franchise for Denver. He even recommended and rejected certain investors.

3.   *Standard Industrial Classification Manual*, Washington, D.C.: U.S. Government Printing Office, 1972.

4.   The concept is taken from Chamberlin, *op. cit.*, p. 3.

5.   J. K. Galbraith, *The New Industrial State*, Boston: Houghton Mifflin, 1967, pp. 8-10.

6.   *Economic Report of the President 1989*, Washington, D.C.: U.S. Government Printing Office, 1990, p. 399.

7.   In U.S. v. Grimaud, 220 U.S. 506 (1911), the Supreme Court held that Congressional enactment of administrative rules is not a delegation of legislative authority.

8.   J. M. Landis, *The Administrative Process*, New Haven: Yale University Press, 1938, pp. 30-38.

9.   K. C. Davis, *Administrative Law Text*, St. Paul: West, 1985, pp. 139-214.

10. R. L. Heilbroner, *The Nature and Logic of Capitalism*, New York: Norton, 1985, pp. 42-78, 141-43, and 197-99.

11. Galbraith, *op. cit.*, pp. 46-85.

12. D. Bell, *The Cultural Contradictions of Capitalism*, New York: Basic, 1974.

13. P. F. Drucker, *The Concept of the Corporation*, New York: John Day, 1946.

INDEX